MAY 2 6 2009

DATE DUE

MAR 0 3	1995	MAR 0 4 1996	
MAR 1 5	1995	MAR 1 2 1998	
		G 0 6 1999	
APR 0 3	1995	DEC 1 5 2000	
SEP 1 0	1995	JUN 0 6 2001	
FEB 2 6	1997	DEC 2 7 2001	
		FEB 0 6 2002	
AUG 1 2	1997	FEB 0 3 2004	
SEP 0 9	1997	MAY 2 7 2004	
DEC 1 6	1997	NOV 0 4 2004	
		FEB 0 3 2006	
FEB 0 4	1998	MAY 1 3 2008	

242.2
THR

365 more
meditations for
women

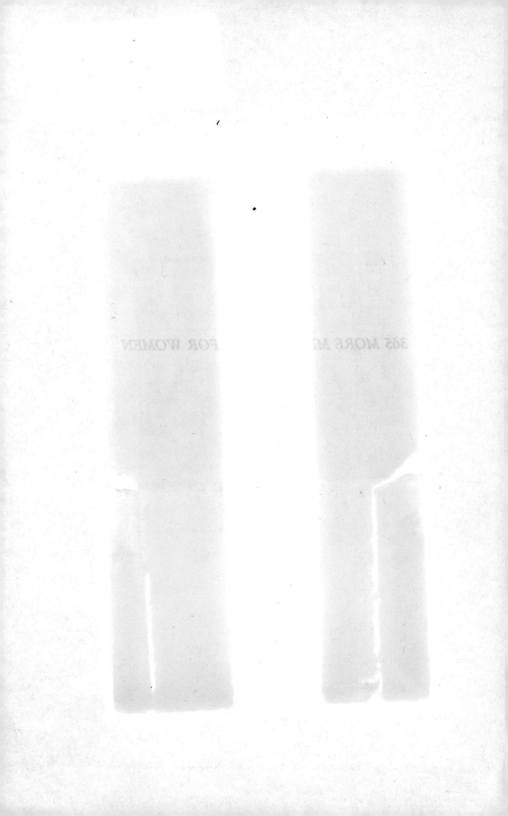

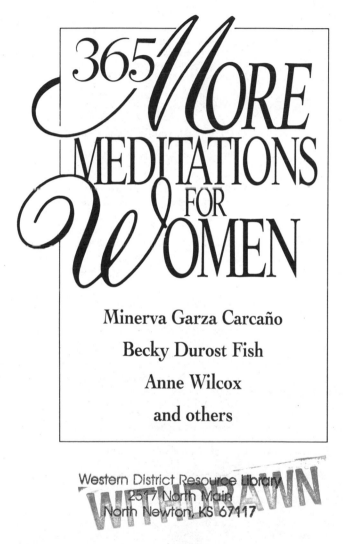

365 MORE MEDITATIONS FOR WOMEN

Minerva Garza Carcaño

Becky Durost Fish

Anne Wilcox

and others

DIMENSIONS

FOR LIVING

NASHVILLE

365 MORE MEDITATIONS FOR WOMEN

Copyright © 1992 by Dimensions for Living

94 95 96 97 98 99 00 01 02 03 04 — 10 9 8 7 6 5

This book is printed on recycled, acid-free paper.

Library of Congress Cataloging-in-Publication Data

365 more meditations for women / Minerva Garza Carcaño . . . [et al.].
    p. cm.
ISBN 0-687-41888-7 (alk. paper)
1. Women—Prayer-books and devotions—English.   2. Devotional calendars.   I. Carcaño, Minerva Garza.   II. Title: Three hundred sixty-five more meditations for women.
BV4844.A14   1992
242 ' .2—dc20   91-33363

Scripture quotations labeled KJV are from the King James Version of the Bible.   Scripture quotations labeled JB are from *The Jerusalem Bible,* copyright © 1966 by Darton, Longman & Todd, Ltd., and Doubleday and Company, Inc. Used by permission of the publisher.   Scripture quotations labeled GNB are from the *Good News Bible*—Old Testament: Copyright © American Bible Society 1966, 1971, 1976; New Testament: Copyright © American Bible Society, 1966, 1971, 1976.   Scripture quotations labeled NIV are from the *Holy Bible: New International Version.* Copyright © 1973, 1978, 1984 by the International Bible Society. Used by permission of Zondervan Bible Publishers.   Scripture quotations labeled "Rieu" are from E. V. Rieu, *The Four Gospels: A New Translation from the Greek* (Baltimore: Penguin, 1953).   Scripture quotations labeled TLB are from *The Living Bible,* copyright © 1971 by Tyndale House Publishers, Wheaton, IL. Used by permission.   Scripture quotations labeled NRSV are from the New Revised Standard Version of the Bible, copyright © 1989 by the Division of Education of the National Council of Churches of Christ in the United States of America. Used by permission.   Scripture quotations labeled "Barclay" are from *The Daily Study Bible* by William Barclay, published by The Saint Andrew's Press.   Meditations for April 3, 5, 10, 11, 19, 20, 22, 23, and 24 are adapted and excerpted from *The Sanctuary for Lent 1991* by LeNoir and Barry Culbertson. Copyright © 1991 by Abingdon Press. Reprinted by permission.   The lines from "voices to voices,lip to lip" are from *IS 5* by E. E. Cummings, Edited by George James Firmage, by permission of Liveright Publishing Corporation. Copyright © 1985 by E. E. Cummings Trust. Copyright 1926 by Horace Liveright. Copyright © 1954 by E. E. Cummings. Copyright © 1985 by George James Firmage.   September devotionals by Anne Wilcox are excerpts from the 1988 and 1989 issues of *Today's Christian Woman,* a publication of Christianity Today, Inc., Carol Stream, IL.

MANUFACTURED IN THE UNITED STATES OF AMERICA

CONTENTS

FOREWORD

Welcome to *365 More Meditations for Women*. The book you hold in your hand is a collection of personal spiritual writings by twelve different women, each of whom has contributed one month's worth of meditations. Thus this book is not only a journey through the year but also a series of encounters with twelve women and their individual ways of relating to God and to life.

The meditations in this book follow no set pattern. Some writers incorporate phrases or selections from Scripture; some end each meditation with a prayer; others use prose alone. But in their various styles, these writers share common themes: a strong sense of values, belief in God as the source and meaning of life, and recognition of the value inherent in daily meditation.

Because the writers tend to begin and end their segments, you will have a real sense of the beginning and end of each month. The contributors themselves represent various age groups and life-styles. Among them are women who work primarily outside the home, inside the home, or who are retired; daughters, mothers, and grandmothers; residents of the East Coast, the West Coast, and the Heartland.

It is our hope that the discipline of daily meditation and the thoughts that will be triggered by these particular pages will make every day more meaningful for you.

Minerva Garza Carcaño is District Superintendent of the Western District of the Rio Grande Conference of The United Methodist Church and frequent contributor to several periodicals. She lives in Albuquerque.

LeNoir H. Culbertson is pastor of College Grove United Methodist Church in Tennessee. She holds a doctorate from Vanderbilt Divinity School and is the mother of two children.

Becky Durost Fish is former editor of *Virtue* magazine. She is a full-time freelance writer and editor and lives in Bend, Oregon.

Martha Whitmore Hickman has written books for children and adults, including *Fullness of Time: Short Stories of Women and Aging*. She has taught creative writing classes and has worked with children in a variety of settings. She lives in Nashville.

Mary Ruth Howes is senior editor at Guideposts Books in New York. She was born in China to missionary parents and has had a long career in religious publishing. She lives in Jersey City, New Jersey.

Maxine Dowd Jensen is a freelance writer and author of four books, including *The Warming of Winter*. She has taught writing classes, is a soloist, and has been a co-sponsor for youth groups. She lives in Lee's Summit, Missouri.

Anne Killinger, who was trained as a concert pianist and once taught piano at Georgetown College in Kentucky, is a housewife who writes hymns, anthems, and children's musicals. She resides in Birmingham.

Marjorie L. Kimbrough is the author of *Accept No Limitations: A Black Woman Encounters Corporate America*. She has also written several programming languages textbooks, taught both technical and religious material on video tape, and conducted seminars and training courses. Currently an instructor in Religion and Philosophy at Clark Atlanta University, she is married and the mother of two sons.

Rebecca Laird is a professional writer and editor with a special interest in spirituality and social justice. She is author of several books, including *Robinson Rabbit, What Do You Hear?* She is a licensed minister in the Church of the Nazarene. She lives in San Francisco.

Phyllis A. Tickle is director emerita of St. Luke's Press in Memphis. She is the author of several books, including *The Tickle Papers,* and the editor of *Confessing Conscience.* She lives in Lucy, Tennessee.

Shirley Pope Waite is a freelance writer, speaker, and instructor. She teaches "Writing to Sell" and "Writing Your Memoirs" through area community colleges, and conducts workshops at Christian writers' conferences in the Northwest. Shirley also leads women's retreats. She lives in Walla Walla, Washington.

Anne Wilcox is former Bible study columnist for *Today's Christian Woman* and author of two books, including *A Woman's Workshop on Ruth.* She has one daughter and lives in Seattle.

365 MORE MEDITATIONS FOR WOMEN

JANUARY

Letting the Light Shine

MARJORIE L. KIMBROUGH

JANUARY 1   **CAN THEY SEE THE LIGHT?**

As the new year dawns I think of New Year's resolutions and
the rapidity at which they are broken and forgotten. So, rather
than promise to lose weight or read twelve books, I have resolved
to let others see the Light. The Light, of course, is the Light that
came into the world to shine on all persons. It is the Light to
which John bore witness. It is even the Light about which David
wrote when he said, "The Lord is my light," and it is the Light
sung about in the spiritual, "This little light of mine, I'm gonna
let it shine."

We as Christians talk about the Light, but can anyone see the
Light in us? Christians ought to bear witness to the Light. As
there are opportunities, and, believe me, every day there are
opportunities, we need to talk about the Light. We ought to say a
good word for the Lord; we ought to tell what he has done for
us; but, most of all, others ought to see the glow of the Light in
our eyes and on our faces. When others look at us, can they see
the Light?

Although David was referring to God when he wrote, "The
Lord is my light," we know that all David wrote also applies to
Jesus, the coeternal and coexistent Son of the Father—God from
God, Light from Light, God with us. And so I resolve to live this
year as though the Lord is my Light. That means that I will not

walk in darkness, for he will light my way. Others will make note of the confidence with which I move, and they will see the Light that surrounds me.

This year I resolve to let the Light of Christ shine everywhere I go. I will greet friends and strangers with a smile; I will do something to help someone each day, even if that something is to whisper a prayer on that person's behalf; I will praise and worship God each day, and I will ask him to surround me with the love and Light of Christ. This is a resolution about which I not only feel good but also know I can keep. This year they will see the Light in me. What about you?

JANUARY 2   VIVIDLY IMAGINE

Some years ago I ran across this quote:
"Whatever you vividly imagine, ardently desire, sincerely believe, and enthusiastically act upon must inevitably come to pass."
I don't know who wrote it, but I do know that the first time I heard it, it changed my life. You see, I really believe it. Let's analyze it.

To vividly imagine means to see clearly. In this new year, is there something that you can clearly see happening in your life? Although some people say that they'll believe it when they see it, I know that when they believe it, they *will* see it, vividly imagine it. Right now vividly imagine something you want to happen this year. Can you see yourself doing it or being involved in it? That's the first step.

Second, you must ardently desire it. Do you *truly* want this thing to happen? Do you want it so much that you can see it, taste it, feel it taking control in your life? Would its happening satisfy that burning desire, that passion that you have for its accomplishment? If so, you've mastered the second step.

Third, do you sincerely believe that you can do it? If you can see it and want it but you don't believe that *you* can do it, it will never happen. You must believe it in your heart. You must be honest with yourself; do you have what it takes, or are you only dreaming? If you sincerely believe that you can do it, the third step is yours.

The fourth step is to enthusiastically act upon whatever it is that you want to happen in your life this new year. This means that you cannot sit around day after day dreaming about it—you must get up and hustle. To act is to work. As you work, are you enthusiastic or lethargic? Do others see the joy in your working or do they see the drudgery? Can they see that you are enthusiastically working with the help of the Light? If so, then whatever it is that you want to happen this year must inevitably come to pass!

JANUARY 3   EXPECT A MIRACLE

Now that we have clearly focused on a goal for this new year, let me propose a formula to guarantee its accomplishment.

Success = Engage + Enlist + Exert + Expect + Endure

Engage in planning. Before you begin to do anything, make plans. It has often been said that those who fail to plan, plan to fail. You will not fail this year. Set deadlines and checkpoints for the accomplishment of your goal. Evaluate your progress by doing a quarterly assessment at the end of March, June, September, and December. As you approach the end of each quarter, ask yourself whether all the elements of the formula are in place.

Enlist the necessary resources. If you are not equipped to accomplish your goal alone, seek help. If you need to learn how to do something, enlist an instructor or check out a book from the library and do a little self-instructing.

Exert the required effort with energy and enthusiasm. Never move listlessly toward your goal. As the Light shines in you, you ought to have a source of energy. Let it show. Remember that you promised to enthusiastically act upon your goal. Let us see it.

Expect a miracle. Claim your victory. Publicly announce it to everyone you meet. That will encourage you. Show your faith. "Be not faithless, but believing" (John 20:27).

Endure to the end. No matter what happens, never give up. Remember the words of gospel songwriter and preacher James

Cleveland: "I don't feel no ways tired. I've come too far from where I started from. Nobody told me the road would be easy. I don't believe he brought me this far to leave me." He won't leave you. Endure to the end!

JANUARY 4   GIVE HIM PRAISE!

It is cold and damp outside today, and I feel the need for God's warmth and comfort. Whenever I feel this way, I find that if I give him praise, his love and comfort surround me and I am warm. So I dedicate today to praising God.

One of our choirs at Ben Hill United Methodist Church, The Majestic Choir, sings a song with these words:

"If I don't praise the Lord, praise the Lord,
The rocks are gonna cry out.
I don't want no rocks, no rocks cryin' in my place."

It would be a shame if the rocks had to cry out for us. Oh, how good God is! I just want to praise his holy name! I don't want the rocks to have to cry out for me!

Just think about God's goodness. Could you have survived without him? Stop now and count your blessings. You are alive and still have the opportunity to serve him. You have a reasonable measure of health and strength; you are intelligent enough to read and understand these words; you are aware of the Light and others may see it in you. You are blessed. Praise God!

I thank and praise him for my family. I have a kind and loving husband; I have two fine, young adult sons, free of drugs and infirmities; I have other family and friends who love me. I am wonderfully blessed. I give him praise!

I praise him that I never experience loneliness, for I always feel his presence. I know that he so loved the world that he gave his only Son, Jesus, who is my personal Savior. I know him and love him. He is my Light. Praise God! Thank you, Jesus!

All day I will remember his great goodness to me and I will give him praise. On this cold and damp day, I feel warm all over.

In recent years, one of the study themes for United Methodist Women was "Hallelujah Anyhow." When I first heard this theme, I was intrigued. It made me remember that no matter what may happen, God is still to be praised. Then I thought of my friend Beverly.

Beverly is a beautiful young woman who was suddenly struck by tragedy. One July, without warning, her husband had a massive heart attack and died, leaving her with two teen-aged children. A few months later, her mother was diagnosed with Alzheimer's disease, and her brother died of cancer. Then she was mugged while shopping for Christmas gifts for her children; and, just before Christmas, her house burned to the ground. She and her children were spared, but all of their possessions were lost—even those special, personal items that had belonged to her husband. They moved to an apartment while their house was rebuilt, and slowly, they acquired replacement clothing and household items. Before they could move back into their house, all of the items they had replaced were stolen. Hallelujah anyhow!

How could Beverly continue to praise God in the midst of all this adversity? Believe me, it was difficult. Sometimes Beverly would say that she just didn't think she could bear it. Then she would say that she had been raised to believe that God would not put more on her than she could bear. My job was to be there for her, to listen, to encourage, to show her that God was still able to bless, comfort, and keep her. She needed to see the Light in me when she felt surrounded by darkness.

In his letter to the churches of Galatia, Paul wrote, "Bear ye one another's burdens, and so fulfill the law of Christ" (6:2). Although we cannot completely bear the burdens of others, we can assist them. We can be in prayer with and for them, and we can praise God when they do not feel like it. Although we may cry with them, we must rejoice with them. In the words of the apostle James, "Count it all joy when you meet various trials, for you know that the testing of your faith produces steadfastness. And let steadfastness have its full effect, that you may be perfect and complete, lacking in nothing" (James 1:2-4). Count it *all* joy! Hallelujah anyhow!

JANUARY 6   MARRIED BEFORE CHILDREN

Today is the day I volunteer at Grady Hospital. Grady is the Atlanta-area county hospital, and I volunteer every week. I work in pediatric therapeutic recreation, reading to and playing games with children under twelve. Each time I go, I think of Brenda.

Brenda was an eleven-year-old patient who had broken her hip. I often sat by her bed and talked with her as we read books and played games. Brenda seemed fascinated by the fact that I came to the hospital every week even though it was not my job and I was not being paid. One day Brenda asked me three questions, "Do you have children? Are you married? Were you married before you had children?" The order and content of her questions told me a lot about Brenda and the environment in which she lived.

I later discovered that Brenda was the oldest of her young mother's three children. She lived in a small house with her mother, siblings, aunt, cousins, and grandmother. None of the women in the house had ever been married, and all of them had children. So, I was a real novelty to her. I was a married woman with children, and I had married before they were born. Brenda dreamed of the presence of a man in her family. She told me that she wanted to marry before she had children so that her children could grow up in a real family with a father.

I wonder how many of us take for granted having a family and being married before we have children. With so many people living together without the benefit of marriage, will there be other children like Brenda asking those three questions and dreaming of a real family with a father? We women can help to make it unnecessary for Brendas in the world to ask such questions by marrying before we have children and striving to make our marriages work.

Brenda and I visited each week during her three-month hospital stay. I could see that she needed a role model. She needed someone for whom her dream of the ideal family had worked. She needed to see the Light. I hope she saw it in me.

JANUARY 7   THERE ARE SCARS

I love to bake and I am famous for my chocolate chip cookies, but I never bake them without thinking of my youngest son, Marty. When Marty was a year old, he was in the kitchen with me while I was baking cookies. I poured myself a cup of coffee to drink with some of those fresh cookies, and while I was taking them out of the oven, Marty reached for that cup of coffee and spilled it down the front of his shirt. His screams pierced my heart, and I turned to see steam rising from his shirt. Panicking, I called the fire department, and then I called my husband to take me to the hospital. I tried to remove the steaming shirt and found that the skin on Marty's chest was removed with it. After many anxious moments pacing in the hospital emergency room, the doctor who treated Marty said, "It will heal, but it will leave a scar."

We all have scars—scars of accidents, sports, and childhood games—but our real scars are on the inside. These are the scars of injustice, meanness, hatred, betrayal, and misunderstanding; and often they are not visible. Think now of your own scars—not only the ones you have sustained, but also the ones you have inflicted on others. Do they still hurt? Do they itch? Are they healing?

As you interact with people today, remember that they have scars. You may never know the depth, anguish, or pain of those visible and invisible scars, but keep asking yourself if there is anything you can do for them to help them forget about their scars and forgive the ones who caused them.

Christ, our Light, accepts us with our scars, our hurts, and our anguish; and he loves and forgives us. And because of our own scars, we can love, forgive, and understand others. Thanks be to God, for he comforts us in every situation and heals us through the scars that Jesus bore. "But he was wounded for our transgressions, he was bruised for our iniquities: the chastisement of our peace was upon him; and with his stripes we are healed" (Isaiah 53:5).

Some days I feel as though I just don't have enough time to do all that I have to do. When this happens I think of the story of the nursery school children, ages two to five, who moved a mountain. Their mountain was eight tons of sand for the nursery school sandbox. The sand had been dumped in the street rather than in the sandbox, and it had to be moved. Although the nursery school teacher was very upset and did not know how she would get all that sand from the street to the sandbox, the children simply began to move the sand with tiny shovels and cans, singing as they worked. They attacked a large, almost impossible task with the tools they had; they persisted until the job was completed, and they did it with a singing spirit. They moved a mountain!

I keep reminding myself that having enough time is a matter of time management. Although there have been many books written on time management, I have decided that the procedure is quite simple. You assess the job to be done; you divide it into steps that can be accomplished with the tools and information available; and you approach it with joy. That's exactly what the nursery school children did! So, before you or I decide that we do not have time to do whatever it is that has to be done, let's assess the total job, divide it into small, shovelful jobs, and get started with smiles on our faces and songs in our hearts.

I'm sure that as the nursery school teacher watched those children working and singing, she saw the Light. Isn't it interesting that when our Lord was asked, "Who is the greatest in the kingdom of heaven?" he answered, "Except ye be converted, and become as little children, ye shall not enter into the kingdom of heaven" (Matthew 18:3 KJV).

We make the most of our time when we plan, organize, prioritize, rejoice, persist, and evaluate. We can move mountains, a shovelful at a time, if we really want to and if we have a singing spirit. "And a little child shall lead them" (Isaiah 11:6 KJV).

It has been very foggy in Atlanta this year. Airplanes have been delayed; there have been numerous automobile accidents; and many people seem depressed. The weather does affect our disposition, and I wonder if we Christians shouldn't have sunny and bright dispositions no matter what the weather.

But the dark and foggy conditions remind me of how much we physically depend on light to guide us. Even when we travel on very familiar roads, the darkness and the fog make us apprehensive. The corner that is just a few yards away seems to be miles away. Sometimes we follow the lights on the car ahead of us and hope that the driver does not run off the road—for if he or she does, we will certainly run off, too. If it were only clear and bright, our traveling would be so much easier and our dispositions so much brighter.

Similarly, our traveling as Christians on the road of life would be so much easier and our dispositions would be so much brighter if we were only guided by the Light. Jesus described his followers as the light of the world. He told them that their light should not be hidden under a bushel, but instead, should be put on top of the hill so that it gives light to the whole world. The light of a Christian ought to make the way clear so that others can see. Christians can be an example to others—they can take the lead and guide as the light, allowing others to see their light and follow without fear of running off the road of life. They can influence others who might not stand for right if they had to stand alone.

The Light that we Christians follow can also warn us. It can guide us away from danger. The Christian's warning light is like the warning lights on my car. These lights let me know when something is wrong and remind me to have my car serviced as soon as possible. If the Christian is guided by the Light, then he or she should be aware of danger and should be able to apprise others that there is danger ahead.

The Light that guides the Christian cannot be selfish, for it cannot shine for one person and be invisible to others. As the Light shines, God is seen and given the glory. Light draws attention; it causes others to notice. But the attention should go beyond the individual to the source of the light. And the true source is God.

So, when that fog hampers my vision, I will look to the Light and let it shine through me. That will brighten both my spirit and my way.

JANUARY 10   KEEP LOOKING

In his book *Tough Times Never Last, But Tough People Do*, Robert H. Schuller, pastor of the Crystal Cathedral in Garden Grove, California, tells of his childhood on a small farm in Iowa. His family was poor and understood the devastation the Midwestern weather could have on their livelihood. One summer the worst became a reality when a tornado destroyed their farm, but the family had to be grateful that all of them escaped unharmed. When they returned to survey their damaged property, they found part of a sign that used to hang on the kitchen wall. Originally the sign said, "Keep looking to Jesus," but after the damage the sign simply said, "Keep looking."

What a wonderful motto! "Keep looking." No matter how tough times get, we must keep looking. We know that as we look we will see Jesus, for he is our Light, our Hope. Ordinarily, we would never keep looking in the dark; we would want some light, and Jesus is that Light. If we just remember to keep looking, we know that we will find Jesus and that he will guide us.

The words *keep looking* ought to be words of encouragement for us this year. Even if we do not accomplish all the goals that we set, we must continue to keep looking. As the great black educator Dr. Benjamin Elijah Mays said,

It must be borne in mind that the tragedy in life doesn't lie in not reaching your goal. The tragedy lies in having no goal to reach. It isn't a calamity to die with dreams unfulfilled, but it is a calamity not to dream. It is not a disaster to be unable to capture your ideal, but it is a disaster to have no ideal to capture. It is not a disgrace not to reach the stars, but it is a disgrace to have no stars to reach for. Not failure, but low aim is sin.

Keep looking!

Many years ago I read a magazine article about a little girl who asked the question "Why was I born?" The child was answered by several people representing different cultures and religions, but the answer that impressed me most was given by playwright and public official Clare Boothe Luce. This was her answer:

You were born to know, love, and serve God. You were born to know Perfect Truth, Perfect Mercy, Perfect Love, and to be loved by God. And Mama and Papa aren't perfect, as you will discover one day; but, he who made you is. Seek him. We will help you, child, as best we can, for this is what we were all born to do. And if we don't try to do it together, it were better for us and for you that you had never been born.

The beginning of the year is a good time for me to rethink that purpose, for surely we were all born to know, love, and serve God. This year, what will we do to know God better? Will we read books, study the Bible, attend classes, worship and pray more often and with greater intensity? How will we show that we love him? Will we feed his sheep? Will we let others see the Light in us? And what will we do to better serve him? Will we lead a commission, teach a class, sing in a choir, visit those who are sick or in prison, feed the homeless? This year will we fulfill our purpose for being?

"And Mama and Papa aren't perfect." We may as well admit that we are not and have not been the best examples for our children. We are not even good examples for ourselves. The admonition to "be ye perfect" never enters our minds. But we must keep reminding ourselves and our children that God is perfect and that we must constantly seek him.

We must help each other in our quest for God, for this is what we were all born to do. We are challenged to seek God together so that our lives are not wasted separately. We thank him that before we ever begin our search for him, he already has found us. We are found by him. He is our Light and will give purpose, meaning, and direction to our lives. He will make valid our purpose for being. We were born to know, love, and serve him.

JANUARY 12   LET HER GO!

When I was working in corporate America, one day my secretary was late to work and was very distressed. When I asked her what the trouble was, she replied that her grandmother had suffered a severe stroke and the prognosis was not hopeful. After expressing my concern, I listened to her talk about the many wonderful experiences she had had with her grandmother. It was obvious that she loved her grandmother very much and was committed to visiting her each night and each morning before reporting for work. She was always tearful and discouraged because the doctors had told her that her grandmother could not live much longer.

One morning I decided to have a talk with her. I asked her if her grandmother was a good person, if she had lived a full life, and if she knew Jesus Christ as her personal Savior. When my secretary answered positively to each of these questions, I said, "Then let her go! She has an opportunity to be with the Master." I asked her if she believed in the Resurrection and if she believed Jesus when he said, "I go to prepare a place for you . . . that where I am, there ye may be also" (John 14:2-3 KJV). I told her that it was time for her grandmother to claim her place, the one that Jesus had prepared especially for her. I said, "Let her go, and then celebrate her life and thank God that you had a chance to know and be loved by her."

The next day my secretary's mother called to inform her daughter of the grandmother's death. The office workers all looked for me and asked me to be with her when her mother gave her the news. I walked into her office just as her mother's call was being transferred. She looked up at me and said, "You know, don't you?" I said, "Yes, and I hope you have let her go."

I put my arms around my secretary and let her cry, but I knew that she was letting her grandmother go to be with Jesus. We can let go with tears of rejoicing when we know our loved ones have walked in the Light.

"Now when they saw the boldness of Peter and John, and realized that they were uneducated and ordinary men, they were amazed and recognized them as champions of Jesus " (Acts 4:13 NRSV). The boldness of Peter and John marked them as persons who had been with Jesus. Somehow once we have been with Jesus, we are not the same. There is a certain boldness, a confidence that not only marks us as Christians but also marks us as winners. Although Peter and John did not have a formal education, they knew who they were, what they wanted, and to whom they belonged. They were winners.

Just what are the marks of a winner? First, a winner knows what she wants to win. A winner has clear, set goals. She knows where she is going. As the Cheshire Cat said to Alice in Lewis Carroll's *Through the Looking Glass,* "If you don't know where you're going, any road will take you there." A winner knows what she wants to win, for she has seen the Light and is guided by Jesus.

Second, a winner looks like a winner. A winner has that boldness and confidence that lets others know she has been with Jesus. She doesn't drag her feet or bend her back when she walks; she is always neat and clean; she has the assurance that she is loved, for she is loved by God. She looks like a winner.

Third, a winner believes she can win. A winner knows that God is on her side and that if God is for her, it doesn't matter who is against her, for God never fails. A winner knows that where her knowledge ends, God's knowledge begins. He is the keeper of knowledge. Peter and John were uneducated, common men, but they had knowledge of Jesus. That was enough. God would lead them to whatever else they needed.

Fourth, a winner never quits. A winner hangs in there until there is nowhere else to hang. A winner knows that a "no" from God may not be a denial but simply a delay. A winner is willing to go all the way, to commit totally, and to win against all odds.

When they saw the boldness and the winning spirit of Peter and John, and you and me, they knew we had been with Jesus.

JANUARY 14   COULDN'T HEAR NOBODY PRAY

As the birthday of Martin Luther King, Jr. approaches, I think of all the struggles African Americans have faced since first making that journey from Africa to America as slaves. I wonder if they could have survived slavery without faith in God. The stories of the deliverance of the Israelites from bondage in Egypt; of Daniel in the lions' den; and of the Hebrew children in the fiery furnace had inestimable influence upon them. If the God they served had delivered all of those before them, surely he would deliver them. Their firm faith was the key ingredient in their physical and spiritual survival of two and a half centuries of slavery.

The story is told of a slave, John, who lived in southern Kentucky. He was known for his long hours of prayer and praise. It was said that John would pray when he "couldn't hear nobody pray." Like Daniel in Babylon, nothing would prevent John from turning his face toward Jerusalem in prayer.

When the time came for John to be sold, the master who was to buy him was determined to stop John from praying. The master did not want to own one of those "praying fools."

John advised the man not to buy him, for he was duty bound to pray. Even though the master told John that he would beat him if he caught him praying, John, like Daniel, continued to pray.

One day the master learned from the slave's own lips that he had been praying. The master decided to teach John a lesson, and he tried his best to kill John by beating him with a lash. Being tired from the beating he had given John, the master lay down to rest, but he found that he was sick and comfortless. It seemed that John's God had convicted the master of his wickedness. Finally the master sent for John and asked John to pray for him. John did pray for him, and the master saw the Light of a new life. From that day forward the master felt that the best investment he had ever made was when he bought John.

John was thrown into a den of lions and they did not harm him, for they were blinded by the Light that shone in him.

JANUARY 15   I HAVE A DREAM

Today is the birthday of the Reverend Dr. Martin Luther King, Jr.—and a holiday in most states. He probably is best remembered for his "I Have a Dream" speech delivered in Washington, D.C., during the Civil Rights Movement of the 1960s. Dr. King dreamed of an America where people would not be judged by the color of their skin but by the content of their character. He dreamed of a land of justice and freedom for all; and although he knew that he would not get there with us, he believed that we would get there. He had seen the Light, the glory of the coming of the Lord.

Even today the mission we so often hear is to keep the dream alive, but I wonder whether or not we need a new dream. We cannot keep Dr. King's dream alive. We must have dreams of our own. If we do not live in that land of justice and equality and freedom for all, then we must dream about it ourselves and never stop until we wake up to discover that we are living the dream. Dr. King was not the only one who could have a dream.

If Dr. King were alive today, he would ask us to give an account of our dreams, not his. He would ask us, "What have you done in my absence? Did I die for nothing? Have you moved toward freedom and justice for all? Are you finally at peace or are you still fighting pointless wars?"

In every generation there is a Light bearer, a prophet, a drum major for justice. Where is ours? Can we see the Light?

JANUARY 16   NOBODY KNOWS

While I still have the struggles of African Americans on my mind, let me tell you the story of the composition of one of my favorite Negro spirituals. The spirituals were and are a great source of comfort to countless African Americans. They provided the strength that the slaves needed to survive the numerous injustices of slavery.

In Augusta County, Virginia, lived two slaves known as Aunt Ailsie and Uncle Anthony. Their old cabin was a realm of melody, for there was always singing coming from within. One day Aunt Ailsie gave birth to a child, and the glad father used every moment he was not working in the fields for his master to make a cradle for his newborn child. When the cradle was finally finished, the father could hardly contain the joy he felt as he carried it home. He could just see his baby in it, and he could just hear the songs he and his wife would sing as they rocked their child. When he reached the cabin, he found it empty! Both mother and child had been sold to slaveholders in the deep South.

Poor Uncle Anthony's reason for existing was gone. He searched the hills, forests, and fields for his family. His master could not force him to work, no matter what threats or lashings he promised. Finally, a white man who felt sorry for Uncle Anthony bought him and set him free to look for his lost loved ones. The last account of Uncle Anthony was that he was seen somewhere in North Carolina, still searching and singing his own composition:

Nobody knows the trouble I see
nobody knows but Jesus;
oh, nobody knows the trouble I see
glory Hallelujah!

We see that this man, a slave who saw the Light, produced a song that leads us all to the Light. Glory hallelujah!

JANUARY 17   **YOUR BEHAVIOR OR**
                                    YOUR NAME?

Although there must be many stories about Alexander the Great, there is one that I find particularly interesting. Alexander was a very proud person, one who believed that he could conquer the world. He felt that everything associated with him should be honored and respected.

It is said that a thief was brought before him for punishment. When Alexander asked what he had done, the thief replied that he had been caught stealing. Then Alexander asked the thief, "What is your name?" The thief replied, "My name is Alexander." In shock, Alexander the Great said, "Then you must either change your behavior or change your name!"

Alexander the Great knew that a thief's behavior dishonored his name, and he wanted only honorable behavior associated with the name Alexander. Alexander the Great never lost a battle. He built a vast empire, studied people, and was able to make friends of those he conquered. Even Napoleon recognized Alexander as his model hero, a supreme general and statesman. Surely, no one named Alexander could be a common thief.

I wonder whether or not we, as Christians, want only honorable behavior associated with our religion. What if we were told to either change our behavior or change our religion? How many of us would have to change?

Alexander the Great lived before the birth of Christ, so he did not have the example of the Light that we know. Alexander was, however, a source of light to those he knew. He required and expected the best of people. He wanted the world to change and people to be educated. He was described by the Greek historian Polybius as a man of a "superhuman elevation of spirit." Like Christ, Alexander lived only thirty-three years.

Those who walk in the Light have no need to change either their behavior or their name.

JANUARY 18   TWO IDEALS OF WOMANHOOD

About three miles from Jerusalem on the road to Jericho is the town of Bethany. Two sisters live there. You know them; their names are Mary and Martha. They represent for us two ideals of womanhood: intellectual insight and practical duty.

Mary is a woman of intellectual insight. She loves to study and to learn. She is sympathetic, understanding, smart, and curious. If she lived in today's world, she would be called a career woman. But she is a special career woman because she has seen the Light; she knows and loves the Lord.

Martha is a woman of practical duty. She's a good housekeeper. She loves to cook, sew, and entertain. We all love to go to Martha's house because she makes us feel at home. Jesus loved to visit with Martha too.

Today Jesus is to have supper with Mary and Martha. Martha is busy with the practical tasks, for she wants her house to be a spotless, shining mansion fit for King Jesus. She also wants the food to be a delicious feast.

It's a warm day in Bethany, and Martha feels drops of sweat roll down her face as she makes the preparations. Then she remembers something. Where is Mary? Mary should be in the kitchen helping her. But Mary is sitting in the garden, under the shade of a tree, at the feet of her Lord and Master, listening and learning about the meaning of existence.

Can't you imagine how this scene looks to Martha? She's hot and tired, and there is Mary looking quite cool and comfortable. In a burst of anger Martha says, "Lord, don't you care that my sister has left me to serve alone? Tell her to help me." Martha's feeling is natural, and Jesus understands. He knows that it is necessary for someone to cook because he is hungry, but he also knows that Mary needs to learn and share with him. He says, "Martha, Martha, you are careful and troubled about many things, but you need one thing. Mary has chosen the good part which shall not be taken away from her" (Luke 10:38-42).

The things that Martha was worried about would not last forever. The food would be prepared and eaten and the house would get dirty again, but the knowledge that Mary was gaining from Jesus would last forever.

The ideal of womanhood combines the spiritual and intellectual insights of Mary with the practical duties of Martha. The Light shines through both the spiritual and the practical.

JANUARY 19   **SING UNTO THE LORD**

She was born in New Orleans, Louisiana, and she once sang the blues along with the recordings of Bessie Smith. She was offered fortune and fame to sing in nightclubs, but she knew that she was born to make a joyful noise, to sing unto the Lord. Rather than use her powerful voice to belt out the blues, by faith and courage she sang only to glorify God.

Her name was Mahalia Jackson, and her extraordinary voice was first recognized nationally in the 1930s when she sang "He's Got the Whole World in His Hands" during a cross-country gospel tour. Somehow Mahalia knew that the Lord's music would feed her, and she beautifully communicated his message in song.

Her records sold in the millions, and because the Light poured out from her soul as she sang, the queen of England, the king of Denmark, and the president of the United States requested personal performances of her.

During the 1960s she became a symbol of the civil rights movement as she stood with the movement's leaders singing "We Shall Overcome." She considered it one of the greatest honors of her life to be asked to sing "Precious Lord" at the funeral of Dr. Martin Luther King, Jr.

Chicago's 4500-seat Aire Crown Theater was filled to capacity one hour before Mahalia Jackson's funeral began. That was a testimony to her courage and Christian witness to the Light. In the movie *Imitation of Life* she sang "Soon I will be done with the troubles of the world," and now she's gone home to live with God.

JANUARY 20 WORKING WITHOUT SHAME

"Study to shew thyself approved unto God, a workman that needeth not to be ashamed, rightly dividing the word of truth" (II Timothy 2:15 KJV). This verse is very familiar to me; studying has always been a big part of my life. I've always wanted to be well informed, intelligent, knowledgeable about life and the subjects with which I deal. Whether it was in my job or in the classroom, I wanted to know what I was doing and what was required. I found it interesting to observe teachers and supervisors, for some were equipped to instruct while others did not seem to know what they were doing. I could not help but feel shame and embarrassment for those who were not prepared.

The Sunday school teachers and Bible study leaders in the small church in which I grew up were willing servants of the Master, but they were not equipped to instruct. With smiling faces they would always say, "Let's read this verse and discuss it." They had not really studied so that they would not be ashamed of the way they handled God's Word. They meant well; they were just uninformed.

Even as a child it was obvious to me that teaching Sunday school and leading Bible study involved more than reading a verse and discussing it. We must study to show ourselves approved unto God, workers who can handle the word of truth without shame. At an early age I accepted that challenge, and I vowed that I would teach with insight and lead with knowledge. Whenever I am asked to teach a class or lead a Bible study, I spend hours in study and research. I never want to be ashamed of the way I handle God's Word. And it's amazing that when I commit to leading the class, God always leads me to the Light. I gain insights and knowledge that previously had been hidden.

How can we lead others to the Light if we do not know the Light? How can we know the Light if we do not study and learn all we can about it? Paul's charge to Timothy applies to all of us, for none of us wants to be ashamed before God. Make a commitment today to study so that you can work without shame.

JANUARY 21   PLAY THE PRINCESS

The story is told of a princess who ruled over a small and very poor country. Her subjects had little hope for the future and feared that they eventually would be taken over by a strong and cruel king who ruled in a neighboring land. Just as her subjects were about to submit to the cruel king, the princess dressed up in her most regal attire; and with her sparkling crown on her head and a bright smile on her face, she rode through the town blowing kisses and shouting words of encouragement. The people were so moved by her faith in their ability to survive and continue as an independent country that they worked even harder and resisted the cruel king.

The princess played her part with a zeal that defied the circumstances in which the country found itself, and her majesty and warmth gave the people the courage to go on. Once the people saw the princess, the Light surrounding her gave hope to all. The people felt that if she could be so calm and confident, then things could not be as bad as they had seemed. Her country survived.

I wonder if we are not sometimes called on to play the princess. If my family were struggling, if my husband were without a job, if my children or parents were sick, I hope I would respond in this way: I would dress up, prepare a delicious meal, and let my loved ones know that I have faith in them and in our ability to survive. What a lift we could give ourselves if we would just try to raise others' spirits when our Light has grown dim and needs to shine. We look and feel better, and we offer that positive attitude to others.

I can imagine that the princess's subjects felt compelled to find work, resist being overtaken, and secure their country for such a regal and hopeful princess. In the same way, I can imagine our families being encouraged and strengthened by such reassuring, faith-filled women. I can even imagine us looking in the mirror and being encouraged to reach our own personal goals and dreams. Playing the princess helps all of us to respond to the Light.

JANUARY 22   PLAIN VANILLA

When I was working in the data processing industry demonstrating software systems, we always referred to systems that were used exactly as they were sold as being "plain vanilla." This simply meant that if a system was to automatically produce pay checks, for example, all it had to do was calculate the salary based on the time worked and deduct the taxes plus any other deductions. It did not have to calculate taxes in several different states or pay differentials based on working partial shifts at different pay rates. The system could quite easily, without any modifications, handle a salaried or hourly employee who worked a single shift in a single state. We loved clients who had plain-vanilla systems.

Children seem to be plain-vanilla people. They are uncomplicated, without modifications, and it is easy to love them. I think of the beatitude, "Blessed are the pure in heart, for they shall see God" (Matthew 5:8 KJV). It is the children who are pure in heart, innocent, and they are the ones who can see God.

Again I remember that Jesus said, "Except ye be converted, and not become like little children, ye shall not enter the kingdom of heaven" (Matthew 18:3 KJV).

People who are pure, plain vanilla seek to lift up God, to help others see the Light. They have no hidden agendas, for they are surrounded by Light. They do not attend church to network with others who are popular in the community. Neither do they work on committees or attend Sunday school to be recognized or rewarded. They are pure.

Adults often are fooled by those who are not plain-vanilla people, but children are not. Have you ever noticed how difficult it is to fool a child? A child can see God in us or see no God in us, because those that are pure in heart can see God. They can see, and they respond to the Light.

I wish that more of us were plain vanilla!

JANUARY 23   1-2-3-4-5

I have a friend whose birthday is today, January 23. The interesting thing is that she was born in 1945, so her birthday is 1-23-45. Because the numbers in her date of birth are in order, it seems to me that her life should be orderly. She ought to be highly organized; she ought to be disciplined in all areas of life. But she is not like that.

I guess I would like everyone to be organized, disciplined, and orderly. I don't like to waste time looking for things, so I try to have a place for everything and always keep everything in its place. I like to have a calendar of scheduled events—at least a mental list of things to do each day—and a daily period of priority setting and reevaluation of tasks. My friend feels that the amount of discipline I like is too confining.

I know that each of us is different and that some of us are more disciplined than others. But it is important to set goals, to evaluate the things that consume our time, and to keep our affairs in order. We accomplish so much more when we do. I suppose that if my birthday had been 1-23-45, I would have felt justified for wanting to be highly organized.

But think about it. If you had a schedule that included time for reading and Bible study, watching one or two favorite television programs, spending time with family and friends, accomplishing household chores, and still getting plenty of rest, wouldn't life be ideal? Well, it can be done, but it can't be done by wishing. Try it just for today. Make a list of five things to be done. Scratch them off as they are completed, and place those that have not been completed on your list for the next day. Never carry tasks over more than twice. If you have not done it in three tries, it's not very high on your list of priorities. We do what we want to do.

The Light seems to surround disciplined people. They get so much done for the Lord. 1-2-3-4-5.

JANUARY 24   I REMEMBER DADDY

This is the day of my daddy's birth, and I remember him. He was not a perfect daddy, but he was mine. He was the son of a minister, he wanted to be a baseball player, and he dropped out of college after two years to get married. He worked as a railroad dining car waiter, and he traveled the route from Oakland, California, to Chicago, Illinois. He was at home one week and on the road the next week for as long as I can remember.

Daddy loved poetry, and when he was at home he would read poetry to me for hours. Edgar Allan Poe was one of his favorite poets. Although I enjoyed the poems, the important thing was that my daddy was spending time with me. I tried to learn the poems from memory so that I could say them with him as he read.

Somewhere between waiting tables in the dining car and reading poetry at home, Daddy started to drink. I am sure that, at first, the liquor was relaxing after "walking all the way to Chicago and back," as he always said. But soon he became dependent on it. Liquor is funny that way, for it is a drug that can become addictive.

The liquor finally cost Daddy his life, for the wages of sin is death, and the way he was drinking was a sin.

I wonder if unfulfilled dreams led Daddy to drink. I wonder whether it was an escape or an excuse. At the time, I was very young and not strong enough in my own faith to pray with him and refer him to the Master. I wish that my Light had been bright enough to shine for him.

Today I remember him and the love we shared. I celebrate his birth and pray he found the Light.

JANUARY 25   A-C-T-S

Prayer is an element of worship—worth-ship, or giving worth to God—that should never be omitted. A prayer alone can be a complete act of worship, and it is essential that we learn how to pray.

One summer many years ago I met Dr. George A. Buttrick, a theologian who specialized in prayer. He offered me a pattern of prayer that he said, if dutifully followed, would change my life. He was right; so permit me to share it with you.

In the morning our prayer may be a brief affirmation of faith like the Apostles' Creed. In addition to this affirmation, we may make a petition for guidance, joy, and strength. We may also pray for those nearest us and for ourselves.

Through the course of the day we can throw "spears of prayer" in the direction of God. This means that we continuously thank God for the many blessings he has bestowed upon us.

The most important prayer comes at night, so that we retire with thoughts of communion with God. Dr. Buttrick feels that this prayer should not be less than ten minutes. It should have as its components the letters of the word *Acts*, *A-C-T-S*.

The *A* is for adoration; we must adore God and tell him that we do. The *C* is for confession; we must confess our sins and unworthiness before him. The *T* is for thanksgiving; we must give God thanks for his great goodness to us. And the *S* is for supplication; after adoring, confessing, and thanking we can petition or ask God for whatever we as disciples can ask in good faith. Dr. Buttrick advises us to pray first for those we love least, then for those we love most, and for ourselves last. If we follow this sequence, our prayers for ourselves will be brief because we will have been praying a long time. We must pray seeking the will of God, knowing that his will is always joyous. This means that we pray in faith that God's will will bring us joy.

36

I praise God for Dr. Buttrick and his advice on prayer, and I thank God for the Light that surrounded Dr. Buttrick and me as I sat, listening and learning as he taught.

JANUARY 26   WINTER STORM WATCH

Today Atlanta, Georgia, is under a winter storm watch. This means that Atlantans are looking for snow and its accompanying hazardous driving conditions within the next twenty-four hours. Snow in Atlanta is usually no more than two to four inches, and it rarely stays on the ground more than one or two days. So why the storm watch?

Atlanta is a hilly town with many narrow roads, bridges, and overpasses; and because it does not snow very often, Atlanta has limited snow removal equipment. When Atlantans are warned of an incoming storm, they prepare for two to three days indoors. They buy all the bread on the store shelves, all the dozens of eggs, all the cartons of milk, and most of the cookies and snacks. Then they go to the video store to rent movies so they will not become bored and will always have something to do. Because of the fear of power failures, they buy batteries and make sure that they have at least one radio or television that can be operated with batteries. They are concerned about and prepare for their physical comfort and their social contentment.

I am always amazed when this happens. I wonder why they don't keep enough food in their houses for emergencies, and I wonder why they need radios and videos to entertain them. In the midst of all of this preparation to provide for physical and social needs, I never hear of preparations to provide for spiritual needs. I don't hear of people planning to spend the storm watch in prayer and fasting. I never hear that there has been a run on Bibles and religious study books. I never hear that people are using this unexpected free time in celebration of our Lord.

Then I remember that we were charged to always be ready, for we do not know the hour or the day that God will require our souls. Are you ready today to meet the winter storm watch of life? Is there Light enough to guide you through the storm?

Every time I read the first sixteen verses of the twentieth chapter of Matthew I am reminded of how human we all are. These verses represent one of Jesus' paradoxical parables—the normal, human assumptions are reversed. In the parable laborers are hired to work in a vineyard. The laborers who were hired early in the morning had agreed on a fair wage for a day's work. These laborers were not aware that those who were hired three hours later, six hours later, nine hours later, and even eleven hours later, were hired for the same wage.

When it was time to be paid, those who had been hired last, in the eleventh hour, were paid first; and they were paid the wage that those who had been hired first had agreed on. Those who had been hired in the ninth, sixth, and third hours were all paid that same wage. So when it was time to pay those who had worked all day, they expected more. And it seems reasonable to me that if we had worked longer we might have expected to be paid more.

However, Jesus uses this parable to teach us that all laborers who work for the Kingdom are the same. There are no different rewards for those who happen to be fortunate enough to have worked longer at kingdom building. God's grace is the same for all, and it is offered equally to all. It was so easy for the laborers, as it is for us, to compare themselves to the other workers. We often feel that we work harder and longer than others; but, if we have agreed on and are paid a specific wage, we have no complaint. Our employer may simply choose to be as generous with others as with us. Even if someone else is paid more, does that make us worth less? Certainly not in the eyes of the Master.

An early calling has no wage benefit in kingdom building. Those who have had the privilege of an early calling should be able to tell those latecomers of the joy they missed by responding so late. How wonderful it is to see and respond to the Light at an early age, but how blessed we all are that we don't have to respond early to be saved. Thank God that even if we are the last to answer, we can be the first to make it into the Kingdom!

During this winter season I think of the best-selling book by Carole Jackson, *Color Me Beautiful*. According to this book, my season is winter. This means that I look best in the vivid, primary colors of red, yellow, or blue and in the cool, icy pastel colors often found in a glittering snowflake. My neutral colors are white, black, gray, and navy. In addition to the primary colors mentioned, I also look good in green, purple, and burgundy.

Of course the purpose of this book is to help each of us to be as beautiful as we can be. When we are wearing the colors that best complement our own seasonal palette, our inner beauty is reflected in our outer glow. In other words, sometimes our outer beauty helps others to see the Light in us. If we truly reflect the Light, we are always beautiful.

Each of the seven fruits of the spirit is associated with a color, and almost all of these are winter colors. I wonder whether we reflect that fruit when we wear that color. Let's think about it.

The fruits of the spirit are *love*, which is associated with red; *goodness*, which is associated with orange; *joy*, which is associated with yellow; *peace*, which is associated with green; *faith*, which is associated with blue; *gentleness*, which is associated with indigo; and *patience*, which is associated with violet. Our favorite color is probably an indication of the strong presence in our lives of its corresponding spiritual fruit. We ought to develop all of the fruits so that no matter what color we wear or prefer, we will be beautiful and others will see the Light.

JANUARY 29   LEAP OF FAITH

A few years ago I saw a television program entitled "Leap of Faith." It was the true story of a woman who had been diagnosed as having terminal cancer. She was given very little time to live, and she was told that nothing could be done to save her life. Rather than accept this grim outlook, she decided to fight. That's when she took her leap of faith.

She began to seek unconventional and unproven treatment. She underwent hypnosis and, during her therapy, sought to fight and beat up the bad cancer cells. She would get up in the middle of the night and breathe out the bad cells and breathe in good ones. She even submitted to acupuncture; she literally did everything she could to beat her dreaded disease.

The interesting thing was that her husband supported her in all her methods, no matter how unconventional they seemed. He got up with her in the middle of the night and together they went outside in the cold air to kill the bad cells and to breathe in good, fresh ones. He helped her take her leap of faith.

But other relatives did not. They thought she was being ridiculous and told her that nothing she was doing would help. They advised her to prepare to die. But she would not listen to them. When they came to visit, she put them out of her house and told them that if they were not for her, supporting her and believing in her leap of faith, then they were against her. With great determination she explained that she had no choice but to remove all of their negative vibrations from her presence.

How many times have we dared to take a leap of faith, to go against safe conventions, to risk ridicule and failure? Do we dare tell others to take their negative thoughts elsewhere? Do we have enough faith to succeed against all odds? Well, this woman did, and she beat that cancer. The Light within would not let it live. Praise be to God!

JANUARY 30   MORE THAN THESE?

A little girl once asked her grandmother if she loved her as much as she did the other grandchildren. The grandmother explained that she had a corner of her heart especially for each of her grandchildren and that she loved them all the same. As additional grandchildren and great-grandchildren were born, the grandmother's heart just kept getting bigger so that more corners could be added. Loving hearts are like that—there's always room for one more.

Every time I think about that little girl's question, I wonder whether the child really wanted to know if her grandmother loved her as much as the others or more than the others. You see, we all want to be the favorite, the one who is the recipient of the most love.

Even Jesus asked Peter, "Lovest thou me more than these?" (John 21:15 KJV). Although Peter answered affirmatively, Jesus asked him a second and a third time if he loved him. You see, Jesus needed to determine the extent of Peter's commitment to service. Those who love the most are required to work the hardest. Those who love more than these must let their Light shine the brightest. Those who love more than these will feed his sheep.

When the little girl asked her grandmother if she loved her as much as she did the others, that little girl wanted her grandmother to feed her, to show her the affection that only a grandmother could give. That little girl wanted her grandmother to make a commitment to service. She wanted to see the Light of love in her grandmother's face. She needed to be assured that her special corner would not be given away. If all else failed, that little girl wanted to know that her grandmother's open arms would welcome her in love.

If we love more than these, we give more. We let our Light shine more. Do you love him more than these?

JANUARY 31   BE ENTHUSIASTIC!

We began this month and this year with excitement and enthusiasm because we were beginning a new year. It is important never to lose that enthusiasm.

When my oldest son was about to enter his senior year in high school, all the students began to think about who they wanted for student body president. My son said that many suggested that he run for senior class president, but he wanted to run for student body president. He had never held office before, and his reputation was that of a very smart but not very gregarious student. He asked me what he should do. I asked him what he really wanted. He responded, "I want to be president of the student body!" So, I told him to go for it.

He immediately began to work hard—putting up posters, handing out pins and ribbons, and preparing his campaign

41

speech. Although he would not let me hear his speech, on the day it was to be given and the voting was to take place, he came to me and said, "Mom, I don't want a sermon, but if you were to give me some advice before I give my speech, what would it be?" I thought for a minute and then I said, "Be enthusiastic! Nobody wants a dull leader!"

That evening when I returned from work, all of the children in the neighborhood stopped me and said, "Mrs. Kimbrough, you should have heard Walter. He really fired us up! We're anxious to make our school the best!" Well, I didn't even need to know the results of the election, for it was obvious that he had won. The members of the student body could see the Light shining brightly and enthusiastically in him. We always win when others can see the Light in us.

This year, let us be enthusiastic in everything we do so that others will know that we have been with Jesus. Just as nobody wants a dull leader, so also nobody wants to live a dull life. Get excited about your life being led by Jesus. "Let your light shine before others, so that they may see your good works and give glory to your Father in heaven" (Matthew 5:16 KJV). Ask yourself daily, "Can they see the Light?"

FEBRUARY

Day by Day

MARTHA WHITMORE HICKMAN

FEBRUARY 1   **REST IN THE LORD**

The January cover of a national magazine blocks out each of the twelve calendar months with characteristic words or symbols. For the month of February, a person with a furrowed brow is saying, "What? January can't be over already!"

I suppose that comes to all of us—the surprise that the month we anticipated, after the rush and excitement of Christmastime, to be a fresh start into the new year and perhaps a more placid mode of life has slipped away before we caught our breath. It's February already!

But wait. Maybe now is the time—not the first of January—to begin resting into and savoring a more quiet way of life. No spectacular holidays mark the short month of February—though there is Valentine's Day and the birthdays of Washington and Lincoln. Maybe this is the month for *breathers*. When I was a child in Massachusetts, we always had a week off at the end of February. A vacation in the deep hinge of winter.

So perhaps this month can be that for us—a bit of a hiatus, a resting time. Behind us are the rush and miracle of Advent and Christmas. Ahead of us is the promise of spring—but also the anguishing drama of Holy Week, the slogging through of

---

*February devotions © 1992 by Martha Whitmore Hickman.

43

despair before we arrive at Easter. But for now, let us breathe deeply, savor the apparent sleepiness of earth, perhaps feel some empathy with the hibernating creatures of the forest, and, as much as time and circumstance allow, try to rest in the Lord.

FEBRUARY 2   CANDLEMAS DAY

As I look at a calendar that lists almost every conceivable observation, I note that this is Ground Hog Day and Candlemas Day. Ground Hog Day I know well—that pleasant myth, brought to America from Germany and Great Britain, about the groundhog's awakening from his winter sleep. The groundhog sticks his head up into the February air, and if he sees his shadow, he is frightened and buries himself for another six weeks of winter. But if the day is cloudy, he emerges and spring is on its way. It is a nice amusement that may help us not to take ourselves too seriously.

The other observance, Candlemas Day, offends me to the core of my feminist heart. Historically it was a festival honoring the purification of the Virgin Mary after the birth of Jesus. The inferences are clear: childbirth is unclean, and a purifying ritual (male-directed, I'm sure) to re-establish Mary's acceptability before God is necessary.

In the old rituals of the church there was a derived observance of "the Purification of Women After Childbirth"—which certainly demeans women in one of their most exalted functions and suggests that, somehow, women are solely responsible and at fault. In early observances, candles blessed by priests were given to the poor in memory of Simeon's words to Mary that Jesus would be "a light for revelation to the Gentiles and for glory to your people Israel" (Luke 2:32 NRSV). One feels Simeon's elation as he sees the revelation of God in the infant Jesus. It is a nice observance, even though its origin may make one wince. Perhaps, as with many symbols in Christian history, we can take the good stuff and let the bad stuff go.

44

A friend with whom I share the meditations that I am writing for this month asks me, "What is your unifying theme?" It's a good question. Puzzled and disconcerted I say, "I don't have one, other than 'Februaryness'"—which, in some ways, is the gift of an uneventful month. That is, some random thoughts that have gotten pushed aside during the more programmed months—fall, Christmastime, Easter, summer vacation—are able to surface. Images that have hovered close to consciousness can, perhaps, come forth to claim their due.

During February in my part of the world, the earth lies quiet and fallow—though underground much is happening, and in the South the rhododendron buds are already bulging. Unless Easter comes early, this time of year is called "ordinary time" in the church year. I love it! As I get older, it is often "ordinary time" that I yearn for—time to savor the quieter aspects of life, to reflect on the daily gifts of life, to pay attention to what might be passed over, to avail oneself of small opportunities for service and love. There are letters we've put off writing and phone calls we've intended to make to people who need a sympathetic ear. There are gifts for ourselves, too—a walk in the woods, a special book we've wanted to read, a browse through a favorite store.

In Thornton Wilder's play *Our Town,* Emily is offered the chance to return to earth for a day, and she asks that it be just an ordinary day. The special days are too wrenching, the emotional weight too poignant, too heavy to bear.

So, welcome to "ordinary time"! Maybe we can share it together.

FEBRUARY 4   **GOD SO QUICKLY**

How else to observe this month of February, this often wonderfully quiet month, than with freedom to choose the objects of our attention in ways we may not have in the busier months of the year?

It is a time for nesting and for savoring our nests, assuming that we are fortunate enough to have a nest. In February I think of images of homecoming: childhood images of cold, snowy dusk when, tired and chilled from an afternoon of sledding, I'd come into the warm kitchen of home, to not only the physical warmth but also the warmth of my mother's presence; adult images of bringing children home after some kind of taxing adventure and experiencing the relief of getting back to our familiar setting. Even now, as I come into the house with a load of groceries, I take a moment before putting them away to enjoy the way light comes in the window, to enjoy the security of home. Experiences of homecoming—whether to one's own home, one's church, or wherever one is assured of love and welcome—have always seemed good metaphors for coming home to God.

As I anticipate this month, I expect a bit of random wandering through the associations I have with what it means to be a spiritual person—in my case a Christian—living in a world often attuned more to outer strife than to a search for inner or outer peace. Always—but especially now—I hope to listen for promptings from any source. Often it is in the unexpected moment, the unplanned event, that God speaks to us most clearly. "Sometimes there's God so quickly," says Blanche DuBois in Tennessee Williams' play *A Streetcar Named Desire*.

FEBRUARY 5   **THE GUEST ROOM QUILT**

When I was very young we had in our guest room an old spool bed with a log cabin quilt as its coverlet. I don't know the origin of the quilt; I never asked. It was just there, part of the given of home.

The quilt was put away on a high shelf when my brother was born and the guest room became his room—eventually with sturdy twin beds so he could have a friend over or my grandfather could share the room when he came to visit.

But the infinite coziness of quilts adheres to that memory— the small patches of mysterious origin, the bright pieces of speckled red, blue plaid, small brown flowers on a cream background. My sister has the quilt now, and it is a nice continuity to visit her and again see the quilt spread out on a guest-room bed.

There has been a resurgence of interest in quilts—quilts as art as well as witnesses to an earlier time, a less frenetic culture. The patterns have wonderful names—"Wedding Ring," "Nine Patch," "Dresden Plate." Sometimes quilts portray historic events. They are a good thing to ponder in February, to snuggle under in imagination as well as in fact. They warm us in many ways, with their variety, their beauty, their patterns.

Frederick Buechner speaks of our lives as having plots, although sometimes discernible only as one looks back over time. The image of a crazy quilt comes to mind—patches of uncertain conformation, making a wondrously patterned warm cover. It is a good symbol for taking one day at a time, in the expectation that if there is a pattern to our days, it may be hard to discern it now. But later, maybe later, we'll see what we have made, what we hold in our hand.

FEBRUARY 6   CORNELIUS REVISITED

When browsing in the Bible (which is sometimes more profitable to me than following some schedule of readings), I am sometimes struck by a previously unnoticed aspect of a particular story or passage. It is as though the most outstanding features of the story have been assimilated and I am therefore free to notice some of the subtler things—as with a new acquaintance: Now that I know your name, where you live, maybe even what you do for a living, I can begin to notice some of the subtler (and often most rewarding) aspects of who you are.

This morning I was reading the story of Cornelius in Acts 10. It is a complicated story, full of parallel events and serendipities and visions entertained and responded to, and the outcome is well known: Peter, a Jew, accepts an invitation to go to Joppa to speak to a group of Gentiles, who are subsequently converted to Christianity. The graphic image of the strange collection of animals being lowered on a sheet and the image of Peter (who had thought it was unlawful for a Jew to associate with Gentiles) hearing the words "What God has made clean, you must not call profane" and interpreting them to mean that the gospel is for all—this is a key moment in the development of the church.

But what struck me this time was that when the angel came to Cornelius to urge that he send messengers to invite Peter to come, Cornelius—who is described as "a devout man who feared God with all his household" and who "gave generously to the people and prayed constantly to God"—stared at this messenger "in terror" (Acts 10:4).

One might think that a man so oriented toward God that he "gave generously to the people and prayed constantly" would feel at ease, comforted, and assured in the presence of God's messenger. But instead, he was terrified.

I don't know just what this says to me—perhaps that any genuine encounter with the holy has its fearful aspects, and that our fear might keep us from acknowledging "the God who comes to us." At any rate, it establishes a human commonality to this chosen centurion who, at probably the key moment in his life, "stared . . . in terror" and then went on to follow the angel's leading into special blessedness.

FEBRUARY 7   AN EASY GIFT

One of my roles in the world is to affirm children. I have done this as writer, as parent and grandparent, and as friend.

It is easy for me to quickly establish a passing connection with children—a smile at a child in a restaurant or an airport, a wave through the front windshield at a child peering out of a car's rear window while we are at a stoplight. (This can go on for several blocks, to the point where an adult face appears, checking on the cause of the child's obvious attention.) Sometimes I am able to distract a fussing child—acknowledged by the obvious empathy of a nearby face—so that the parent will look around in relief and curiosity to see what is easing the child's distress.

I suppose that connecting with young children is easy for me because the child in me is never that far away. So it is not to my credit—I don't go out of my way; it is just that I notice children and I delight in being, for a moment only, an enhancer of life for that particular moment of his or her life.

But one of the by-products in which I also delight is the way in which this acknowledgment of a child seems to make the parent—who notices the smiling attention of a stranger—become gentler, more appreciative, more savoring of the child, too. I suppose, in a way, this is a kind of positive reinforcement. If my child is someone in whom a stranger invests attention and delight, the child becomes more special in my eyes as well. It is an easy gift for me to bestow, and it feeds me, too. How fortunate when our small gifts of gracious presence are also gifts to ourselves.

FEBRUARY 8   BECOME AS LITTLE CHILDREN

I have been thinking more about children and the witness and challenge they are to us. Sometimes their vulnerability is unbearable—as one reads of cases of hideous child abuse or sees news photos of children with distended bellies and haunting eyes. How can we allow conditions like this to prevail in the world? The politics of national and personal neglect, the descending spirals of poverty and illness, and poor stewardship of land and resources and power afflict their terrors on the weakest, the least able to protect themselves.

There are, on the other hand, people whose lives are given to enhancing the lives and well-being of children. These people seem to have such an innate understanding of and love for "who children are" that to be in their presence is to value children's lives and sensibilities even more than one might value otherwise. And one senses that children, in the presence of these individuals, become their best selves, too—self-confident, attentive, caring.

I remember hearing Fred Rogers ("Mister Rogers") speak at a national conference of children's workers. He speculated that perhaps Jesus spent as much time with children as he apparently did not because he had any particular teaching agenda or wish to "do them good," but because he "delighted in their presence." Of course, the children could tell that. The radar of children is unfailing, without guile.

May we honor the example of Jesus and, to the extent that we are able, become ourselves "as little children"—transparent, available, attentive to our immediate world.

FEBRUARY 9   A MATTER OF BEING

Yesterday I had a lot to do, and being an inveterate listmaker, I made my list—as though somehow the intention declared assures the deed done. I should know better by now!

But there was the car that had to be taken to the shop. And then there were the phone calls to find out what was wrong, and more phone calls to see if it had been fixed yet.

And there were calls for a couple of application blanks and for straightening out a bill—which required leaving a message and then being called back.

And then my husband called—he is usually careful not to interrupt my work time, but he needed some information from his desk drawer pertaining to our next summer vacation plans.

When I got to the Y to swim, they'd closed the pool because of trouble with the filtering system. And so on.

But then—there was the nice young man from the shop who brought the car back. As we were returning to the station, he told me about his two young daughters—ages seven and nine. And there was such affection in his voice that it gladdened my heart.

And we did get the financial matter straightened out. And the day rolled on, and it was dinnertime and then bedtime.

Today I started over again. I'm grateful for the cycles of each day and for sleep "that knits up the raveled sleeve of care"; and I'm grateful that today I can start again, riding along on my particular sea of faith and uncertainty, of solitude and sociability. It doesn't really matter—does it—in these quieter February days, whether all the list gets crossed off today or whether some of it is left for tomorrow, or even next week. It's just another evidence that life is a matter of being as much as of doing, and that sometimes the being is easier to attend to—to notice, even—if the doing doesn't click itself off too efficiently.

FEBRUARY 10   THEY'RE ONLY THINGS

I have spoken of February as a time for relishing our nests, which includes, of course, the things we have gathered about us. From time to time I wonder whether I am too dependent on some of these things—not elaborate, expensive things but my own particular household gods, the *lares et penates* as they were defined in high school Latin class. In my mind I catalog them: family photos; gifts my children have given me—an appliqued camel, a particular mug, a tin biscuit cutter made in a metal shop class; other things—a tiny yarn llama my husband left on my pillow before one of his trips with the words "I love you" on a scrap of paper beside it, my slotted jug-bank into which I put my childhood pennies, a small ceramic pin tray my grandmother gave me, my great-grandmother's silver berry spoon. Am I too attached tó these things? Do I define myself by them?

Several years ago on a warm September afternoon a thief broke in and took away almost all our sterling silver and a few pieces of antique jewelry that had been passed down in the family. Of course, I was upset—this was an intrusion into my sanctuary—but not too much. "They're only things," I said to my sympathetic neighbor who came to offer shared indignation and consolation.

But had the thief taken a lot more, or created havoc through useless vandalism, I'm sure I would have had unresolved anger to deal with. I remember hearing a theologian discussing this issue and saying, "We try to sit loose to our possessions"—to enjoy them now but be willing to let them go when circumstances decree it. I think that is my attitude. But I can't imagine what it would be like to be without a home—not only without shelter and warmth but also without the layers of security and association and love symbolized by these treasured objects.

So, let me enjoy them, but not be addicted to them, acknowledging again that though foxes have dens and the birds of the air have nests, there are many who have no place to call home, no place to lay their heads. Our ultimate security, as Jesus taught us, lies elsewhere.

FEBRUARY 11   BALANCING ACT

Who looks over your shoulder? Who looks over mine? Whose approval do we covet? Whom are we trying to please? Whom do we want not to irritate or estrange? Whose music do we dance to?

In a society as complex as ours, in lives as complex as many of our lives, we have many audiences, many who respond to us: young children, who probably think we're perfect; adolescent children, who probably think we're hopeless; adult children, who stand apart from us in their own space and mode but whose histories with us—and ours with them—continue to resonate, adding overtones and undertones to all our dealings with one another; spouses; business associates; church members; and professional colleagues—our particular circle of friends.

But these categories, too, divide into smaller units. My husband said that when he was young, finding his way in the world and participating in many diverse groups, one of his nightmares was that all of his friends would get together! Even adult children have different relationships with parents—birth order and gender affect aspects of those relationships.

To whom do we speak? And do those to whom we'd like to speak want to hear us? If not, we'll have to spend much of our communication energy trying to get their positive attention. Sometimes it may be worth it, and sometimes not.

I think of these issues as a writer. To whom do I want to speak? Am I content with the constituencies that are naturally mine? Do I want others? How much does it cost to court them? And will they come if I do?

I have a friend who says, "Live your life from the inside out." To maintain the integrity of who one is while at the same time honoring the reality of the particular world in which one lives and can best function seems a constant balancing act, and the checking of the weights in that balancing act is a kind of prayer.

FEBRUARY 12   **REMEMBERING LINCOLN**

At age ten, I traveled with my family to Washington, D.C., for the first time. I can still remember my exhilaration when my mother announced one night at dinner, "Daddy and I are going to take us all to Washington during spring vacation." I could hardly sleep for excitement. My announcement of the forthcoming trip to my fifth grade classmates—and my teacher—became the basis of a punctuation lesson: the necessity of placing a comma between Washington and D.C.

But among the thrills of Washington—monumental government buildings, escalators and air-conditioning in department stores, a trip to Williamsburg, and meeting cousins I'd never met before (and being startled when an apparently fine, wholesome cousin of my mother included in her offered refreshment to my then-teetotalling family "a nice, cold beer")—was that first glimpse of the Lincoln Memorial.

My uncle, always one for drama, arranged for us to have our first glimpse of the memorial by moonlight. It was—in the more reserved sense of the word—awesome. I shall never forget it—the man sitting high in his chair, the light playing on the huge figure, the surrounding columns.

Lincoln has always been, I suppose, the easiest president for us to love—at least those of us growing up north of the Mason-Dixon line. We remember his humble beginnings; that craggy, sorrowful face; the agonizing issues surrounding his presidency; the sadness in his personal life; the horror of his death.

And then, of course, we remember his words. "Words," Elie Wiesel has written, "can sometimes, in moments of grace, attain the quality of deeds." This is a long hope I have. Because I spend so much time with words, I sometimes wonder about the value of words attaining the quality of deeds in a world where there is so much work to be done.

FEBRUARY 13   POWERFUL SYMBOLS

I am more and more impressed with the power—even the necessity—of symbol and story to express the most profound truths of life, of faith. I suppose the supreme example in the Christian faith is Jesus—not a theory of limitless love but a person who loved limitlessly. The same is true for Holy Communion—not a theory of how we are organically related to Christ but a taking in, a swallowing, of food and drink that become part of our bodies, a way of keeping us alive.

We all have our own personal symbols. On a windowsill in the room where I write—among more obvious "collectibles" including a small hand-woven lion and lamb, a crystal butterfly, and a soapstone bird—are a lump of coal and two, smooth black stones.

The lump of coal was given to me by a young boy whose family we visited. It is gleaming and beautiful, with its rough, jagged slopes catching the light. It speaks to me not only of that pleasant visit, but also of my own history. My grandfather's family in England were coal miners, so this is that family revisited, reaffirmed.

I picked up the small, smooth black stones on the shore of the North Atlantic—on the coast of Iceland—on a cold, bleak day when the wind blew so hard that we had to hold our coats around us to keep them from flapping like Superman's cape. The stones have been rounded by tossing in the ocean, grinding against sand and rock. They call to mind that wonderful gaunt coast, the imagined journeys of these stones—and, yes, the daily abrasions that perhaps smooth away some of our own rough edges.

So, remember the importance of symbols in embodying life and faith:

"You are Peter, and on this rock I will build my church" (Matthew 16:18 NRSV).

"I am the vine, you are the branches" (John 15:5 NRSV).

"This is my body, which is given for you. Do this in remembrance of me" (Luke 22:19 NRSV).

FEBRUARY 14   LOVE LETTERS FOR EVERYONE

Valentine's Day, traditionally celebrated as a festival of love and romance, also honors Saint Valentine, who, during his imprisonment for defending his religious beliefs, made friends with the jailor's daughter and who, on the eve of his execution, sent her a note thanking her for her kindness. He signed it, "Your Valentine." It is a touching story and an odd progenitor for what has become such a commercialized occasion—a bonanza for greeting card manufacturers, candymakers, florists.

Still, romantic that I am, I'm not eager to banish or decry Valentine's Day, though even for me it has had its stresses— those years in elementary school when I wondered how many of the valentines being dropped in the box would come to my desk.

I think some effort now is made in schools to assure that everyone gets at least a modest number of valentines. But it used to be a more blatant popularity indicator, and it could be painful. My mother told me—not once but a number of times—how in her childhood one sent valentines only to a few most favored friends. "One year," she said, her dark eyes still hurting from the memory, "I didn't get any. Not one."

I'm sure I had my share of disappointments—as well as delicious triumphs—on Valentine's Day. I endorse all efforts to spare any child hurt feelings over not being chosen. And if one may put a Christian overlay on the love and romance of the day, perhaps it is that in the reality of God's grace—God's love for us—we all are chosen, we all are sent love letters, and no one is left out: "I have called you friends . . . You did not choose me, but I chose you" (John 15:15, 16 NRSV).

FEBRUARY 15   THE PEARL OF GREAT PRICE

As I get older, I am more aware of the need to narrow my range of activity, to cut down on what doesn't seem to be most compatible with who I am and what I do best. A few months ago I accepted membership on the board of directors of an agency with whose goals I was highly compatible—an agency that supports families during the time a family member is in prison. I have visited prisoners and families and I have written a children's book about a child with a father in prison. So I felt at home in this enterprise. Furthermore, it would ease my conscience about being socially involved—I would not be just an observer, a writer who watches from the sidelines and writes, often indirectly, about contemporary life.

But then it began to be apparent that this board was not a good fit for me. The meetings cut into my morning writing time. To function well, I would need to apprise myself in detail of the financial aspects of the agency—a time-consuming task. I was asked to help organize fund-raisers, for which I had no aptitude or interest. After a mutually understanding talk with the director, I resigned.

I have been on boards of directors whose overlap of interests with mine was less than this, and I have been comfortable with that. But I am older now, and time is precious. My sense of my own vocation, my gifts, is stronger. It's a matter of stewardship, of doing the best with what I do best.

The Bible is full of stories. Some of them speak to us and some don't; some speak to us at some times and others at other times. It is now that the parable of the Pearl of Great Price comes to me as comfort and directive: "Again, the kingdom of heaven is like a merchant in search of fine pearls; on finding one pearl of great value, he went and sold all that he had and bought it" (Matthew 13:45-46 NRSV). So, my prayer is this: "Help me to know what is mine to do, and then to do it."

FEBRUARY 16   **DEEP WATER TRUST**

I am thinking of images of trust.

Recently, while swimming at the local YMCA, I noticed a young man in a red swimsuit walking around the rim of the deep end of the pool carrying a small boy against his chest. Their arms were wrapped close around each other. I recognized them as a young father and his son who are members of the church to which I belong. I watched for several minutes as the father turned the corner by the deep end, approached the diving board, walked to the end of the board, and, with the child still in his arms, jumped into deep water.

In a few seconds they surfaced—the child laughing and brushing water from his eyes; the father using his free arm to stroke toward the ladder at the edge of the pool where he could climb out.

Perhaps it was my vulnerability at the time that caused me to be so affected by this sight of father and son jumping into deep water. I recently had gone through one of those frightening sequences of possibly ominous symptoms and tests. The tests proved negative; I was fine. But the memory of the experience and the disappointment that I'd not handled the fear better coalesced with the image of the father and the child stepping into deep water to become a powerful image of the God in whom it is safe to trust. I thought, The next time I'm faced with a crisis, I'm going to remember this father, his arms wrapped around his child, walking out over deep water and jumping off with the justifiable confidence that they'll come up again.

"O Most High, when I am afraid, I put my trust in you" (Psalm 56:2-3 NRSV).

FEBRUARY 17   MORE THAN WORDS

Yesterday I went to the memorial service of a woman whom I did not know well but who had been one of the "saints of the church." Long before I met her I heard her name—as an advocate of justice for women and for racial minorities. In her retirement, she moved to the city where I live, and I saw her from time to time. I didn't know that she'd been ill. When I read of her death and the memorial service, I decided to go—not so much out of personal loss as to honor "one of the family."

Even so—even with no personal emotional tie to the person whose life and death we were noting—I was impressed by how glad I was to have a friend slip into the pew beside me and whisper, "Okay if I sit with you?" I needed someone to be with through this occasion of solemnity and joy and sorrow—and the reminder that I, too, will make this journey through the passage of death.

I remember another friend telling of a memorial service for a man who died of cancer in the prime of his life. The service was in a church, and the man's widow and children sat in a pew close to the front of the chancel, with several rows separating them from the next pew of worshipers. My friend told how, as the service was about to begin, a signal passed along the pews and two rows of friends left their seats and moved quietly forward to sit immediately behind the bereaved family.

My heart leaps at the support in this gesture. How we need one another, not only in the words we say—often not with words at all—but also with our physical presence. We are the word made flesh—our flesh, full of our own grace and truth, offered in solidarity, in risk and in love.

FEBRUARY 18   MOUNTAINTOP EXPERIENCES

We are more than midway through the month of February. Perhaps the quiescent nature of the month—not the height of winter, not yet into spring—is beginning to pall. But wait, the ground is stirring. It won't be long.

And there are heralds of spring. Unless Easter is very late this year, the beginning of Lent—Ash Wednesday—will fall in February. And before that, on the Sunday preceding Ash Wednesday, will come Transfiguration Sunday.

Transfiguration Sunday: the original "mountaintop experience"—archetype of all those pairings of exalted moments of religious intensity and the subsequent need to "return to the valley" where the world awaits our attention.

According to the story, which appears in three Gospels, Jesus took Peter and James and John and went up on a mountaintop. Suddenly "he was transfigured before them, and his face shone like the sun, and his clothes became dazzling white" (Matthew 17:2 NRSV). Then Moses and Elijah appeared and spoke with Jesus, and a voice came, saying, "This is my Son, the Beloved" (Matthew 17:5 NRSV). Astonishing! Is it any wonder Peter suggested they stay, so they could continue to be transported by the assurance of God's being, God's reality—not to mention the assurance of life beyond death in the presences of Moses and Elijah!

No, Jesus said that wouldn't do. And after the vision faded, they went back down and Jesus again began ministering to the crowd. But surely the disciples now had a whole different mentality. Even in the darkest time they could summon up this sacred memory, hold it against the desolations that might follow, remind themselves of it, and so restore their faith, their hope.

And so do we—with this story and with our own cherished sacred memories, our own mountaintop experiences remembered.

FEBRUARY 19   THE BEST PART OF WAKING UP

The weather forecast last night was for snow—one to three inches by early morning. Waking early, I look out the window.

The brown grass, silvered by the first light of morning, is what I see. In this mid-South city, snow stops traffic, causes slow-ups and accidents. We have a trip to make late in the day that will be much harder if it snows. "No snow yet," I say to my husband, "but the sky looks ominous."

An hour or so later we have had breakfast, he has left for work, and I am at my desk. I have read the paper. The world outside is grim, and it still may snow. I turn with particular longing to some spiritual reading, choosing a journal I have read before. (Douglas Steere reminds us that nowhere more than in spiritual reading is variety unimportant. Indeed, favorite readings acquire a history of layered meanings that make them especially valuable as nourishment for the spirit.)

But my spirit doesn't quiet. Instead, a tune runs randomly through my head—except these tunes are never random. They are psychic codes. Sometimes they are only fragments of songs; but, if I listen, they give me a leading clue—they ask the right question. I have learned to pay attention.

The song this morning puzzles me. It's an advertising jingle—"The best part of waking up"—extolling a particular brand of coffee. What kind of clue is that, I wonder—beset by anxiety about the weather and the world situation.

The song suggests its own question. "All right, then, what *is* the best part of waking up?"

And the answer that comes is disarmingly simple, but able for the moment to waft away stress and the threat of storm: "Just being alive." It is a gift for any day.

FEBRUARY 20   A SIGNIFICANT FLIGHT

As I anticipate the beginning of Lent I think of images of trust.

One of the things no one ever told me about having children is that one of them might go into aviation. I suppose it should have come as no surprise. My son always has had an interest in machines and an almost intuitive understanding of how things work. At one and a half, he identified by name the sound of a motorcycle two blocks away. As an adolescent, he spent his allowance to learn to fly a sailplane. Then, after a couple of experimental tries at other vocations, he decided to "go for it." He borrowed the money for flying lessons and a post-graduate course in flying and then started up the vocational stream—instructing, flying cargo, flying commuter planes, flying with a major airline.

But one of the moving moments of my life (in more ways than one—it was in an airplane, after all!) was flying with this son for the first time—in a small three-seater airplane that was so light that you would bump your head on the ceiling if the plane hit an airpocket.

I did have a moment of misgiving when, readying for takeoff, my son pulled a sheet of paper from under the instrument panel and began to read it. I have done a lot of sewing in my day, and the function of the pattern instruction sheet came to mind. "Are you reading the *instructions?*" I asked with alarm in my voice.

No, it was the take-off list, and this was required procedure.

So we took off, up into the sky, and I was not surprised that tears sprang to my eyes. This child whom I had carried, in my body and in my arms, was now carrying me! It was a good image of trust. It was one of the sacramental moments of my life.

FEBRUARY 21   **ASHES OF HOPE**

Ash Wednesday, the first day of Lent, often comes in February.

When I was growing up in the industrial Northeast, Lent was not often observed among Protestant Christians, though I was aware that many of my Roman Catholic classmates had the custom of giving up something for Lent—chewing gum or eating candy. I was just as glad that my tradition called for no such deprivations!

But in later years, Protestants have made more observations of Lent—such as occasions for special services and special studies. I've been glad of this seemly preparation for the profoundly painful and then profoundly triumphant occasions of Maundy Thursday, Good Friday, and Easter Sunday. Perhaps we can appreciate better the life-transforming joy if we have walked through some of the lowlands of anguish and apparent defeat.

One of the services that means the most to me is the service on Ash Wednesday, the beginning of the forty days of Lent. In our church, it is a brief service held in the early evening. There is the reading of Scripture, prayers, a few words of preparation, and then, as each in turn kneels opposite the kneeling pastor, the imposition of ashes, made from burning some of last year's palm branches. "Dust you are, and to dust you will return."

It is a sober statement, a physical reminder of our own mortality. More sobering still, perhaps, is hearing these words recited as the ashes are placed on the forehead of a loved one.

Yet one remembers, in hope and gratitude, other loved ones whose bodies have already fallen to decay. And one remembers that the message of Ash Wednesday, of Lent, of Holy Week, and of Easter turns the sting of death into the triumph of resurrection!

FEBRUARY 22   AN ORDINARY HERO

Washington's birthday, I suppose, is still observed in elementary schools, though the civic season lumps it with Lincoln's birthday to make Presidents' Day a three-day weekend—providing getaways, cluttering airports, and giving retailers another occasion for a sale.

Who was he? Surely the stories children hear about Washington embroider his life rather than deal with the basic threads—the warp and woof—of who he was. There is the story about the cherry tree which gives children a model: don't lie. There is the recognition that his extreme height, in comparison to other men of the time, was one of the reasons he was a good leader: he could be seen! There is the conjecture that the reason he's so sober in Gilbert Stuart's famous painting is that his wooden false teeth were of fragile attachment, which would cause one sitting for a portrait to keep his mouth shut. These are not awe-inspiring stories about our first president, the father of our country. I'm sure scholars do better by him. But for the man or woman or child in the street or classroom, there is in

Washington little of the giant moral stance or the poignant, tragic face of Lincoln—with whom he must now share the day.

But Washington did have the plantation at Mount Vernon, and to go there and smell the boxwood and sit at the top of the slope and look down toward the Potomac is to experience George Washington as statesman, as a presence in the early days of the republic. And there is the other famous painting of Washington, standing in the prow of an apparently ill-equipped boat as the small company of soldiers crossed the Delaware.

Washington the hero is made known to us through the real and imagined details, the images and stories of daily life. In this way Washington is like Jesus, the image of God, who, among more cosmic attributes, ate and drank, wept, cherished his friends, and delighted in the presence of children.

FEBRUARY 23   RISKING IN FAITH

Even if one has not grown up with the tradition of giving up something for Lent, it is a good time to think about simplifying our lives, to think about what we cling to and what we give up, sometimes out of choice, sometimes out of necessity. I have mentioned the wisdom of not being addicted to one's personal treasures—a favorite piece of furniture, a collection of books, even an abundance of family photographs. The dangers are not only that we may lose our treasures by fire or theft or feel overrun by our possessions, but also that we may move to smaller quarters when we get older.

What will be hardest to eliminate, to give away or discard? As I contemplate the already crowded drawers of my desk and try to wedge in another file folder, and then another, I acknowledge that among the hardest things for me may be incompleted projects—nebulous dreams of what else I might do.

Long ago I gave away the scraps of cloth for a pieced quilt. Years ago I wrote to a cousin telling her not to save the cello for me any longer—I'm never going to learn to play it. A dream relinquished.

Harder for me to relinquish will be the notes for extended writing projects I've thought about pursuing and now know that

I never will—or the manuscripts I've not been able to sell but have kept on the shelf, thinking some day.

Can I give up these things? I'll have to, some day—and will probably feel freer, though a little sad—to have done it.

But the astonishing gift of Easter, for which Lent prepares us, is that the most devastating apparent failure turned mysteriously into triumph. It doesn't mean that all our failures will become successes. It does mean to me that risks taken in faith are worth taking. Because who knows?

And it means that somehow the triumph of Easter sweeps through all our failures, saying, *I love you. I will care for you. I will be with you. That's what matters. You'll see.*

FEBRUARY 24   GIVING UP FRETTING

One of the vocational hazards of being a writer, especially a reflective writer, is that sometimes the habit of reflection goes to extremes. If, as Plato said, "The unexamined life is not worth living," then perhaps the overexamined life can be equally hazardous to fullness of life. I remind myself of this, or try to, until I forget my good intention and go spinning around and around on my worry-track.

There's always something to fret about—a manuscript that isn't going well, the state of the publishing industry, the state of the world! One's children (though they are grown, established, and now your good friends) are always good subjects for fretting—not only about current concerns but also about remembered incidents when we didn't act with the utmost wisdom.

Possibilities for fretting about friends and acquaintances are endless. We keep going over and over a difficult conversation in our minds, wishing we'd then had the insight we have now. We mull over the difficult turn a relationship has taken.

It is hard to know how much of this is our wish to control and how much is a genuine regret that we've not been able to do as well as we'd like. But it's not hard to know that this kind of running in place, this kind of hovering over sore places, does no good. Sometimes we *can* redress an old wound. But, more often than not, we have no choice but to let bygones be bygones and to try not to cling to what we should let slip from our hands.

I heard a sermon not long ago that touched on this kind of foolish replaying of old hurts and worries—which is really, I suppose, a kind of distrust of life, of God. Somewhere in the development of the preacher's thought were the words, "Let it go. Just—let it go." It has been helpful, and I invoke it often when there seems to be no available solution. (Sometimes a solution isn't even called for.)

Maybe this needless fretting is one thing I can happily give up for Lent. For a lot longer, too? Maybe, but these few weeks are a good beginning.

FEBRUARY 25   IMAGES OF LIFE'S JOURNEY

Outside my window a female cardinal perches on a wire stretching from the corner of the house to the telephone pole. She sways there a moment in the light breeze, then drops on a swooping arc to the ground and flies off out of my sight. She is unprotected, free from any pattern I can see. I am enamored of her image this morning, as I sit at my desk surrounded by the weighty matters of my own body, this office, this house.

I think of another image that never fails to intrigue me, to set my imagination adrift. It is, of all things, the experience of going through an automatic carwash!

There is, for one thing, the intent focusing of attention during the experience—being sure the windows are closed tight, driving onto the ramp at just the right angle and just far enough. Then, once secure in this cocoon of glass and metal, one is witness to such a display of power—the rushing water, the whirling brushes, the machinery thumping on the roof. One is a voyeur to all this violence and adventure, but perfectly safe. Still, invariably, the walls appear to move backward—surely some mysterious transportation of energy is doing the fearful unexpected. The mind is called to remember: It is an illusion; never fear.

Then the rush of water stops. The brushes recede. The lighted sign reads: Exit Slowly. One goes out into the world again, this mini-drama having refreshed the mind and spirit as well as the car.

The vulnerable bird on the wire, the protected person going through the maelstrom—these are images to savor of the variety of our journey through life.

FEBRUARY 26   LONGING TO LIVE

One of the things I know about myself (and don't particularly like) is that I have a low threshold of health anxiety. A mysterious twinge that lasts more than ten minutes, an irregular heartbeat (Is it caffeine? Is it that seven people are coming for the weekend? Or am I on the verge of a heart attack?), or a change in any of the customary rhythms of my body and I am trying to be poised as the doctor tells me I have a fatal illness.

Not only would I not be poised at such a moment, but I also would not be poised even thinking about it—even though I know that these recurrent anxieties are part of my legacy from a long, nearly-fatal childhood illness. That period of illness also gave me its gifts: Keen observation (Someone has said, "Sickness sensitizes a person for observation, like a photographic plate"); a sense of the preciousness of life and a delight in the gifts of sight, touch, taste, smell, hearing; a special rapport with children, because I have dwelt in childhood with a particular intensity.

Anyway, there it is, and what am I to do about it? One thing I want to do is to forgive myself, because I, for whom faith is a central lodestar of life, am so easily panicked at the thought of the loss of life. I believe in a loving God, in a life beyond death, in the assurance that "nothing can separate us" from God's love— perhaps death least of all. Then, why do I panic? I see people, read their testimony, who are serene in the face of imminent death.

But wait. Maybe I will be, too—if I get through the stages of denial, anger, bargaining, depression, acceptance. But it will take some time. The human response, as with all other animals, is to be fearful enough to mobilize for preservation. And I know that there have been times when, before the tests were in, I felt the cloak of love and freedom from fear creep over me, and I felt I would be fine, whatever the outcome.

It is an act of faith that this blessed assurance would, in time, come to me again. It also comforts me to know that Jesus loved the world in all its quandaries and gifts and prayed in the garden, "If it is possible, let this cup pass from me" (Matthew 26:39 NRSV). Let me escape this if I can. It is a different story, of course, but the acknowledgment of a wish to avoid anguish, to stay with life, speaks to me, too. I think of it, as we head toward Easter.

FEBRUARY 27   STEPPING PAST OUR COMFORT ZONE

On a television show, a group of women speak of their *comfort zone*—and of the effort and reward that accompanied their pushing themselves past their usual level of comfort. They were speaking of mountain climbing. The thought of groping in a string of rope-bound climbers up the face of cliffs holds no allure for me! But I thought of a time when, as a child, I balked at leaving my own comfort zone and what I learned from that.

It was February, spring vacation. My sister and I were to travel by train a day's journey to visit an aunt and uncle. My father would take us to the train in the early morning. My aunt and uncle would meet us at the journey's end. No train changes were called for. My mother had packed us a lunch. We had our tickets. Nothing to do but get on the train.

We were wakened before first light to get ready to go. My sister, a year older, was confident and eager. I was terrified—I don't know why. Perhaps it was just the uncertainty of it all—going on our own, and the night still dark.

We dressed, then I bade my mother (who was staying home with the younger children) a tearful good-bye. We set out on the drive to the station. I'm sure I pleaded with my father not to make me go.

He, wiser than I, put us on the train, kissed us good-bye, and left. I waved to him out the window, through my tears.

Within twenty minutes I was fine. And by the time we reached our destination, I was jubilant with the adventure, so relieved my fear had not dissuaded my father from sending us on our way—though it must have been hard for him, too, being the tenderhearted, loving parent that he was.

I still have no wish to climb mountains, and I am reluctant to leave my own comfort zone. But I am grateful to remember a time when an adventure seemed terribly fearful, and I would have turned away—and, once launched, how I loved the whole thing. Perhaps those of us who are fearful are more than ordinarily exhilarated when, by choice or by force of circumstance, we are able to step past our fear.

As I get older and want to cling to the securities of what I am used to, let me remember that morning when I didn't want to go, and trusting in the wisdom of others who loved me, I went. Perhaps these are "nudges from God" to help us enlarge our lives.

FEBRUARY 28   LIFE'S SEASONS

I'm going to speak to a group of women about "The Seasons of a Woman's Life." The occasion has me thinking about my own seasons. Hovering on the edge of senior citizenship, I have a long way to look back.

The years of childhood are imbued in my mind with a kind of security and coziness, which was true overall but which surely had its lapses. There were times of health crisis, times of disappointment (a friend who had promised to come and play didn't come), times of anxiety (I thought my brother, whose care had been entrusted to me, was lost), and times of loneliness (those Sunday afternoons with their bittersweet tenderness when I would get out my watercolors and paint—there was no television then, and for my family Sunday afternoon was a time of quiet).

And then these were the tumultuous years of adolescence followed by the uncharted years of young adulthood; worries about popularity; the heady excitement of college and the receding barriers of available knowledge; a first job; falling in love; getting married; and bearing children and tending to their growth.

Then came the bonanza, or so it seemed, of beginning a second career as a writer when the children were launched into school and the recognition that the delay in starting this career meant an apprenticeship when I was already well into middle age.

More recently there have been the marriages of children, the utter joy of grandchildren, and the pleasures of undistracted time with my husband.

The seasons are paced out: spring, summer, fall, winter. Now, in what I suppose might be considered the winter of my life, it doesn't seem at all as though I'm heading into some port of closure, some dull and ominous finish. "I live one day at a time," as the song puts it—"I dream one dream at a time."

These are good days, good dreams. Some of them, perhaps even long-delayed dreams, come true. And here at the end of February I am reminded how our faith tells us that in life-seasons as well as in nature, past the creaking gray silence of winter, is the promise of a whole new riot of life! "For now the winter is past, the rain is over and gone. The flowers appear on the earth; the time of singing has come" (Song of Solomon 2:11, 12 NRSV). So let it be for us!

MARCH

Gold in the Old

MAXINE DOWD JENSEN

MARCH 1   **WINDS OF CHANGE**

The one who . . . creates the wind . . . the LORD, the God of hosts, is his name!

—Amos 4:13 (NRSV)

March is fickle. Chicagoans, especially, know about the wind.

Wind or no wind, I'm a crazy walker. I stroll in the rain, relishing its tears on my cheeks. I plod through virgin snow. To me, it's as if I walk alone with God. The silence, the apparent absence of any living being, brings me a step closer to my Creator.

However, more than either of these, I like striding against a stiff wind. It's a challenge.

When I moved to Arkansas, I found gorgeous springs—springs that I reveled in—and the songs of myriad birds, but I missed the saucy insolence of Chicago's March wind.

Wind plays a psychological part in our lives, too.

Numerous layoffs and plant closings in the early part of the year may have stirred up a whirlwind for you. The death of a mate, a parent, a child, or a close friend sometimes blows open unexpected and unwanted doors.

Winds of change. They come for every one of us. But the

God who created us and the wind can provide courage and protection. He changes not. He's the same yesterday, today, and forever.

Oh, Lord, who changest not, thank you for the differences in my life, for the gentle times, the quiet moments, the challenging periods, and the open doors when I find one closing behind me. Guide me during this month. Use me for your service.

MARCH 2   THE IMMEDIACY OF THE MOMENT

(Read Genesis 12:1-5.)

Perhaps three words from my lips that both my mother and my husband disliked the most were, "In a minute." And, when I was younger, they issued from my mouth with great frequency. "Procrastinator" described me and, sometimes, I put off things longer than a minute.

I always ran. There never seemed to be enough time for my many interests. Yet, I crammed them in.

Before my marriage, I agreed to many singing engagements. I rushed down to Northwestern evening school. I couldn't refuse to go to the basketball game scheduled for the teenagers for whose youth group I was cosponsor. In all of these, I hurried.

Though I read the Bible daily and picked up many insights for controlling and guiding my life, it wasn't until after the deaths of both my mother and husband that I began to appreciate Abraham and the message his experiences held for me.

I found the most impressive advice in my NIV Bible beginning with Genesis 12. God told Abraham to leave Ur. He left. God gave other instructions, and immediately or the next morning Abraham carried them out. Because of this passage, I now take more thought for my projects.

It has not been easy for me to realign my life. My singing, my writing, and my youth work have all been important to me. So, day by day, I decide which task should take precedence. Like Abraham, I expect, rely on, and receive God's leading.

So can you.

MARCH 3   THE DISAPPEARANCE OF ILLNESS

(Read Exodus 23:20-23*a*, 25.)

Recently, I began retracing my steps in a Bible given to me one Christmas by my mother. Since I always mark my Bibles with dates and comments, I've enjoyed rereading some of the happenings and statements of those earlier days.

Another habit of mine, when I was younger, was to choose a verse for the coming year from whatever passage came next in my reading on New Year's Eve. One December 31, my verse for the year became Exodus 23:25.

The past year had not been a good one for my mother. The doctor had forbidden her from going up and down stairs and from taking her two-mile walks every other day. He'd told me to find an apartment on the ground floor. She didn't obey him, but I looked for a new flat.

Ground-floor apartments were scarce, and landlords wanted prospective tenants to pay a bonus. I couldn't afford the latter. I'd become our breadwinner at age eighteen. At twenty-one, I'd paid for my father's funeral and for two operations needed by my mother after his death. So, we had no savings.

As I kept searching for a first-floor apartment, I felt that Exodus 23:25 was a verse I could count on.

One day, a janitor and member of our church told me that I might be able to rent an apartment in one of the buildings where he worked. I did. The walk from the entry hall to the apartment door was only five steps, and the apartment even had a back porch where mother could rest in the fresh air.

As I read my notes in that old Bible, I thanked God for the year he took sickness away from our home. I look forward to finding other memories. They will be there.

Does the leather on your Bible still smell fresh? Do the gold edges continue to glisten? Or do you mess yours up, too?

MARCH 4   LITTLE THINGS MEAN A LOT

(Read Leviticus 11:44.)

Often in life we can cope with the big things. It's the little things that trip us.

As I'm writing this, I've not been to church in the past four Sundays.

Of course, I've had a reason for three of these. The roads were covered with ice. So, why did I feel guilty when I read this Leviticus passage? Probably because only light snow lay on the ground yesterday and my notation on the meaning of sanctify read "set apart for the service of God." To me that includes regular attendance at church.

I've asked God's forgiveness, even though he knows that my husband drove in this kind of weather in Chicago and that when I lived alone in Arkansas, everything came to a standstill when it snowed. No school, no church, not much of anything moved.

However, the snow that fell last Saturday night was different than the snows of the weekends before. Previously, it was either preceded or followed by sleet. Yesterday, no sleet lay underneath or above the snow. But, I saw the snow and yielded to the temptation to stay home. My guilty feelings arrived when I watched it disappear just before Sunday noon.

Maybe you think this is a minor matter—too insignificant for God to be bothered by it. But the Bible says that if we are faithful in little things, God knows he can trust us in the big ones.

The Lord has never failed me; I want to be equally trustworthy whenever possible.

Lord, help me to be careful about the little things.

MARCH 5   DAUGHTERS, DAUGHTERS, DAUGHTERS

(Read Numbers 26:33; 27:1-8.)

I just received an announcement of the birth of a third daughter to a couple who have no sons, and I thought of Zelophehad. He had five daughters; no sons.

The sadness in his heart then might have been greater than it would be today. Sons were needed more then. They grew up to help fathers with their work. Sometimes they rose to the level where they sat in the gates or became leaders of their tribe. A son was a special arrow in the quiver of a man.

In that day, every name had a meaning, and Zelophehad's sorrow was evident in the name he gave his first born. He called her Mahlah, or *sickness*.

When Noah came along, I can picture Zelophehad walking through the fields, perhaps snatching off heads of grain in his disappointment.

I believe Zelophehad mellowed a bit when Hoglah arrived. Her name means *partridge*. I know I smile when I see a line of quail marching across my front lawn.

Then came Milcah, *counsel,* and Tirzah, *pleasantness.*

In these names Zelophehad gave to his girls, we can see the growth of a man. I like to think that those who preceded Tirzah made such an impression on Zelophehad that he rejoiced when she was born. And, had he lived, how proud he would have been of them!

These girls dared to approach Moses and ask for an inheritance, saying how faithful to God their father had been. Previously, only young men were inheritors.

Perhaps Milcah spoke for them. As a good *counsel,* she told of her father's life and made a good case for herself and her sisters.

When Moses approached God about their request, God agreed with the girls. They are part of the reason you and I enjoy the privilege of an inheritance today.

MARCH 6 — TEACH YOUR CHILDREN TO FIND TIME

(Read Deuteronomy 6:4-7.)

Today everyone rushes. Perhaps no one rushes more than a mother.

A woman who works outside the home returns to a myriad of tasks; the woman remaining in the house has those same chores plus chauffeuring Bobby to Little League, Tiffany to ballet class, and picking up Dad at the train. When can we find time to teach our children to love God with all their heart?

After my youngest daughter married and had her first baby, a long-time friend of the family moved next door to her. This woman had an injured arm, and my daughter drove her many places because the woman would say, "I just can't handle my car except for the few blocks to the beauty shop."

Then my daughter bought a condo a short distance away. A week after her move, she telephoned me. "Guess what?" she said. "Edith drove herself all the way out to the new mall. Can you believe it?"

"Yes, we usually can do what we *want* to do," I said.

I wanted to learn to be a writer, so, in spite of my other responsibilities, I saved my pennies for courses at Northwestern University.

When friends asked, "How do you find the time to go to evening school?" I'd reply, "I go to find time to write." It sounded like a paradox.

Children are the most precious enigma God puts in our hands. My sister-in-law believed this. When her children interrupted with questions, she turned off the iron or stood the mop on end. She listened and answered. Her house isn't a model for housekeeping, but three of her children graduated from college and all have become interested and interesting adults.

All of us can find time to do what we really want to do. The non-essentials can wait.

MARCH 7   WHAT A YEAR CAN HOLD

(Read Joshua 3:5.)

One New Year's Eve, I claimed the promise of sanctification for the next year—for the last part of the year, that is.

I'd heard of some faiths in which sanctification was an important process, but I didn't know what it meant. I needed to find out before I could claim the wonders.

On one of the blank back pages of that old marked up Bible, almost too indistinct now to read, I wrote the meanings of sanctify.

But, I wondered, "How can I attain this level? How does one become sanctified?" I began to check the Bible verses containing that word.

I found that we are sanctified, not necessarily in the following order, by the Word, by faith, by the Holy Spirit, by the sacrifice of Christ and of God the Father, and by prayer.

I knew I could use strengthening in all of these, except those already provided me by the Lord. I began the New Year determined to be a better Christian. God did the rest.

In February, I was among the twelve service representatives of the city's telephone company to be chosen to work on the debenture issue. This five-week stint resulted in a promotion to a better-paying job—and one that proved easier to do.

Then, in May, under unusual circumstances, I met and began dating one of the nicest men I've ever known.

God is no respecter of persons. When we follow the Lord's instructions, great and welcome surprises can happen for us.

Lord, touch the parts of my life where I need to draw closer to you.

MARCH 8   WHY NOT YOU?

(Read Judges 6:12-16a.)

Today I received a thank-you letter from a reader who was led back into the book of Deuteronomy with a set of my meditations that appeared in *These Days*. In the letter, the woman said she'd been "widowed three times all with prolonged serious illnesses." She went on to tell me she'd asked, "Why me, Lord?" and that the Lord had replied, "Why not you?"

I'm a widow. I have two friends who've been married three times each. One lost her first two husbands to death; the other has just lost her third husband the same way.

Psychologists tell us that no trauma affects individuals as severely as the death of a spouse. I believe them. There are too many of us who ask God, "Why me?" I also believe the answer should be "Why not you?"

We Christians are *in* the world though not *of* the world. Therefore, we are subject to the same temptations and problems and losses as everyone else. If this were not so, there probably would be thousands more who profess Christianity for the sole purpose of avoiding earthly trials.

However, we possess not an accomplice to aid us in

wrongdoing but an accomplice who is joined with us in solving any situations we face.

With God, we can stand up to any trial, any loss, any temptation and come *through* it a stronger, better Christian. Our Lord can replace the bitterness of mourning with joy (Isaiah 61:3).

Lord, God, in this my hour of loss, assure me of your presence with me.

MARCH 9   ANOTHER HEART

(Read I Samuel 10:1-9, 26.)

I assume you are a church-going believer or you wouldn't be holding this meditation book in your hands. However, if I think this way, I may be overlooking someone, and I don't wish to do that.

But I'm a writer. I like to picture what my readers look like and what may be in their hearts.

Perhaps, like Saul, you are tall, well-built, and eye-catching. Though I think David had red hair in his younger days, I can't picture Saul's coloring. Nor can I picture the color of your hair.

I'm assuming again, but because you are reading this I believe you know a group of people whose hearts God has touched. One or two may be in your workplace. Perhaps they surround you in your women's society. You may know someone in a choral group or sit beside someone in an evening class. Or one may be a dear, God-loving lady in a nursing home where you visit.

Of one thing I'm sure: you would not be reading this book unless some woman or women, at some time, had touched your life for God.

Are you aware that if you haven't walked as close to God as you should or would desire, God can give you another heart, as he did for Saul—a heart open to the words he left behind for all of us?

He's as close as a prayer. Good things can come to pass for you when he is your Savior and Lord.

Oh, Lord, hear my prayer. Give me a new heart to serve you.

MARCH 10 ANOTHER WAY

(Read II Samuel 22:30-31.)

People don't always choose a direction for their life that someone else believes is the right one.

Once I read a book titled *I Leaped Over a Wall*. The story told how a nun came out of a convent and returned to life outside those walls.

When my friend Viv revealed she wanted to enter a Poor Clare Monastery, I was devastated. I tried to talk her out of it.

"You're so good with children. You have so many ideas for promotions and parties. You've nursed your mother for two years. There are so many other orders that you could enter where your talents could be used. But, *that* one?"

Viv had a problem. While caring for her mother, she had passed the maximum age for entry. But she kept trying.

As I prayed for her to come to her senses, I remembered my father. He was the oldest and smartest son. My grandfather wanted one of his sons to be a doctor, and he chose my father. After working his way through college and medical school, my father rebelled. So, one day I said to Viv, "It's not for me to criticize what God may be leading you into. I'll pray for the Lord's will to be done."

A month after I married, Viv married the church.

I've visited her a number of times. The Reverend Mother Abbess has given my book for widows to those seeking help in the convent. The sisters pray for my continued writing success. I see Viv's eyes, the smile on her face, and the lift in her voice that even comes through in her letters. She is in God's chosen place.

It's not for us to select another's vocation. We can suggest. We can pray. Then let's leave it to our Lord.

MARCH 11 A GUARDIAN ANGEL?

(Read II Kings 6:13-17.)

A few weeks before Judith Anderson's mutilated teen-aged body was discovered in an oil drum in Montrose Harbor, my mother and I had moved to the Chicago neighborhood from which Judith disappeared. At about the same time, the newspapers told of a rape that happened near a corner I had to pass every morning. Though I knew these occurrences were few in this area, I'll admit I felt a bit squeamish.

The week after the Anderson killing, as I started down the block adjacent to my corner apartment building, a large Doberman pinscher exited from between two houses. Now, ever since I'd been jumped by a German shepherd when I was eight or nine, I'd possessed a fear of unknown dogs, and often I sent a prayer to heaven when I felt threatened. I did so this time.

The black dog walked down to busy Central Street with me (the street where Judith supposedly had been waylaid). He crossed the street alongside of me and continued four more blocks before I turned south on Laramie. Then he turned around to go back.

During the two years before my marriage when I lived in this neighborhood, that dog walked from between those two houses and kept me company every morning. Sometimes he walked in the parkway a bit before me. At other times he'd be behind. Occasionally, beside me.

After several weeks, I told my mother, "I think he's my guardian angel. No one who sees us together will try to attack me. They'd think he's my dog."

Have you ever walked dark, threatening streets, entered an empty apartment, or heard strange sounds and been afraid? Don't you know that God is only a whisper away? Surely, as with Elisha and his servant, the hosts of God will protect us. Trust in the Lord.

MARCH 12   FIRST WOMEN'S LIBBER?

(Read I Chronicles 7:20-27.)

Imagine my surprise when I read I Chronicles 7:24. Was Sheerah the first feminist? I think so.

I called my first set of meditations for *These Days* "Gold in the Begats." I included Sheerah. She fascinated me. She was the only daughter among nineteen brothers, nine of whom she never knew. She lived in a day when women didn't do the things that men did. But God's word includes an aside after her name, telling of her three cities.

I had to find out more.

Although Sheerah's name is never mentioned again, Gideon chased and conquered an enemy between Gibeon and one of her towns, and Solomon rebuilt two of them.

After "Gold in the Begats" appeared and I began getting letters, Sheerah also surfaced again. She began pestering me with questions such as, "Why did I decide to build a city?" "How did I learn to construct one?" "What problems did I face in getting men to work for me and getting cooperation from the sellers of the tools and supplies I needed?"

I couldn't help myself. I had to research her era and write a novel telling her story. It turned out to be the most exciting writing I've ever done. I could hardly wait to get to my desk each morning to find out what would happen next.

Surely you must have some dreams, some unfulfilled desires. Think of Sheerah, and don't be afraid to try to realize them.

I haven't sold my Sheerah novel yet, but, one day, I will!

You can use Sheerah as a model of determination against tremendous odds. Don't be afraid to try your "thing." You, too, could be as successful as she was!

MARCH 13   WISDOM FROM GOD

(Read II Chronicles 1:9-12a; 9:23; and James 1:5-7.)

My best friend through high school and junior college had a method of studying that was different from mine. She crammed. When I crammed, everything became muddled. So I had a stock prayer. It went something like this: "Lord, help me to remember everything I've learned, and don't let the teacher ask anything I don't know."

My friend and I made nearly identical grades.

As I matured, I realized lots of things seemed like mazes to me. It wasn't until I memorized the first chapter of James that I fully realized God could give me wisdom to make right choices.

Exactly a month before my husband died, my early pension

became effective. Later, my boss said that he could rescind it so that I could return to my job. He'd not yet selected a permanent replacement. I declined, because retirement gave me the chance to try to fulfill my dream of writing full time.

However, the night I sank into my chair to read the news after entertaining two estimators regarding moving charges and the tax consultant who prepared my income tax forms, I wondered if my prayers had led me to the right choice. Was I foolish to try to write, hope to manage some travel, and move from Chicago to our vacation home?

I read the paper back to front—a habit probably left over from when the comics were on the last page. Almost immediately, I came to the investor's column. As I began to read, I thought, *This sounds like me, but I didn't write it. He has the same desires.*

Then I read the answer. It started, "I don't want to snow you. It won't be easy . . ." and it ended, "Go to it. I think you'll have a ball." To me, it was God's vindication of my choice.

When we expose our hopes and options to God's all-seeing eyes and ask for wisdom, it will be supplied.

MARCH 14   THE ANGEL OF THE LORD

(Read Psalm 35:1-5.)

I woke up this morning telling God, "I love you." Often, I awaken with these words, and I praise the Lord for special things. Today I praised the Lord for health and the husband God led into my life.

Then I turn over on my back, lie there looking up at the ceiling, and remind him of all the friends I have who need special attention today. Gert and Sally just buried their husbands. Aunt Mary, one hundred years old this past December, will lay her last child to rest today. Anne, a dear friend, cares for a sick husband.

Last, I sit on the edge of the bed and think of the possible problems of my day. *I must spend time with the devotions I'm writing. And I have to start putting my income tax figures together.*

After this, I sit on the edge of the bed for my morning devotions. Today I got no further than the fifth verse.

I know the sparkle rushed into my eyes and a smile wrinkled my cheeks as I pictured the angel of the Lord chasing after all my requests.

Strange! I'd never noticed this phrase before. But, then, that's the Bible: fresh every morning, new every night.

In my mind's eye, I could feel the breeze as the white garments swirled behind *my* angel. I heard a faint rustle of wings. Did a right hand go up to steady a halo?

I'm a dreamer, and I'm glad of that, because God often reveals something in a new light to me—something I can muse about.

Will it help you today, or tomorrow, to picture *your* angel chasing after *your* problems—hurrying to make life a little safer or easier for you?

I hope so.

MARCH 15   THE IDES OF MARCH

Julius Caesar called "Speak . . ." and ". . . speak once again," and the soothsayer replied both times, "Beware the ides of March."

In the ancient Roman calendar, the fifteenth day of March was designated "ides." Julius Caesar was warned about the ides of March; it proved to be a bad day for him.

When I studied Shakespeare's writings, I laughed at March 15. I thought of the groanings and moanings that used to take place just before that date. That's when income taxes were due. Is that why the IRS changed the deadline to April 15? If so, the change doesn't help much.

The Bible warns us against soothsayers and fortune-tellers. These people possess a fascination that lures many, to be sure. Today there are other prognostications that should be believed.

Television commercials, for example, warn us of the dangers of drugs and alcohol. Programs in schools and organizations and videotapes tell the story of how harmful things can look and feel so good. Even a popular song says, "If it feels so right, how can it be so wrong?" But the end result of many harmful things isn't often revealed. The end is the same as the end for Julius Caesar on the ides of March—spiritual or physical death, or both.

We should heed the advice of Jeremiah 6:16: "Stand ye . . . and ask for the old paths, where *is* the good way, and walk therein, and ye shall find rest for your souls" (KJV). The sad thing is that people still say, just as the last portion of the verse records, "We will not walk therein."

Have you forsaken an old path? Perhaps it's *only* the path of going to church regularly. However, even forsaking this could result in spiritual death.

MARCH 16 THE HAND OF THE LORD

(Read Ezra 8:22.)

The hand of the Lord lay upon Ezra. In chapter 8, we find this hand extended toward others. I especially like the Modern Language Bible's translation of Ezra 8:22, "the hand of our God protects all who seek him . . . ."

I imagine you remember my Doberman pinscher protector. If, like me, you go back over your life, you'll recall times when God protected you. Two other events in my life stand out in my memory.

On my first trip alone after my husband's death, I headed for Lexington, Kentucky. I started about 5:00 A.M. By the time I reached Paducah and the first four-lane highway on my journey, I'd driven many miles at 35 MPH. At Bardstown, my watch said 4:00 P.M. and I thought, *only sixty more miles*.

Just as I got up to speed, my purse lurched off the seat. I grabbed for it and then watched as I headed down a ditch, through a barbed wire fence, and into a cornfield. The car was badly damaged; I sustained only a fractured right arm. God's hand?

A few years ago, I got dressed to go to our monthly Musical Moments meeting. As I reached for the back door knob, I felt my hand being stayed. I decided not to go.

About 7:30 P.M., wind began to shake my porch canopy, rain beat against my front windows, lightning lit up my rooms while thunder crashed over my head. I went to bed after the lights went out, knowing I could roll off one side and pull the mattress on top of me. A tornado was in the area.

The next day, I learned the program lasted until nine instead of the usual eight. The tornado had hit a quarter of a mile east of me and then moved down the highway into town. Had I attended the meeting, I would have driven directly into its path.

The hand of God? I believe so.

MARCH 17   THE LETTER "I"

(Read I Kings 3:5-10.)

Several weeks after I began vocal lessons with an elderly Swede who'd studied in Italy, he asked, "Your parents are from Ireland, aren't they?" I answered, "No, they're not."

A short time later, he asked again. I said, "I'm of Irish descent, but why do you ask?"

"Because of the way you sing the letter 'I.' Don't lose it. It distinguishes your voice from others. Every great singer has possessed such a feature."

I thought, *He's getting old. What does he know?*

But when I sang in Wisconsin, a little woman with a thick Irish brogue said the same thing about my pronunciation of the letter "I."

Again I shrugged this off, until my teacher died and I began to study with a younger woman. One day she said in an exasperated tone, "I don't know what you do with your 'I's,' but you don't sing a clean one. You must change it."

Since I felt Mr. Blomquist was a better teacher, I never tried to change, but I began to wonder, *What do I do with that letter?*

A few years ago, I visited Ireland and spent an evening at a dinner and vocal concert at Bunratty Castle. I listened intently. Then I heard it: the same letter "I." When I spoke to several of the singers, they, too, had been unaware of what they were doing. I did not hear the letter spoken in the same way that it was sung.

I thanked God for the distinctive Irish sound that pleases many, but then I wondered about my speaking. Do I "follow the truth at all times—speaking truly . . . and so become more and more in every way like Christ . . ."? (Ephesians 4:15 *TLB*) Do you?

Lord, make me more like you in every way, so that all may know my descent.

(Read Nehemiah 4:6.)

I like Nehemiah. He possessed qualities that many women have.

First, he showed an interest in people—in the Jews who had escaped captivity—and he wept and mourned and fasted and prayed because of his concern.

Like many of us, he put on a happy face for his employer, Artaxerxes, but his sadness over the fate of his people showed through one day. Hasn't your sadness shown through, even though you may have tried to hide it?

He also prayed without a thought of where or when it might be appropriate, and he did something some of us forget to do. He prayed *before* he attempted things or sought solutions to problems. I, too, have found that praying before saves me trouble.

When his employer granted his wish, he inspired those in the city of his father to rebuild the walls. In my life, I've often been an encourager. Haven't you?

Nehemiah didn't hesitate to speak up. When Sanballat and Tobiah and Geshem insisted Nehemiah meet with them, Nehemiah refused. He kept on with the job he felt had been entrusted to him by God. Like Nehemiah, everyone in the story had a particular job to do. So also each of us has a sphere of influence owned by no one else, and some of us stand firm in our spheres just as Nehemiah did.

In chapter 5, verse 7 lets us know he even talked to himself. I've done this, too. Haven't you?

It pleases me that he gave credit to the proper parties: "So built *we* the wall . . . for *the people* had a mind to work" (my emphases). I also like the way he closed his book: "Remember me, O my God, for good."

I like the book of Nehemiah. If you have never read it in its entirety, I hope you have enjoyed this "taste" enough that you will do so now.

(Read Psalm 37:1-5.)

My mother was a worry-wart. So I'd tease her about her favorite Bible chapter, Psalm 37. "Mother," I'd say, "how can a scripture that tells you to 'fret not' be the one you like best, because you're always fretting?"

Of course, I knew some of the reasons she worried. All our relatives lived a minimum of five hundred miles from us. Things happened at night in the big city, and every weekend of my dad's three-and-a-half-year illness I worked from 4:00 P.M. to midnight at a second job. After his death, whenever I could afford it, I went to night school. I also was accepted in Chicago's Swedish Choral Club, and we had evening practices and orchestra hall concerts. This meant that I was on public transportation and the streets late at night.

Probably all of us have a worrier in our family. Instead of being upset when they fume, we can help them.

Early in my teens, I began a "trick" to help my mother—and she never caught on. I gave her an expected return time of an hour later than I thought I'd make it. That way, I had the extra hour. If I came home when I believed I would, she was happy. I was early. If my errand kept me later, I could phone to extend my time.

Whenever possible, I left a name and number where I could be reached in case she needed me. Often I invited her to come along. We enjoyed our trips together. In these ways I succeeded in saving her many wasted hours of fretting.

If your worrier is someone you love dearly, or even a casual friend, you can succeed by making life more enjoyable and less traumatic for them. Think of the various ways.

MARCH 20   I TALK TO EVERYBODY

(Read Proverbs 17:1-5.)

Today I scanned the sports headlines and read that a tennis player I dislike was ousted at a prestigious tournament—one he had won the three previous years. I was glad. I didn't even remember I'd read the last half of Proverbs 17:5 just this morning. At least not until I smirked at the headline one more time.

Did the Holy Spirit remind me? He does this to me. This time I wondered why I sometimes dislike people I don't even know.

After I scrutinized my feelings, I realized it's people in the sports world who cause me to rejoice when they falter. I talk to strangers, ordinary people, and I rarely find one I dislike. Would I think differently of these stars if I could converse with them? Would I come to dislike my favorites if I knew them?

During my late teens, an attractive girl began attending our church. Her light blond hair suited her deep blue eyes and alabaster skin. Her clothes fit well and were exquisite. She entered and left never speaking to anyone.

My friends thought she was stuck up. But I talk to everybody. I soon found out shyness, not aloofness, caused her actions. I also discovered that she made all her clothes, which showed her proficiency.

I introduced her to a young man (to the displeasure of my friends who knew the boy). I sang at their wedding. We are still friends and she and her husband complement each other as I knew they would.

We need—I need—to pry beneath the surface. Many times people are wonderful when we get to know them.

Lord, help me not to judge by face value. Help me probe beneath the surface.

MARCH 21   OLD AGE

(Read Ecclesiastes 12:1-5.)

My fourth book has recently appeared in bookstores. I can really like the name because it wasn't my idea, though it's something I might say: *"Old" Is Older Than Me.*

Ecclesiastes paints a poor picture of old age, but one that doesn't have to be true for everyone. Yes, old hands may tremble, and often the backs of older people are bowed. But medication can help the first, and a walking stick can help the second. If we brush, floss, and go regularly to the dentist, we may keep all our teeth. Cataracts can be removed, retinas patched up, and glaucoma halted.

True, we may need hearing aids and more sleep than when we were younger. Our fears, especially in big city environments or isolated areas, may increase. We may not be able to do as much, and our desire for certain pleasures may slacken. But, *we don't have to give in to age.*

Have you ever thought that each day you live brings you that much closer to heaven?

Perhaps you believe your life has been a failure. Mary Pickford, long ago star of the silent movie, once was asked at a party to give her philosophy of life. After hearing her, a guest who was an editor asked her to write an article about how she looked at unhappy experiences as a beginning rather than an end. The article evoked so much mail that it was later published as a little book: *Why Not Try God?*

Among the things Mary wrote were the words, "you may have a fresh start any moment you choose for this thing that we call 'failure' is not the falling down, but the staying down" (from *Light from Many Lamps*).

MARCH 22   JOY FOR MOURNING

(Read Isaiah 61:3.)

I've moved recently from a place where I lived for seventeen years. There are numerous things I miss, but none reach deep inside me more than the loss of my birds. Brown thrush, gold and purple finch, meadowlarks, snow birds, cardinals, bluebirds, blue jays, robins, humming birds, and others clustered around my feeders and made their nests where I could watch their families grow.

Usually I surveyed them from the deck at the back of my home or from my study window where many nests cropped up in the arborvitae just outside.

One year I hung three flower baskets across my front porch. As I watered them one day, I scared a tiny wren from her nest. So the next year, I was more careful when watering.

Then one day I noticed a large mourning dove ensconced among my shocking pink petunias. Faithfully she sat. Rarely did I enter or leave by my living room door. I warned expected friends, and I probably glared if a salesman appeared at the front.

Then, one day, she was missing.

I watched for her return before I climbed my little step stool to peek. There lay two jelly bean eggs. As I cleaned the nest out, I dropped one of the eggs. There wasn't even the semblance of a growing embryo. She had known. She had flown away to the future.

Immediately, I thought of younger women. *If they should lose a baby, will they go forward not looking back?* As I prayed, I thought of Isaiah 61:3 and whispered, "God, if or when that happens, please replace their mourning with your oil of joy."

MARCH 23   **NEW EVERY MORNING**

(Read Lamentations 3:22-25.)

I don't know about you, but there have been mornings when I didn't want to open my eyes. When I first read Lamentations 3, the verse that stood out was not one of those in our reading for today but the 27th verse, where it said it was good to bear the yoke during your youth. I didn't agree with that.

In my eagerness to get ahead so that I could support my family better, I took a position where I dealt with an angry public. But I was supposed to stay calm and pacify them. I fully believe this is what brought about my asthma. The seasonal shots didn't alleviate my symptoms; the medication caused a deep sleep from which I hated to awaken.

Always one who seeks a solution to a problem, I decided to visit relatives in Washington state and friends in Colorado at the height of the hay fever season. My mother went with me.

I found relief from my symptoms and a prospective job in both places. All I had to do was advise them when to expect me. Moving to Colorado was out, because my mother couldn't stand the altitude. But she didn't want to live in Washington, either. "I wouldn't know my way around. I don't know anyone but Ann and Will," she said.

I wrestled and prayed. Then I told her, "Unless I can find relief, we'll be moving to the Pacific Northwest."

Then, through prayer and a fellow employee, I finally located an allergist who helped me. Once again I realized that "great is thy faithfulness" is true of my God.

Are you troubled today? Seeking a way out of a bad situation? Pray, then get up tomorrow expecting to see the Lord's mercies.

Thank you, Lord, for your constant love and care for us.

MARCH 24   A WRITER'S GIFT

(Read Ezekiel 3:19; 9:2*b*, 11.)

Sometimes God speaks to me in the strangest ways. I'm sure this happens to you. Such was the case in these verses from Ezekiel.

A few years ago, a letter came which began, "I've been wondering, ever since I saw a quotation from a piece by Maxine Dowd Jensen, whether you are the Maxine Dowd I knew in Austin High School." I'd attended Austin my freshman year. I looked at the signature. I'd known only one Gertie, and I had met her that year. Her maiden name revealed that it was my long ago chum.

She wrote that she'd been trying to find me ever since to tell me, "Your witness bore fruit sooner than you thought." I was confused. Ezekiel 3:19 describes "witness" as my church believed it. However, never had I spoken this way. I've felt my life and my praise of God should show my beliefs. As it turned out, I'd bubbled over with joy when we met. She felt I was a Christian, and she wanted what I had.

I was busy with hospice duties when the letter arrived, but I remembered what a writer friend had told me. She'd said, "Max, you can touch more people with your pen than you can ever help one-on-one." Gertie's letter may have proved that to me.

Ezekiel had another gem for me. I was thrilled to find these words: "one man among them . . . with a writer's inkhorn by his side"—a man who could say, "I have done as thou hast commanded me" (KJV).

89

If you are a writer, reexamine your priorities. Can you do more with your pen? If the answer is yes, begin to weed out the less profitable occupations and replace them with the talent God has given to you. It's a special one!

MARCH 25   UNDER THE FIG TREE

(Read Micah 4:4-5.)

When I was a teen I wondered about many things I read in the Bible. One of these was when Christ told Nathaniel he'd seen him "under the fig tree." From time to time, I'd try to picture what Nathaniel did under that tree. It couldn't have been something bad since Christ didn't seem to be rebuking him. Nor did Christ refuse him admittance into the special group of twelve. Micah 4:4 says that many shall sit there, and when they do, "none shall make them afraid."

Recently my minister mentioned Nathaniel and his fig tree in a message, so I asked him about it.

He said that "under the fig tree" meant to study the Scriptures, to be seeking answers, to be interested in holy things. In theological seminaries it has become a catch phrase: "I can tell you've been 'under the fig tree.' "

How many times does God see us there? Is it only when we have cause to be afraid?

I'm determined to spend more time there—not just when I'm worried or in some other kind of need.

How about you? Do you want to know more about God and obtain answers to the mysteries in the Scriptures?

Lord, help me to spend more time with you, learning and understanding the messages your word has for me so that others may know I've been alone with you.

MARCH 26   A BROKEN MIRROR
AND A PRAYER FOR PATIENCE

(Read Romans 5:3.)

When I was eighteen, two things happened that I'll never

forget. I broke a mirror and I prayed for patience. Both were mistakes, and for the next seven years, it seemed like I paid for both.

I'd planned to enter Northwestern University in the fall, but my father was brought home from work, never to return again.

A man in my church lied to me. As a result of that lie, I took the job he offered. I was fired at the end of the week. He wasn't the owner.

My mother, in her attempt to help me financially, contracted strep infection. Her fever lasted five weeks. I prepared lunch for my father and instructed him to make sure that my mother gargled. After work, I attempted to ease my mother's nights by caring for my father.

My father died three and one half years later, and before I could finish paying for the funeral, my mother needed two operations. I worked seven days a week to keep us afloat.

I couldn't understand why all these things were happening. I didn't believe the seven years of bad luck could be attributed to the breaking of a mirror. I was a Christian. I believed God would supply all our needs, so I lived by faith.

Then, one day, I discovered Romans 5:3: "tribulation worketh patience." I brashly looked up and said, "God, I'll never pray for patience again," and I never have. Somehow, some way, I seem to acquire it in certain situations, and with Habakkuk of old, "I will rejoice . . . the Lord God is my strength." He was my strength during my seven-year ordeal, and he continues to strengthen me.

He can do the same for you.

MARCH 27   UNFINISHED BUSINESS

(Read Haggai 2:1-5.)

Some of us have unfinished business in our lives, just as the restored remnant saw only part of the temple. Haggai's task was to encourage the people to complete the project.

As a child, I started many handcraft pieces and stopped before they were through. When a hard task confronted me, I sometimes gave up. My mother had an adage she hoped would spur me on: "God helps those who help themselves." Haggai had a similar one for his people: "be strong . . . and work: for I am with you." When I read it, I thought of my mother.

It took me twenty years to finish my first afghan. I started it before I ever began working, so I didn't have enough money to buy all my yarn. After getting a job and seeing my fellow employees knitting at noon, I dragged it out again. When I was transferred to another office, I put it away. But after marrying, I knew my husband needed something to cover him when he napped on the sofa. So I finished it, twenty years later.

Other things are unfinished in our lives. There may be a sister from whom we are estranged. Our parents may have fought against our marriage and we have turned our backs on them. A former friend may not even know the reason we stopped seeing her.

Unfinished people business can poison our lives, make us less than we should be, stop us from doing certain tasks.

Why don't we decide to be strong and work toward a reconciliation? God will be with us as he was with Haggai and the restored remnant.

MARCH 28   TWO BRAVE WOMEN: JAEL

(Read Judges 4.)

Some of us skip over stories of lesser known Bible women. Therefore, when we read Judges 4, we remember Deborah but we don't remember Jael, whose name means "wild she-goat."

Jael was the faithful wife of Heber, the Kenite, who severed himself from the other Kenites and became a friend of the enemy. He was among those who showed Sisera that Barak, Sisera's enemy, had gone up to Mount Tabor. Jael left with her husband.

We can imagine her quietly serving when Sisera was a guest. We discover that Sisera noticed her. Why else would he, when his army was routed and destroyed by Barak, have fled to the tent belonging to Jael?

Jael invited this tired, foot-weary man to come in. When he lay down, she covered him with a mantle. When he asked for "a little water," she opened a bottle of milk and gave it to him.

If we read between the lines of this story, we can assume that Jael did not agree with Heber's decision to leave the Kenites. Her heart belonged to her people and her God.

After Sisera lay sleeping, she took a tent stake and a hammer and lived up to her name. She smote him to the ground with the nail through his temple, killing him.

Deborah had told Barak that a woman would "see to" Sisera, and as Barak approached the house of Heber, Jael met him and showed him his fallen enemy.

Sometimes we are called upon to do unusual deeds to save someone. As Deborah and Barak sang praise to God, we, too, can praise the Lord for the abilities and courage he gives to us.

MARCH 29   TWO BRAVE WOMEN: JUDITH

(Read Judith 9.)

Like Jael, Judith required great courage to perform a difficult deed for the sake of her people. When Nebuchadnezzar sent his general, Holofernes, to surround her town and starve it into submission, she resented the decision of the councilmen to bow to the call of the majority of citizens to surrender within five days if no help came.

This beautiful widow devised a plan to save her people. She convinced Uzziah to open the gates for her, and she and her maid began their journey to the enemy camp. Along the way they met an Assyrian patrol. Judith's cunning and beauty persuaded the men to accompany her and her maid to Holofernes' camp.

Holofernes was impressed by Judith's wise speech and physical beauty, and she and her maid remained in camp for three days. On the fourth day, Holofernes invited Judith to a banquet for his personal attendants. After dinner and drinking, Holofernes fell into a drunken stupor. When the attendants left, Judith took Holofernes' sword down from the bedpost and killed him.

Then Judith and her maid went out together as they were accustomed to do for prayer, and they made their way back to their city. The enemy was cast into confusion by Holofernes' death, and Judith's city survived.

I doubt that I would have been as brave. What about you?

MARCH 30   ASK FOR GUIDANCE

(Read Joshua 2.)

Just as there is evil in the best of us, so also there is good in the worst of us.

Rahab was a harlot, a prostitute. Yet God used her and rewarded her for hiding two spies sent by Joshua.

Do we categorize people? How would we treat a harlot?

One of my teenagers came to me one night with a problem. Although I was co-sponsor of their youth group, they knew I never revealed what they told me in confidence.

As soon as she began to speak, I knew from my extensive reading that she was dealing with a personal issue that she was not yet even aware of. I sent a fast message to heaven saying something like, "Lord, don't let me look shocked, and help me to guide her."

I listened for nearly three hours. I didn't know until later that this is what professionals are taught to do: listen, not probe.

She took two of the three suggestions I made at the end of our talk. However, evidently she never took the most important one: to trust the Lord as her Savior and let him help her.

I'm sure you've often heard the phrase, "Hate the sin but love the sinner." If we would be like Christ, we must think on this.

Lord, if I ever have the opportunity to counsel a troubled individual such as Rahab, help me to ask for your guidance and try to lead them to you, the solver of all our difficulties.

MARCH 31   A LIFE VERSE

(Read John 3.)

Have you ever thought of adopting a life verse? You are never too old to choose. In fact, your verse may change at various stages of your life.

I always sang as a child and my mother would repeat, "You're just like your Aunt Becky. She couldn't carry a tune in a bushel basket either." However, when I committed my life to the Lord, he not only set my heart strings singing, but he tuned my vocal chords as well. So it was no wonder that I loved the verse in Isaiah which said, "Behold, my servants shall sing for joy of heart."

At about age sixteen, I decided I should read the whole Bible. The Old Testament might prove as dull as people said, but it was God's Word, too. One day I found my spiritual birthday was the same as the beginning of the Feast of Trumpets. My eyes lit up at that information!

However, as I matured, I felt I needed a life verse. No one that I remember had ever spoken to me about it, nor do I recall even hearing the expression. But I wanted a verse to guide me my whole life through.

I began my search.

None seemed to fit my inmost desires, my goal, until I reread John 3. I've forgotten the circumstances now, but verse 30 leapt out at me: "He must increase; but I must decrease." It became my personal slogan.

Oh, I've fallen far short of my aim at times. I know I haven't always pleased God or my fellow men and women. However, it's been my ultimate desire ever since that special day.

God has a verse especially for you.

Lord, help the reader of these meditations to love your Bible more and to discover a special verse for her life.

APRIL

Isn't It Wonderful!

LENOIR H. CULBERTSON

APRIL 1   **GOD'S FOOLISHNESS**

April Fool's Day! This is the day that your shoe stays untied, and that spider keeps crawling on your shoulder. Foolish fun indeed! But on this day I would like to think of the foolishness of God. How foolish (from the perspective of "winning" and "success" in the world) of God to *so* love the world that he would give his only Son. How foolish and how wonderful!

I remember as a high school freshman experiencing an earthly taste of this magnificent "foolishness." My older brother had come home from college on spring break. As the little sister, I felt pretty unnoticed in his full agenda of visiting with old friends, until one afternoon he came bursting into the house, shouting for me and pulling me toward his mud-encrusted jeep, saying, "I want to show you something."

This initiated a two-hour trek toward Holston mountain, from paved road, to gravel, to dirt, on to weaving and bumping through ravines and trees. It was beginning to get dark and I was getting cold and tired. I couldn't see that we were getting anywhere in particular, when suddenly, he threw the jeep into reverse, backed up a few feet, and turned sharply to the left. Leaping to the ground, he motioned for me to come to the front of the jeep. There, visible in the circle of light from the headlights, bravely blooming in the last snow of winter, was one little red trillium. "Isn't it wonderful?" he whispered. How wonderful, indeed!

Not only did a tiny, "insignificant" flower remind me of the hope-filled promise of spring, but I also received a graceful gift of love from my brother. I, even I, in my perception of insignificance, was of value to him.

How did the psalmist put it? "O Lord, our Lord, how majestic is your name . . . when I look at the heavens, the work of your fingers, the moon and the stars . . . what is humanity that you are mindful of us? And yet, you have made us inferior only to yourself" (paraphrase of Psalm 8).

"For what seems to be God's foolishness is wiser than human wisdom, and what seems to be God's weakness is stronger than human strength" (I Corinthians 1:25 GNB). How wonderful, indeed!

APRIL 2   PERCEPTION

Have you ever seen those pictures that illustrate optical illusions? The kind that if you look at it one way you see birds flying and if you look at it another way you see fish swimming? Perception—how we see—makes a big difference in the way we interpret the world and therefore respond to the world.

Jesus came into the world in order to improve our *perception*. He came that we might perceive the circumstances of life, ourselves, and others through the eyes of the kingdom of God. Perception is not a game or a trick, but rather a major contributor to our understanding and experience of abundance in life. This notion came into focus for me as I heard a speaker read a letter from a college student that went something like this:

Dear Mom and Dad,

Since I have been away at school, I haven't been very good about writing, so I thought I'd write now and bring you up to date. First of all, please sit down. You must sit down before you read any more of this.

I'm getting along pretty well now. The skull fracture I got when I jumped out of the window of the dorm when it caught on fire is pretty well healed now. I was only in the hospital for two

98

weeks and I can almost see normally out of my left eye. Fortunately, the fire and my jump were seen by a gas station attendant near the dorm. He called the fire department and visited me in the hospital. Since the dorm was destroyed, he was even kind enough to let me move in with him. It's just a one room apartment, but it's cute. He's a nice guy and we have fallen in love and plan to get married sometime before the baby arrives. Yes, I am pregnant. I know how much you are looking forward to being grandparents!

Now that you are up to date, I need to tell you that there was no dorm fire, I didn't have a skull fracture, I am not pregnant, I am not getting married; and I do not have a steady boyfriend. However, I am getting a "D" in English and an "F" in calculus. I wanted you to see those grades in proper perspective.

Love,
Cindy

Perception can make all the difference! And what is the perception of faith? You are created and valued by God; therefore you can love yourself and your neighbor—life has a purpose.

APRIL 3   IMAGINATION

How marvelous is the gift of imagination! My friend Suzanne told me about a picture her little girl drew for her at age two. It basically consisted of one large purple blob in the middle of the page.

"That's nice, Katie. Can you tell me about it?"

"It's a house and two cows."

"I think I see the house here, but where are the cows?"

"Mom, they're behind the house!"

That's imagination! Victor Hugo once said, "There is nothing like dream to create the future." That's imagination, too, for to imagine is the first step toward making something real.

Thomas Edison had to imagine the light bulb before he could begin the long process of designing one. Alexander Graham Bell had to imagine the telephone before he could ever come close to assembling one. Abraham Lincoln had to imagine a unified nation with freedom for all before he could work toward establishing one.

Imagination is the first step toward making something real, and in this sense the church is a community of imagination. Jesus came into the world, and through his life and death and resurrection, he has called us to imagine the kingdom of God, a kingdom of righteousness, justice, and peace. When we can imagine it as real, we are taking the first step toward living it as real.

But imagination takes effort and demands that we see beyond what is to what may be: God calls us to use our best gifts of imagination to awaken the reality of the kingdom of heaven in our midst.

APRIL 4   FOLLOW ME

Easter! Christ is alive! Christ is risen!

Once there was at least a budding recognition of the reality of the Resurrection. Christ's first words to that frail and fragile group that would become the church were "Go and tell my brothers to go to Galilee and there they will see me" (Matthew 28:10 GNB).

In other words, don't hang around tombs; go to Galilee, the place where the needs are, the place where we were about performing the work of healing the sick, touching the afflicted, and sharing the good news!

What we find, in essence, is that the call of the risen Christ is much the same as the call of the man Jesus: "Follow me." But this "follow me" did have one different quality. The call was no longer a once-in-a-lifetime offer, but now it was an invitation for all lives for all time. It no longer applied just to a few who were willing to roam the dusty hills of Palestine. It was, and is, and will be an invitation for us all: *Follow me! Go to Galilee and there you will see me—go where the needs for ministry are, and there you will see me.*

Perhaps this thought should give us a little push in the midst of our Easter celebrations. Perhaps it should be a reminder that the risen Christ does not hang around too long in the places where the glad hallelujahs are ringing. More likely, he is back on the Emmaus Road, trying to help some confused and lost person find his or her way through the meaning of the promises of the Scripture. He is inviting himself to the house and into the life of a Zacchaeus. He is looking for a Matthew or a Mary Magdalene, trying to open real life to them. He is still looking out across the faces of the crowd with compassion in his heart.

And if we would see him, let us go on to Galilee. Let us follow him along the paths of service in the spirit of compassion. Then, and only then, will the treasure of Easter be truly opened to us. Hallelujah! Christ is risen! Christ is risen, indeed!

APRIL 5   PATTERN OF FAITHFULNESS

As a part of the one-hundredth anniversary celebration of our church sanctuary, each family was asked to bring a scrap of cloth that represented them in some way. For weeks, pieces of tablecloths, bedspreads, old ties, and baby blankets came pouring in. These pieces of fabric were pieced together into a magnificent patchwork banner. Holding all the scraps of varying texture, quality, and size together in harmony of purpose was a large gold cross stitched in the center.

Over and over again in my life, the presence of Christ has brought a sense of harmony of purpose out of what seemed to be a heap of scattered scraps of dreams and hopes and desires. Sometimes in the midst of the storm, I couldn't see either the pattern or the purpose, but I should have trusted that it would come, because faithfully, across the years, it always had come.

"Why are you afraid?" Jesus asked his disciples. "Has not all that you have seen and heard confirmed in your hearts who I am? Do you still not trust my power and my love?" Jesus continues to ask us, "Why are you afraid?"

Martin Luther, during episodes of struggle or doubt, would reportedly touch his forehead and say to himself, "Martin, be calm, you are baptized." The work of God symbolized in baptism has always been to form good worlds out of emptiness, to bring light to the darkness, to bring life where there was death. Oh, to trust that pattern of faithfulness!

APRIL 6   UNLIKELY CIRCUMSTANCES

Have you ever taken the time to read the genealogies of Jesus in Matthew's and Luke's Gospels? I especially like the one in Matthew 1:1-17. At first it strikes one as being a long list of names that were put there in order to be hard to pronounce, but when you begin to think about those names and recall the stories of those lives, that list becomes a profound theological statement. It depicts Jesus as the true heir to messiahship through the royal line of Abraham, David, and the kings of Judah, but it also makes a masterful proclamation of the sovereignty and creative power of God, even the freedom of God.

Take, for instance, the names of the women in that list. It wasn't normal to include women's names in Jewish genealogies. Remember that this was the age when every Jewish male awoke to the morning with the prayer, "I thank thee, O God, that I was not born a Gentile, a slave or a woman." Women had no legal rights and no social standing, and yet here is this parade of women's names. That's extraordinary! Not only are they women, but they also are undesirable persons. This is amazing. Rahab was a prostitute in Jericho. Ruth wasn't even a Jew, but a Moabite, an alien and hated people. Tamar was an apparent seducer and adulteress. Bathsheba was the woman David seduced and then, with incredible cruelty and gross disregard for human life, set up circumstances so that her husband Uriah would be killed in battle.

Matthew is saying in a subtle, quiet, yet profound way: "Listen! Remember how God has been at work in the world in the past? God has taken the most unlikely circumstances, the most unlikely times, and the most unlikely people and, in a profound grace, has shaped them into expressions of the divine will and love, and has channeled through them, amazingly, the grandest of God's blessings for humankind."

In the midst of this Easter season, I recall Frederick Buechner quoting what he calls a "crude German saying": *"Wie Man's macht, ist's falsch,"* which means, "Whatever men do, it turns out lousy." Looking at the cross, one might want to affirm that statement. But think of that list of names and consider the sweep of salvation history. Isn't that how God has often worked—by celebrating great triumph in the lousy moments, by celebrating wisdom in what we consider foolishness, by celebrating liberating opportunities in what we consider desperation? God has taken the most unlikely circumstances, the most unlikely times, and the most unlikely people and, in a profound grace, has shaped them into expressions of the divine will and love and has channeled through them, amazingly, the grandest of God's blessings for humankind.

Lord, take the unlikely circumstances of our time; take us—a most unlikely people—and work in and through us a profound grace.

APRIL 7   THE HURT OF YESTERDAY

On a beautiful, warm, sunny day, a friend of mine was mowing the lawn when suddenly a large maple tree crashed to the ground, crushing the lawn mower just inches in front of him. After taking several moments to recover from the shock, my friend began to inspect the tree, searching for some clue as to why this seemingly healthy tree, for no apparent reason, had splintered right before his eyes.

Before long, he discovered the reason. Years before, someone had used what was then a straight little sapling as an anchor for a clothesline. Over time, the tree grew and hid the metal wire from sight, but nonetheless it continued to cut at the heart of the wood, leaving it weakened. The day came when the weakened center just could not bear the weight of the tree any longer.

Human life is a lot like that. Anger never resolved, some hurt never consoled, some loss never filled, some sin never forgiven—these things cut deep within us, and even when we can put on a smile and say, "Oh, I'm just fine," the constriction continues to weaken the very core of our being. Sometimes our lives come crashing down, not because the weight of today is too great for us, but because the hurt of some yesterday never let us grow properly in heart and mind and spirit so that we could adequately deal with today.

"So do not worry about tomorrow, for tomorrow will bring worries of its own. Today's trouble is enough for today" (Matthew 6:34 NRSV). Perhaps these words of Jesus are a reminder not to worry so much about tomorrow, but they also are a reminder to be sure that we address all that comes to us today.

APRIL 8   SPIRITUAL DISCIPLINES

After years of dreaming, a friend of the family finally made it to the Big Apple to see the New York Yankees play ball. An inning or two passed, and he became curious about a uniformed man who walked up and down his section of seats, shouting, "Skunk eyes! Get your skunk eyes!" Finally he waved the man over, curiosity getting the better of him, and said, "Let me try some of those skunk eyes."

"Skunk eyes?" he shot back. "I'm selling score cards." (Northern and southern accents must be added by the reader!)

I think of those "skunk eyes" from time to time when I feel that God is leading me, often pushing me, to take up some new task or put aside some old routine. "God," I think, "surely I'm not hearing you right. Surely you don't want me to do that?"

How do we know we are understanding the will of God for our lives? What are the steps toward discernment?

In 1947 Albert Edward Day wrote *Discipline and Discovery*, a little book that helped me to more fully understand that spiritual disciplines allow a person's life to remain open to God and thus discover the will and purpose of God.

What are spiritual disciplines? They are simply things we can do that enable us to push aside the clutter of life and make a space for God in our hearts. The traditional disciplines are obedience, simplicity, humility, frugality, generosity, truthfulness, purity, and agape love; but one could also add things such as study, prayer, confession, and worship. The form is not nearly as important as the results—hearing God more clearly and being gracefully empowered to act upon that which you hear. As James Fenhagen noted in his book *More Than Wanderers*, "A life of inner discipline is not only the result of faith, it can lead to faith just as we learn the meaning of love by loving. Our task is not to search for God, but rather to open ourselves to the reality of God's search for us."

APRIL 9   MOMENTS OF LOSTNESS

I was listening to a man speak on the radio recently about his various adventures as a world traveler. On one occasion, he was in Hong Kong awaiting a return flight to the United States when he happened to sit next to a young woman who appeared to be a college student who was out to discover the world but had exhausted her resources. She looked so sad and hopeless that the man began to talk with her. He learned that she had been in China for several months and had scraped together enough money to buy a ticket home—and had lost the ticket. With nowhere to go and no one to turn to, the woman had just been sitting there in the airport terminal for hours, not knowing what to do. As the tears began to flow, the man was moved to compassion and promised to help her. As they stood up to go and talk with the airline officials, the young woman screamed. "Are you hurt?" the man asked. "No!" she responded, "it's my ticket! Here it is! I've been sitting on it all this time!"

How often we are like that in our spiritual journeying. We find ourselves far from home. In desperation and anguish we feel we have no resources to get back to the place we long to be, when the reality is that we've just been sitting on the ticket all along. We've been sitting on the promises of God to accept us and reclaim us as children. In those moments of lostness, what we need to do is get up. In that simple act of moving toward God, we will find God, as the prodigal found his father, running to meet us in order to put clothes on our backs, rings on our fingers, and proclaim to all, "This child of mine who was lost, now is found."

APRIL 10   NEW BEGINNINGS

Whenever I read Luke's account of the Last Supper, I am always struck by the words, "And when the supper was over . . ." When the supper was over, Jesus took the bread and the cup.

As you know, Jesus and his disciples were sharing the Passover together. This was a Seder meal, a symbol and gracious reminder of a gracious and mighty act of God. In the course of this meal, they had recited the Passover story, spent time remembering the afflictions of their forefathers and foremothers in Egypt, blessed and eaten the matzah, bread of affliction, and eaten bitter herbs dipped in salt water to remind them of the tears of oppression. They had already recited the Great Blessing, drunk the hopeful cup of Elijah, and sung a psalm of praise. And the supper was over.

I can imagine the disciples pushing back from the table, settling back—it was finished. Everything was done; and it was at that moment that Jesus picked up the scraps off the table, some bread and some wine, and said, in effect, "It is not over, but just beginning." It was at that moment, when everyone thought it was over, that Jesus did a new thing. He took the old story and gave it a new ending. When the supper was over, Jesus offered a new gift of life and redemption. When everything was finished, from the perspective of most, Jesus opened wide the doors of life anew.

Isn't that the way God so often acts in the life of the world? When we think it's all over, God does something new. God picks up the scraps of our lives, blesses them, and fills them with new meaning. Certainly that is the message of the cross. As Jesus breathed his last with the words, "It is finished," God was already preparing the resurrection.

And is this not the repeated story of grace at work in our lives? At those moments when we think everything is over, when we have done all we can do, we see most clearly God opening the door to new hope, new possibilities, new dimensions of understanding and new abundance in life. Thanks be to God that our endings are often God's beginnings.

APRIL 11   AFRAID TO ASK

I don't know at what point students learn this, but it must be in a standard 101 level course that we learn to smile, nod our heads, and write knowingly in our notebooks when we *haven't got a clue!*

"I didn't know you didn't understand; why didn't you ask me," the teacher will say. We have no good response.

Why are we afraid to ask questions? And, more important, why are we afraid to ask questions of God? Is it an admission that we are not perfect? (God already knows that!) Is it that we fear God will reject us? (God in Christ has promised to be with us "even until the end of the age.") Is it that we think it's not respectful? (Do our children ask a thousand "whys" because they don't respect us or because they come pre-packaged with a thousand questions?) Is it that we don't think God can handle it? (God is not us, God is *God*—creator and sustainer of all things. Perhaps God is even the author of our questions.)

Any teacher can tell you that a key to true understanding is a good question. And how God hungers for us to truly understand, to be released from fears, to move, in God's time, from seeing "in a mirror dimly" to seeing face to face.

APRIL 12   GOD'S EXTRAVAGANCE

When you think of God, does the word *extravagant* immediately come to mind? Today I was taking a walk, enjoying the encouraging warmth of an April morning when I looked at the hillside before me, all lacey in its greens and blossoms, and began to think about green. Right there before me were at least eighteen different shades of green!

In creating the world, God could have made everything brown or purple, but he didn't. Just consider the absolute extravagance of color, shade, and texture displayed in creation! Think of the variety of birds and animals. Think of the endless variety demonstrated in human personality. I think this little poem written by e. e. cummings must have been a prayer of thanksgiving and a hymn of joy:

> What's beyond logic happens beneath will:
> nor can these moments be translated: i say
> that even after April
> by God there is no excuse for May

Children have a refreshing, if not shocking, way of looking at the world. This is so, in part, because they are looking at things fresh and are not yet bound by a host of carefully prepared presuppositions.

I was shocked into taking a fresh look at my faith recently while riding in the car with my four-year-old son. "Mom," he mused, "If there were no earth and no space, we'd all have to stand on God's head. Right, Mom?"

At first I was a little concerned about the state of his religious education, but as I thought about it, I came to wonder if in his young heart he was not trying to express the same kind of affirmation of faith that the writer of Deuteronomy made when he declared, "The eternal God is your dwelling place, and underneath are the everlasting arms" (Deuteronomy 33:27 RSV).

How wonderful to know, beyond a shadow of a doubt, that no matter what twists and turns life takes, regardless of both the predictable and the unpredictable circumstances of life, no matter what, underneath are those everlasting arms of God, bearing us up, leading us forth, and guiding us toward life.

This is the assurance Paul tried to relate to the church at Rome in their time of trial:

> Who will separate us from the love of Christ? Will hardship, or distress, or persecution, or famine, or nakedness, or peril, or sword? No, in all these things we are more than conquerors through him who loved us. For I am convinced that neither death, nor life, nor angels, nor rulers, nor things present, nor things to come, nor powers, nor height, nor depth, nor anything else in all creation, will be able to separate us from the love of God in Christ Jesus our Lord. (Romans 8:35, 37-39 NRSV)

I hope that in the years to come, I'll have the opportunity to say to my son, "See. You were right. No matter what, God always gives us a place to stand."

APRIL 14   **WHAT ENDURES?**

Thumbing through a magazine one day, I came upon an article about two men who, reviving an ancient European tradition, built a beautiful wooden man four stories high and then, on the morning of the summer solstice, burned it.

The message they hoped to convey in this act was that in view of the grand sweep of time and space, the life of an individual person appears so small and fragile, and yet there is, within the human spirit, something enduring. This made me pause to wonder.

Certainly, as Christians, we see in God's gift of Jesus the ultimate indication that God values us as persons, and in the Resurrection we affirm that God claims us for new life; but from this fragment of life in the here and now, what endures? Is there anything that lasts?

Paul's words in I Corinthians 13 filled my mind as I recalled all the things he said would "pass away" and the three things he said would abide: faith, hope, and love. These things last.

How often do I get so busy with living (existing, making it) that I forget about life? How many hours do I allow to be filled with the "stuff" that will not endure? Lord, this day, may I be intentional with my hours and fill them with those things that abide: faith, hope, and love.

APRIL 15   LESSON FROM A SQUIRREL

In the course of a long, intense family struggle, I came to know a woman in one of my congregations very well. Even in the midst of her heartache and suffering, she always seemed to be at peace with herself and with God. I asked her once how she did it—how she made peace with all the conflicting pieces.

She said, in essence, "When there are no easy answers to seemingly insurmountable problems, we need an anchor, a stabilizer, to hold us steady. A regular source of wonder to me is watching a squirrel playing joyfully between trees in our backyard. He climbs fifty feet and races out on a small limber twig that swings down as if he would surely fall. He races down the limb to firm footing, then repeats the performance again and again. His timing is always perfect. When we are clinging to a twig in life's problems, I am reminded that Jesus died for us so that we may hope for what we cannot see. Through faith and hope in Jesus, prayers, and support of Christian friends, I can cling to the twig to reach the firm foundation, giving thanks to God with joy, for I *know* his timing is perfect." All that from a squirrel!

"So we do not lose heart. Even though our outer nature is wasting away, our inner nature is being renewed day by day. For this slight momentary affliction is preparing us for an eternal weight of glory beyond all measure, because we look not at what can be seen but at what cannot be seen; for what can be seen is temporary, but what cannot be seen is eternal" (II Corinthians 4:16-18 NRSV).

APRIL 16   READY TO LISTEN

When my oldest son was five, he came to me and in a very serious tone asked, "Where do tomatoes come from?" I was thrilled at his apparent interest in the world of nature, so I began to expound about how we plant seeds, how the sun and rain unleash the potential of the seed, how the seed sprouts and becomes a plant, and how, over time, the plant produces tomatoes.

When I was finished, he looked at me and shook his head. "No, I mean where do the tomatoes come from that killed those people in Franklin?"

Not being aware of any killer tomatoes in the general area, I felt that I needed to pursue this further. I found out that he had seen a news report concerning the *tornados* that had struck the area and had, indeed, killed a man. I was so busy giving my answer that I hadn't really heard the question, and more important, I hadn't heard the fear and the terror behind the question. He was afraid. He was afraid that a tornado would strike his house and hurt his family, and he wanted to know where they came from.

There are so many times when we as Christians stay very busy answering questions that no one is asking. It is a lot more demanding to listen to the hard questions and the questions behind the questions—the fear, the doubt, the wonder, and the dreams behind the questions. Sometimes it is hard to hear these questions because we know we do not have the answers, but

Jesus stands as our model. Often Jesus responded not with quick and easy answers, but with a graceful and life-giving presence. He did not tell his disciples, "I'll give you all the answers in the next chapter"; rather, he comforted them and empowered them by saying, "Lo, I am with you always." The risen Presence does not demand that we have all the answers in order to qualify for discipleship, but he does invite us to stand with one another as ambassadors of grace and hope. But first, we need to be ready to listen.

APRIL 17   GROWING HIM

While working in a Bible school on the tiny island of Montserrat for a short-term mission trip, some of our American ears had trouble interpreting the British English of the islanders. I remember one team member asking a young boy about his favorite hymn and hearing "Growing Him" rather than "Crown Him."

As the years have come and gone since that trip, as my life has traveled along a pathway of various twists and turns, I have, at times, wished I knew a hymn titled "Growing Him"—not that God changes, but certainly my vision and understanding changes and, I hope, grows.

I have come to understand maturity in Christian faith as coming from conversion that happens over and over again. The word *conversion* comes from the Hebrew *shub,* which means turning—turning time after time away from sin and toward the good; away from brokenness and toward wholeness; away from the darkness and toward the light; away from death and toward life; and, most important, away from my little gods and toward *the* God.

Maybe the closest thing to "Growing Him" is the old Shaker hymn that goes:

> When true simplicity is gained
> to bow and bend we shant be ashamed
> To turn, turn, will be our delight,
> Till by turning, turning
> We come round right.

Following extensive knee surgery, I entered what was to be months of physical therapy. I remember so vividly the day I finally "graduated" to the stationary bike, with the instructions to just rock back and forth on the peddles. Peddling a full 360° turn was weeks away! While I was sitting there, carefully rocking back and forth, another patient walked past and casually declared, "You're not going to get too far!"

I smiled, but inwardly that casual comment hurt. He didn't know just how far I had come or how hard I had worked just to get to the point of sitting on a stationary bike, rocking back and forth.

How quick we are to judge others without knowing the battles they have faced or the struggles they have endured before their life came into our view. How quick we are to judge ourselves by vague standards of "getting there" that may or may not fit our journey. Is the value of a life something that can be judged in terms of destinations alone?

Christ Jesus came into human life to say, among other things, that there is another dimension of value that comes from beginnings: whose we are. We are God's sons and daughters, and wherever we go, wherever we find ourselves, we have a Companion and a Friend.

APRIL 19   NO SHORTCUTS

Upon leaving relatives in Montana on a family vacation, my father decided to take the scenic route south to Yellowstone Park. After traveling miles and miles on a two-lane road with no evidence of human life to be seen, we were all relieved to discover, at last, a small gas station and country store. After filling up with gas, my father asked, pointing down the road, "How far is it to Yellowstone Park?"

"Oh, I guess about a hundred million miles," he said calmly as he hung up the pump.

"What!" my father gasped.

"Well, if you kept going down that road to get to

Yellowstone, you'd have to go all the way around the world."

How often Jesus and his disciples are found "on the road," and how often the disciples are convinced that they must be going the wrong way. And how appealing our shortcuts still look to us today! Surely there is an easier way. Surely there is a way other than the way of the cross and suffering?

But the way of Christ has no shortcuts, for it is the way of love—love of God and love of neighbor—the way of love that bears all things, believes all things, hopes all things, endures all things. Perhaps Paul should have added, "Love is never easy, but the results are heavenly."

APRIL 20   QUICK FIX

I saw a cartoon once that showed a man and a woman standing in a town square. To the left of them was a library with a sign on the wall that read, "Easy Answers." To the right was the Quick Fix Auto Shop. In front of them was a restaurant called "Free Lunch," and behind them was the "Cure-All" Pharmacy. The man leaned over to his wife, smiled, and said, "I think I'm going to like it here."

We, too, dream of the life of easy answers, the quick fix, the free lunch, and the cure-all, but that has never been the texture of a life that follows Christ.

James and John must have thought they had this messiah business all figured out. They understood kingdoms and power, and they also had figured out where their place was in the scheme of things—of course, they were number one! Just when they had it all figured out, Jesus set a child in their midst, thus turning their answers upside down. In the presence of Christ, power meant powerlessness, authority in the kingdom meant servanthood, first meant last, and life meant death.

Have you ever noticed how the presence of Christ always seems to bring comfort, but never comfortableness? That presence, then and now, challenges us with all of our answers, all of our freedoms, all of our cures, and all of our quick fixes to take up a cross and follow.

When I was doing the dishes the other day, I picked up a blue and white plate that my husband and I had received as a wedding present. As I plunged it into the soapy water, I began to wonder just how many times I had washed that same plate. Over the last fifteen years, I'd seen it serve Sunday pot roast, and I'd seen it serve peanut butter and jelly sandwiches. I'd seen it sparkling and new as it came out of the beautifully wrapped package, and I had seen it after it had been under the couch for a week, gleaming with all sorts of colorful mold. I had seen it at its best; I had seen it at its worst. But even at its worst, I'd always been able to submerge it in the suds and make it clean again.

I guess God must wonder about me in a similar way. "How many times have I needed to wash that soul clean?" God has seen me at my best and at my worst. God knows how often I have fallen short, and yet God continues to see another reality of what I may yet become in grace. So when I offer myself to his forgiveness in love, he makes me clean again.

This can be a new day, a new beginning, a morning as fresh as spring, if we pray, *Lord, once again, make me clean.*

APRIL 22   DOING THE BEST WE CAN

The other day, my three-year-old son came into the kitchen dragging the cat in his arms. I was just about to shake my finger and warn him that he must not strangle the cat when he looked up at me and said, in the absolute honesty of a three-year-old, "We must take care of all God's creatures."

It was then that I realized he was doing the very best he could; so instead of scolding, I knelt down and showed him a new way to carry the cat.

Why did Jesus desire Simon Peter, James, John, Andrew, and the others? They were unskilled and not especially influential. They constantly misunderstood and missed the point of the work of the kingdom. Why did Jesus want them? And why does Christ desire us to be disciples? We continue to misunderstand so much, to misuse gifts and persons, to miss the point, and generally make a mess of things. But God must see that we're doing the best we can, utilizing our own resources; so instead of condemning us, God knelt down to the world in the person of Jesus to show us a new way—a better way—to live and love.

APRIL 23   CHANGES

Though the earth should change, though the mountains shake . . . though the waters roar . . . though the mountains tremble—God is a stronghold!
— Psalm 46:1-3 (paraphrase)

It has been said that nothing is as permanent as change, and change certainly is common to us all. We expect some changes with the flow of life, as we move from adolescence to adulthood, from singleness to marriage, from life as parent to life as grandparent. Some changes come "on schedule," but then there are those unforeseen changes that rip and pull at our lives until we hardly recognize them as our own. God's promise is that in the midst of all the changes we expect, as well as the changes that shake us with the fury of an earthquake, God is ever there—our refuge and our strength—a stronghold upon which to stand firm when everything about us appears to crumble and fall.

But that word *refuge* also denotes a habitation—a home, a place not unknown or foreign to us. It is not a distant castle, not a hotel, but a home with which we are familiar, a home to which we have the key to open wide the door—a home where a welcome is always prepared for us. God is a stronghold. God is home.

APRIL 24   CHASED BY A RAINBOW

I was weary. I was exhausted. Making a weekly four-hundred-mile commute between home and seminary got old in a hurry.

One rainy morning, driving my much too ancient VW back toward divinity school, I began to ask myself, Why am I doing this to myself? Who would care if I quit today? Didn't finish school? Didn't become "a preacher"? I could go out and do something "normal"! As a matter of fact, all I could think of were the people who would be really relieved if I quit.

115

I began to look for a place to stop, turn around, and go home, when it dawned on me that it had stopped raining. And then, there in my rearview mirror, filling the glass with a flood of color, was the most magnificent rainbow I had ever seen. I was being chased by a rainbow! I was being pursued by a symbol of the absolute faithfulness of God.

Could I turn away from a God so faithful? *Can* I turn away from a God so faithful? Yes, at times I have, and yet, there always comes that sense of urging from that "great cloud of witnesses"—those who have gone before me—and there is that voice that challenges my weakness, "Let us run with perseverance the race that is set before us" (Hebrews 12:1).

APRIL 25   **NOT VERY HUNGRY**

I was serving Communion one Sunday morning when I approached a boy about ten years old. Watching me lean toward him, the boy threw up his hand and said, "I don't want any today. I'm not very hungry."

What a parable for the way many of us approach the table of Christ, the place where we are called to remember the life, ministry, death, resurrection, and continuing presence of Christ. How many times do we push aside the blessings of God with the words, "I'm not very hungry"?

Why are we not hungry for the true food of righteousness, justice, and purity? Perhaps it is due to the fact that we fill ourselves with spiritual junk food, such as, "But I'm not as bad as they are," or, "Everybody else is doing it," or, "If it feels good, I'll do it."

No wonder Jesus preached, "Blessed are those who hunger and thirst for righteousness for they will be filled" (Matthew 5:6 NRSV). It is hard for the blessings of God to fill us if we don't even know that we are starving.

APRIL 26   **RUNNING**

Sometime during the summer between fourth and fifth grades, I remember sitting at the breakfast table with my family when Bill, a man who helped out on the farm, went racing past the window with Smarty, my brother's dog, close on his heels. A few moments later, here came Bill again, the dog gaining the distance. After the third pass, my father went out on the porch, called the dog, and halted the now panting Bill.

"That dog chasing you, Bill?" my father asked.

"No," he replied. "He was just running the same way I was."

Our pride often makes it difficult to admit that a problem is chasing us. Sometimes instead of making that admission, we just keep running from it as fast and as long as we can, hoping against hope that maybe it will not overtake us. But more often than not, problems seem to have four legs to our two.

Standing upon a foundation of faith, Christ calls us to turn around and name the affliction. We are to use all the creative gifts and skills God has given us to address the problem. We are to call upon the resources beyond us such as prayer, study of the Scriptures, and strong, Christian counsel. And then we are to *know* that in God's time, a new name of grace shall be given to that which pursues us.

A plaque hangs in a church in England that declares: "Fear knocked at the door; faith answered; there was no one there."

APRIL 27   EXTERMINATING ANTS

Knowing how to turn and face a problem is important, but it is equally important to know how to distinguish between a problem and an annoyance.

One of my favorite children's books is Robert Quackenbush's *Henry's Awful Mistake*. In this story, a duck ends up destroying his entire home due to the undesirable presence of a little ant.

How easy it is to allow any inconvenience or any disruption of the normal routine to be a burdensome cross to bear. How much energy we expend exterminating ants when dragons lurk in every corner!

Once I heard someone say, "In terms of time management, never shoot butterflies with rifles. Save your big guns for big stuff."

One spring we discovered a great big pear tree full of blossoms behind our house, but as summer came, the only thing the tree produced were a few hard, inedible pears. "Maybe next year it'll be better," I thought. But the next year brought the same results. We found out that the tree was dying at the roots. It couldn't produce much because it was disconnected from the source of its life.

I couldn't help recalling the words of Jesus: "I am the vine, and you are the branches. Whoever abides in me and I in him will bear much fruit, for you can do nothing without me" (John 15:5-6 NRSV).

I began to wonder about my "root." Did the "fruit" I was producing in my life indicate that I had a healthy connection with my roots?

Branches bear fruit consistent to the species. Is my fruit consistent with my roots in Christ? How about your life? When other people encounter your life, do they encounter "fruit" like that which was produced when lives encountered Jesus? When people know you, really *know* you, do they also come to know that kindness is stronger than cruelty? That mercy is stronger than revenge? That right is stronger than wrong? That hope is stronger than fear? That love is stronger than hate? That God is stronger than the past and that in Christ we and the whole world are being made new? Common roots—good fruit!

APRIL 29   **LIGHT AND SALT**

In the life, death, and resurrection of Jesus, God had a plan. And the plan was *us*—you and me! The plan was that just as Jesus was the light of the world, so also are we to be light. Just as Jesus was satisfying and purifying salt, so also are we to be salt. What a great trust placed within our hands!

But must we not confess that often we have taken our saltiness and applied it in places that were already salty enough? Often do we not add our light where lights are already glowing? It's easier that way. It's safer that way. But doesn't the voice of

God whisper, "Go, in the name of Christ, to the tasteless wilderness—they need your salt. Go, in the name of Christ, and brighten the dark corners of despair and hurt—there are so many out there and your light is needed there."

Where are those places in the world that need your salt and light? You can name them. Go! Infuse your life and let your light shine. The presence and the promise of God will go with you.

APRIL 30   SEEING AND DOING

I started to school in what must have been one of the last two-room school houses in America. There were eight grades, two teachers, two stoves, and sticky floors. My first memories of "status" were getting to read in front of the bigger children and getting to ring the hand bell, which indicated the end of recess. In this setting I started my journey with Dick and Jane and Spot, but I was also initiated into a world that I did not really understand.

Many of the children who attended this school were from families related to a nearby junior college, but there also were the "others" who came from "the knobs" and from tiny farms. Many of these children were literally dirt poor. Some of my classmates were ragged, hollow-eyed, and ashy.

One day in early spring one of the poorest little girls in the second grade got sick. She fell out of her desk and started trembling and chattering her teeth. Both the teachers came in, picked her up, and put her on the low reading table at the front of the class near the stove. Then one of the teachers asked, "Would you give me your coats so we can cover her up?" One by one the children went to the hooks on the wall and brought their coats to cover the skinny, trembling body. She looked dead, except that she trembled so much.

Just a few days before I had gone to town with my mother and had bought a new coat. It was beige with tiny pink rosebuds. I was not of a wealthy family, by any means, but somehow, at this point, my fear got the best of me. I would not put my new coat on *her*. She was sick. She was dirty.

This picture came flooding back to my mind recently when I found myself in a group in which I was the new one. I was an outsider; I was different. As I remembered my hesitancy to help, I first thought, "How quickly we learn to make distinctions." But as I thought more, I came to see that the problem is not that we see the differences between us. (The rich man was convicted of his sinful treatment of Lazarus when he said, "I never saw him.") Yes, we need to see that there are differences—there are the poor; there are the oppressed. But the important work of the Christian is what we do *after* we see.

In the parable of the good Samaritan (Luke 10:29-37), the thing that makes the Samaritan a model for us is that he sees *and* has compassion. Being "moved to compassion" releases an absolute barrage of action verbs: He *went* to him . . . *bandaged* his wounds . . . *poured* oil and wine . . . *put* him on his animal . . . *brought* him to an inn . . . *took care* of him.

Seeing and doing are our work. "But be doers of the word, and not hearers only . . ." (James 1:22*a* NRSV).

MAY

Blessings

SHIRLEY POPE WAITE

MAY 1   **JUMPING TO CONCLUSIONS**

Every May 1, a memory creeps into my mind, one that takes me back to my days as a young mother with a very fussy and difficult eight-month-old son.

He awakened at the slightest sound, so during his afternoon nap, I literally tiptoed around the house.

Then a rash of doorbell ringing began. Neighborhood children would run up on the porch, ring the bell, and hightail it around the corner. Several times the noise woke up the baby.

So when the bell rang one May afternoon, I tore to the door, flung it open and in my loudest fishwife voice screamed, "You kids get out of here, and don't you *ever* come back!"

As I shouted, my hand brushed against the doorknob. There hung a paper basket full of lilacs, tulips, and daffodils. At the same moment, my eye caught the frightened face of little Nancy, our six-year-old neighbor, cowering behind a nearby tree.

What had I done? I wanted to call out an apology but was so ashamed, I just grabbed the basket and closed the door. As I peeked out the window, I saw Nancy crossing the street with a hangdog look and tears running down her cheeks. An apology was in order, of course, but the damage had been done.

Since that long ago May Day, I've tried very hard not to jump to wrong conclusions. I'm afraid I might miss out on a blessing.

For where your treasure is, there your heart will be also.
—Matthew 6:21 (NIV)

May is the perfect time for cleaning out closets, garages, basements, *and* the perfect time for a yard sale.

I recently read an article on yard sales that introduced me to a new French word—*bricoleur*. It means someone who makes use of "odds and ends, the bits left over, and oddly related objects." Long before yard sales were popular, my mother used to comment that one woman's junk is another woman's treasure.

The authors of the article tell of planning their weekends around yard sales, and they give hints for buyer and seller:

Use brief signs with arrows pointing the way to the sale site.
Consider a multi-family sale.
Take care not to mix dissimilar items.
Never guarantee anything.

These suggestions could apply to Christians.

We are "signs" pointing the way to the living Lord.
We invite folks to church, emphasizing multi-family activities.
We take care that we don't mix our theology with worldly ways.

But contrary to yard sale rules, Christians plan *their* Sundays around church, and they *can* make a guarantee—that God will touch people, and turn the junk of their lives into treasure.

Father, help me to be a bricoleur for you as I seek those who feel left out, or unrelated to the gospel.

He's the Lily of the Valley,
He's the Bright and Morning Star,
He's the fairest of ten thousand to my soul.

So goes the chorus to an old hymn by Charles W. Fry. A seventy-five-year-old friend recalls singing "The Lily of the Valley" in Sunday school when she was a girl.

One concordance lists this flower as a description of Christ (Song of Solomon 2:1). I agree.

Lilies of the valley grow at the corner of my house. They became so thick that I decided to transplant some to another area. But they withered and died. Several seasons passed; then one spring I was flabbergasted to see delicate shoots pushing their way up through the soil. They are so sturdy that neither a winter of sub-zero temperatures, droughts, or torrential showers have affected them. The pure white flowers are as lovely and fragrant as ever.

Jesus Christ is also "a fragrant offering" (Ephesians 5:2).

In John's vision, he is on a white horse, followed by armies dressed in white linen (Revelation 19:11, 14).

Furthermore, he is pure—"and in him is no sin" (I John 3:5).

More than any of these—he came back to glorious life after everyone thought him dead, just like my petite blossoms.

That's why May's special flower, the lily of the valley, reminds me of our precious Lord and Savior, Jesus Christ.

MAY 4   **FAITH FOR THE DAYS AHEAD**

Now faith is the assurance of things hoped for, the conviction of things not seen.
                              —Hebrews 11:1 (RSV)

As I write this, we look forward to the birth of a grandson in about three months.

Each evening at prayer time, our five-year-old granddaughter and her daddy talk about names for Jessica's new brother. Our daughter-in-law is buying appropriate clothing for a boy.

It's amazing that today a simple test reveals the sex of a child, and parents can plan accordingly. Of course, it takes the element of surprise away, and I'm not sure I would have wanted such knowledge in advance.

But how I wish I could glimpse into the future in other areas. What will the world situation be when these words are in print? Will my precious children return to their spiritual "roots"? As my husband and I grow older, will we maintain our health, and stay in our own home?

I choose to believe that God is in control, not only of my life and the lives of my children, but also of this hurting world.

That's what faith is all about.

Lord, you're in charge, and I ask that I may be your woman in the days ahead, regardless of what they hold.

MAY 5   CINCO DE MAYO

As minority groups establish roots in America, they bring with them unique customs and cultural observances that enrich our society.

When our church became aware that Spanish-speaking Protestants within the community had no place to worship, a Hispanic congregation was established. It is flourishing and adds a richness to our church family.

One of our regular members, Hispanic by birth, saw another need: that of a Spanish-speaking radio station.

Can you imagine living in Mexico, Germany, Japan, or anywhere in the world where another language is spoken? What a joy to tune to an English-speaking radio station that plays *your* kind of music and that has announcers who talk in *your* language!

Station KSMX went on the air in 1988, just in time to help the Hispanic community celebrate Cinco de Mayo, which commemorates victory in the revolution Mexico fought against the French in the 1860s. The May 5th event features folk dancing, a marachi band, and piñatas for the children.

"Many Anglos think we're celebrating our 'Fourth of July,'" says Mary Lou. "In fact, one of the local supermarkets published a headline, 'Mexico's Independence Day.' I laughed. Our Independence Day is September 16.

"We hope people will have a sense of respect for our customs. Hispanics are proud of their culture."

Our two church bodies have held a joint Christmas Eve service, new member Sunday, and worked side by side during an English language training event.

We have discovered that we worship and serve the same mighty God, and that *alleluia* is understood in virtually every language!

MAY 6   EXERCISING MUSCLES

My husband and I go to the college fitness center several times a week. Over a dozen machines are designed to exercise the various muscles in the body.

I do well on the low and high pulleys and the total hip machine, and I enjoy the seated back. My body is beginning to tolerate the shoulder press, leg curl machine, and the abdominal crunch. (Oh, how I need that for lazy tummy muscles!) I can't begin to master the back/leg extension or the hip flexor. In between these "stations," I ride a stationary bike or jump on a trampoline.

This morning as I made the rounds, I likened my physical muscles to spiritual ones.

My church attendance muscle is very strong, as is my "flash prayer" muscle. My Sunday school and tithing muscles are in pretty good shape. But the Bible reading muscle needs more work, and the praise muscle is quite weak. I haven't begun to master some of those "prayer closet" muscles, especially the "trust God in all circumstances" muscle, or the "let go and let God" muscle.

I periodically set up a new regime of spiritual exercises, but I often spin my wheels as on a stationary bike or get stuck in one spot as on a trampoline.

Persistence will get physical results at the fitness center. I must be just as tenacious in exercising my spiritual muscles. When the old body wears out, I want my spiritual life to be strong and vibrant for the rest of my days.

My ninety-year-old friend is in a nursing home. Her hearing has been poor for years, but she enjoys handwork and reading. Now her eyes are failing, and these simple pleasures are denied her. Yet she remains cheerful. One day I asked her about it.

"Well, dear, I just go to the bank more these days."

Pointing to her forehead, she said, "This bank—the storehouse. I dredge up old memories—the good ones, of course—but they're only the interest that has been accumulating in my bank. And my, they are interesting!"

She paused, as if recalling an old joy.

"Then I turn to the principal—the old Sunday school songs, the hymns, and best of all, the Scriptures I've memorized. They're the principal items in my bank. The Bible says, 'Thy word have I hid in mine heart . . .' but here is where I've hidden it." She again tapped her head.

Leaning back on her pillow, she looked at me intently through her thick-rimmed glasses. "Interest or principal—I draw out any amount I want. There's always an ample supply the next time I go to my mental bank."

She pointed to the well-worn Bible on her night stand. "I sometimes get discouraged. Then I remember Isaiah 46:4. Read it to me, please."

I turned to the underlined passage: "Even to your old age I am He, and to gray hairs I will carry you. I have made, and I will bear; I will carry and will save" (RSV).

On my way home, I wondered about my own spiritual assets. What positive, happy memories did I have for interest? How about God's Word as the principal resource in my mental bank? In this day of financial upheaval, I know that these possessions are the greatest investment for my future.

MAY 8   REST IN ME

Come unto me, all ye that labour and are heavy laden, and I will give you rest.

—Matthew 11:28 (KJV)

---

*This piece first appeared in *Scope* (now defunct) in 1982.

Do people still have visions today? I believe so.

Let me tell you what happened to me. I'd been pushing myself mercilessly, teaching at the community college, trying to meet writing deadlines, leading a church school class, all without shirking home responsibilities. Then I caught a "granddaddy" of a spring cold.

I crawled back into bed one morning, feeling miserable and frustrated. I tried to pray but my thoughts were swirling like dust devils. In my half-waking state, I suddenly saw a chalkboard—like a child's slate of yesteryear. Three words appeared on the slate—*Rest in me*.

I kept saying that brief phrase over and over until I fell asleep. When I awakened, my nose was still stopped up, and my chest tight, yet I felt exhilarated, as if bubbles floated in my brain. All day I repeated the words, "Rest in me! Rest in me!"

The cold ran its natural course, my classes met on schedule, and home chores didn't magically disappear. Yet confusion vanished and I became calmer and happier.

The vision continues to sustain me in similar circumstances today. Resting in him makes the difference.

Lord Jesus, thank you for the promise that we can rest in you.

MAY 9   **LIFE IS TOO SHORT***

The older I get, the more I realize that life is too short to fret about
> frayed washcloths
> burned cookies
> cat hair on the couch
> the ring in the bathtub
> the woman who barged ahead in the grocery line
> the car repair bills
> the cutting remark by my relative.

---

*This poem originally appeared in *Scope* (now defunct), August 1979, and has also appeared in a 1988 issue of *Ideals*.

The older I get, the more I realize that life is too short to postpone

       telling my friend how much I appreciate her
       writing that overdue letter
       finishing the children's scrapbooks
       doing those stomach-firming exercises
       reading the entire Bible in that new version
       writing the poem that's been on my mind
       volunteering to babysit for my young neighbor.

The older I get, the more I realize that life is too short.

MAY 10   YOU CAN NEVER FORGET

We hadn't seen Sandy for more than ten years. This talented athlete was our foster son while he was a senior in high school. During that year, I saw every football and basketball game, including a trip to the state basketball tournament. But after graduation, Sandy dropped out of our lives.

* * * * *

None of the children had called that Mother's Day afternoon. I was feeling terribly sorry for myself when the doorbell rang. A tall moustached young man handed me a large envelope.

"Happy Mother's Day," he said quietly, shifting from one foot to the other. I paused momentarily, then asked, "Do I know you?" He took off the dark glasses. It was Sandy!

I called to my husband, and we excitedly began catching up on the past ten years when the phone rang. Sensing it was a long distance call from our daughter, Sandy whispered, "Say hello to Laurie," signaled his departure with a wave and was gone.

Later I opened the card.

"For my mom with love and gratitude. Moms have a lovely way of giving, helping, teaching and loving."

The inside verse was beautiful, but the words written at the bottom brought tears to my eyes. "You can be thoughtless, but you can never forget."

Last year, after another long absence, we were invited to

Sandy's wedding. At the reception, he introduced me to his new wife as his "high school mom."

* * * * *

Is there someone who has been like a mother to you? Pick up the phone, or drop them a line. You've never forgotten, nor have they.

MAY 11   GOD IN THE MUNDANE

"I'll never be able to memorize our new license plate," I complained to my husband. "GQE 603. How can I remember it?"

I often try to attach a spiritual meaning to ordinary things. Take the cuckoo clock our daughter sent from Germany. It played a German drinking song on the hour. Like a child with a commercial, I went around the house singing:

En Muenchen, steht ein Hofbrauhaus,
Trink, Bruderlein, trink.

Loosely translated, it means:

In Munich, stands a tavern.
Drink, little brothers, drink.

When I realized what I was doing, I changed the words and began singing:

To Jesus Christ, my voice I'll raise,
Praise to the Lord, praise!

But the new license plate was a challenge. Looking at the "GQE" one day, the words leaped to my mind—*God Quickens Everyone.* So much for the letters.

But the numbers? Could there be a third verse of some sixtieth chapter which illustrated this truth? No. How about a chapter 6, verse 3? My search began, and I found it!

"Oh, that we might know the Lord! Let us press on to know him, and he will respond to us as surely as the coming of dawn or the rain of early spring" (Hosea 6:3 TLB).

What quickens the earth more than early spring rain? Or rouses the sleeper more than bright rays of a dawning sun?

Mundane things—from license plates to cuckoo clock tunes—remind me of the great God who has "created all things" (Revelation 4:11).

Use *your* imagination and try it.

MAY 12   HOW DO YOU PLAY THE GAME?

May 12, 1939! More than fifty years ago, but it stands out as clearly as if it were yesterday. I was a frightened young teen from a rural school, headed for the Metropolitan Spelling Bee in Detroit. I wore my lucky pink dress, which I'd worn during four years of competition. My recent growth spurt had turned it into a blouse. Mother laced the sleeves with brown ribbon.

A sea of faces floated before my eyes. Would I spot friends and relatives who planned to cheer me on to victory? Each contestant stood upon the approach of three judges, who had to agree on the correct spelling.

Soon half the fifty-four contestants were disqualified and my confidence soared. After all, wasn't I—as a congratulatory letter stated—"one of the finest spellers in 160,000"? Surely, I would go all the way to Washington, D.C.!

The judges approached again.

"Incandescent," one pronounced.

"Incandescent," I repeated. "I-N-C-A-N-D-E-S . . . ."

Aha, a tricky "C"! Smiling, I quickly added, ". . . C-A-N-T."

The moment the letters spilled out, I knew the "A" was wrong. Then why were the judges conferring?

"Number 37, will you please respell *incandescent?*" With no sound system or tape recorder, someone hadn't heard those last four letters.

A reprieve! It must have been my lucky dress!

I started again. "I-N-C-A-N-D-E-S-C . . . ." A sickish feeling enveloped me.

Then I blurted out, "I spelled it wrong," and dashed off the stage, tears blinding me as I stumbled down the steps.

Later my grandfather wrote in my autograph book these words by Grantland Rice, a sportswriter of that day.

When the one great Scorer comes
to write against your name—
He marks—not that you won or lost—
but how you played the game.

I've tried ever since to concentrate not on the score, but on playing the game.

MAY 13   HOT AIR BALLOONS

You will always have your trials but, when they come, try to treat them as a happy privilege; you understand that your faith is only put to the test to make you patient, but patience too is to have its practical results so that you will become fully developed, complete, with nothing missing.

—James 1:2-4 (JB)

The second weekend in May brings an exciting event to my community. The Hot Air Balloon Stampede, which began in 1975, now attracts balloonists from all over the country. Last year, there were fifty-eight balloonists and close to thirty-five thousand tourists.

On scheduled liftoffs, it is vital that pilots be alert to wind currents and to the air inside the balloon. It must be 125 degrees warmer than the outside air in order for a balloon to rise. There's always the danger of electric wires and other hazards as well.

Some years, liftoff has been cancelled due to high winds. Balloonists, their crews, and the crowds are highly disappointed. But one pilot commented, "Ballooning teaches patience. We can't control the elements, but we still try to have a good time."

I lose patience with God when winds of adversity threaten to blow me off course and I'm not in control. I'm going to start treating these trials as a "happy privilege," knowing that God wants me to be "fully developed, complete and nothing missing." And that includes having a good time!

Lord, too often I pray for patience and I want it RIGHT NOW! Help me to enjoy life as I await your perfect timing.

As our Hot Air Balloon Stampede grows, other activities have mushroomed. Arts and crafts booths and food concessions abound. A golf tournament, horseracing, an air show, a 5K race, skydiving, and an antique car parade are held in various locations. Visitors enjoy cultural shows such as bagpipers from British Columbia and origami demonstrations by Japanese students attending the local community college.

One of the highlights is Nite-Glow, a giant simultaneous light show put on in unision by balloonists. Lighting of the propane burners is synchronized and done in ten second intervals so the balloons don't catch fire.

Both pilots and ground crews must concentrate fully on their individual jobs, never allowing their focus to waver.

Focus—that's what I need. Whether I'm writing a letter, driving a car, teaching a class, grocery shopping, or having devotions with my husband, I'm most likely thinking, "What's next on my agenda?"

As the balloonist focuses on wind currents and his propane burner to make his balloon go upward steadily, I need to turn my mind first to God, then I will have the proper focus for the task at hand.

I like to think of it in this way:

> F - Following
> O - Our
> C - Christ
> U - Upward
> S - Steadily

A good acronym to memorize!

MAY 15   BACK-UPS

"For you are my fortress, my refuge in times of trouble."
—Psalm 59:16 (NIV)

In preparation for a telephone interview with a well-known author, I borrowed a sophisticated phone recorder, not trusting my suction cup device.

While transcribing, I discovered that the second side of the tape consisted of nothing but a loud buzz. I'd lost half my interview! How I wished I'd used the cheaper mechanism as a back-up!

Back-ups are common. The theater hires understudies. Orchestras have second and third chair positions. Virtually every team sport has a bench of back-up players ready to go into the game at a moment's notice.

Our kids learned early on that a bike made excellent back-up transportation when the family car was spoken for. My retired husband serves as backup when he substitutes for an absent teacher.

A back-up can mean a reserve supply, assistance, something or someone that gives moral support.

That sounds like my heavenly Father. How would I ever get along without a reserve supply of his love, his helping hand over the rough spots, and his support in every area of my life?

Lord, thanks for being my refuge in times of trouble, my divine back-up.

MAY 16   BIRTHDAYS

It doesn't matter where we are, or where she is. We always contact our daughter on her birthday. One May 16 we were out of town and forgot to call. We heard about it later, in no uncertain terms!

Memories of early birthdays flood my mind—doll parties, swimming parties, slumber parties, cookouts, trips to nearby sand dunes. During her college days and single-girl working years, there was always a special phone call.

When Laurie taught school for two years in Germany, we called at 10:15 P.M. on May 15, in order to reach her at 7:15 the morning of her birthday.

We called from a campground in Utah, and we made a contact when she was visiting in Nashville. One year we surprised her with a call from England's North Sea Coast. It was a poor connection, but Laurie still heard her parents singing "Happy Birthday" over the miles.

May is such a lovely birth month. Winter is behind, temperatures are usually moderate, and a baby gets a good start before cold weather arrives again.

Our May baby is now in her thirties and happily married, but to this parent's heart, she shall always be my "baby girl."

To our heavenly Parent's heart, we shall always be his dear little ones. He remembers us in a special way, not just on our birthdays, but on the other 364 days of the year as well.

MAY 17   THE ELEVATOR OF LIFE

"For I know the plans I have for you," declares the Lord, "plans to prosper you and not to harm you, plans to give you a hope and a future."
—Jeremiah 29:11 (NIV)

The story is told of a young woman who won a trip to a large city. She had never been out of her native mountains, so she looked forward to staying in a posh hotel and taking in urban sights.

Upon arrival at the hotel, a man said, "I'll show you to your room." She followed him inside a door and was devastated. Why, this was nothing like what she had imagined! No furniture, not even a window. She expressed her disappointment to the man. He shook his head and said, "Ma'am, this is the elevator!"

The story reminds me of a friend's recent experience while attending an international convention. A hotel elevator full of women from the 32nd floor kept stalling between floors. Each time the door opened, the women saw a blank wall. When the elevator finally opened to daylight, all of its occupants got out on the 20th floor and walked the rest of the way to the lobby.

God speaks to me in two ways through these illustrations. I often jump to conclusions before God has a chance to show me what he plans for my life. Second, when I hit a blank wall, I may have to change direction, even if it's more work than I first anticipated.

In the elevator of life, I have a choice—I can push the UP

button and go up in my spirit with the Lord, or the DOWN button and find myself down in the dumps.

Father, how glad I am that you do have plans for me. If changes need to be made in my life, help me to be flexible.

MAY 18   WHERE'S YOUR TRUST?

"Some trust in chariots and some in horses; but we trust in the name of the Lord our God."
—Psalm 20:7 (NIV)

"What's in *that* jar?" I asked myself.

The basement cupboard was full of old treasures. Red clay from my daughter's backyard in Georgia. Stones from Flathead Lake in Montana, beautiful when covered with water. But the gray dirt in the jar?

That evening, I watched a television special on Mount Etna. Villagers tried to save buckets, wheelbarrows, and cultivating tools as they watched lush vineyards being gobbled up by red hot lava.

That's it! Volcanic ash!

It was May 18, 1980. Majestic Mount St. Helens, with bejeweled Spirit Lake snuggling at the base, blew its top. Prevailing winds carried the ash several miles northeast of our town.

But a neighbor experienced the frightening darkness during a fishing trip. "Help yourself," he offered, as I looked into his boat, covered with several inches of the gray matter. "I hope I never go through anything like that again!" I filled a small jar with the heavy ash.

Later I heard a comment made by a survivor who lived at the foot of St. Helens. "You work a lifetime to have a nice home and possessions, and it's all wiped out in a flash."

Another added, "It took five minutes. We lost all our furniture and clothes. It was awful." She held up a tea kettle, all that remained from a $100,000 dream house.

I think I'll put the jar of Mount St. Helen's ash in a prominent place. Maybe it will remind me not to get too attached to my possessions.

Lord, may I always be aware of my real security—your love and care.

MAY 19   YOU'RE IMPORTANT!

"There is neither Jew nor Greek, slave nor free, male nor female, for you are all one in Christ Jesus."
—Galatians 3:28 (NIV)

Dayton Edmonds, native American storyteller and missionary from Omak, Washington, spoke at our church recently. Dayton, from the Caddo Indian tribe, was raised by his grandparents in Oklahoma.

"When I entered high school, I looked forward to becoming part of America's melting pot. But when I plunged into the pot, I was thrown out. I tried a second—then a third time—with the same results."

It all became clear to Dayton on a camping trip. "I was making stew, with meat simmering over an open fire. I tossed carrots, potatoes and onions into the broth. Each vegetable added richness to the stew, yet each maintained its own shape and flavor. Then I saw it! If I omitted any ingredient, the whole pot of stew suffered, losing its savor."

Dayton concluded, "We must each lend our juices to the broth of society. God chose you to be who you are. You're important."

As I glanced around our congregation, I saw Jesse and his Hispanic family; Alicia, an Apache Indian with her children, Strong Eagle and Little Hawk; Patty, a second-generation Japanese American; and Kathy whose unique singing style reveals her black heritage. Our church and our community is richer because of them—*and* folks like you and me. We're all essential ingredients.

Lord, fill me with your love for people who are different from me.

I teach a delightful class, helping senior citizens write their life stories. These memoirs have included those of a woman whose family was possibly the last to go West in a covered wagon, a man who was lost at sea during World War II, and a nurse who was a missionary to Malawi. Men and women have shared the joys and heartaches of the Great Depression, eked out a living on homesteads, taught in one-room schoolhouses in remote parts of Montana, and had childhood Christmases when the greatest thrill was an orange in the toe of a stocking.

Writing one's life story can also be therapeutic. A recent widow told me, "This is helping me work through my grief. As I write about meeting and then marrying Vern, I'm not so lonesome."

Among my students are those who endured traumatic and often abusive childhoods. Many feel the need to share their backgrounds with children and grandchildren, but, of course, not with the class.

I tell them, "If you want me to critique your paper, write 'PERSONAL' on it." I have shed tears as I've read of experiences buried in the hearts of some women for years. But healing takes place as they confront those hidden feelings and write about them.

Perhaps there are readers who have never dealt with a terrifying ordeal from the past. Psychologists attest to the value of writing one's feelings and thus facing them head on.

There's something else you need to know. The Lord promises that he "is near to the brokenhearted, and saves the crushed in spirit" (Psalm 34:18 RSV).

MAY 21   COUNT YOUR BLESSINGS

We enjoy a time of "Show and Tell" in my "Writing Memoirs" class. Students have brought old photographs, childhood toys, mesh purses from the 1920s, ration books from World War II, and mementos from their scrapbooks.

One such treasure was the following piece titled "Count Your

Blessings." It is an authentic Kentucky recipe in its original spelling.

* * * * *

Bild a fire in back yard to heet kettle of rain water.
Set tubs so smoke won't blow in eyes if wind is pert.
Shave one hole cake of soap in bilin water.
Sort things, make three piles, one pile white, one pile cullord, one pile work britches and rags.
Stur flower in cold water, to smooth, then thin down with biling water.
Rub dirty spots on boards, scrub hard, then bile, rub cullord but don't bile.
Take white things out of kettle with broom stick handle and rench, blew and starch.
Spread tee towels on grass.
Hang old rags on fense.
Pore rench water in flower bed.
Scrub porch with hot soapy water.
Turn tub upside down.
Go put on clean dress, smooth hair, brew a cup of tea, set and rest and rock a spell and count blessings.

* * * * *

Aren't we modern women spoiled?

MAY 22   DON'T SPOIL WHOSE DAY?

"Do to others as you would have them do to you."
—Luke 6:31 (NIV)

What a fantastic day! I'd heard a wonderful speaker at a Christian women's group. I'd rejoiced in honest communication with my teenaged son. My daughter, a recent college graduate, called to share the excitement of her first job. To top it off, I was experiencing a respite from chronic headaches.

Feeling euphoric, I walked to a friend's house that evening. Breathlessly, I told her of my wonderful day.

Connie finally got a word in edgewise. She was upset with her husband, dreading the impending visit of a difficult relative, and her boss had been extremely demanding.

"Oh, Connie," I blurted out. "Don't spoil my day!"

A pained look crossed her brow, and I hastily added, "I mean, don't spoil *your* day. Just count your blessings!"

She changed the subject, and our conversation moved to neutral ground.

A few days later, I awakened with a headache. My son snapped at me for no apparent reason, and my husband called from the bathroom, "My razor just went on the blink!" I tripped over the cat (who meowed for her kitty tuna), causing me to break a favorite dish.

Over a belated cup of tea, I mused, "Wait until I tell Connie about *this* morning!"

I could almost hear her say, "Please, Shirley, don't spoil my day!"

Aristotle said, "We should behave to our friends as we would wish our friends to behave to us"—another way of stating the Golden Rule.

Thank you, God, for friends who take time to listen to me. Help me to show empathy toward others.

MAY 23   IN A FOG

When Jesus spoke again to the people, he said, "I am the light of the world. Whoever follows me will never walk in darkness, but will have the light of life."

—John 8:12 (NIV)

I always chuckle when I think of the story of a man driving in fog. Unable to see the road clearly, he followed the taillights in front of him.

The lead vehicle turned and then stopped suddenly. The second driver ran right into the back of the first car. He jumped from his car, yelling, "What do you think you're doing, slamming on your brakes?" Whereupon the first man replied, "What are *you* doing? I just turned into my driveway!"

That little anecdote tells me something. When I'm in a "fog" and not sure of my direction, I must be careful whom I follow!

Today there are many groups clamoring for my attention. Some look so authentic that I might be inclined to heed them. But I must keep my eyes on the One who calls himself the light of the world, for when I do, he promises I'll never walk in darkness.

Father, when I don't know which way to turn, please open my eyes to your light so that I will always follow you.

MAY 24   GREEN EGGS AND HAM

One of my children's favorite storybooks was Dr. Seuss's *Green Eggs and Ham.*

"Is there such a thing as a green egg?" my son asked.

"Of course not! Dr. Seuss uses silly ideas to make his books funny."

Now, thirty years later, a lady from whom I occasionally buy eggs has proudly showed me green ones, which she claims have less cholesterol. These eggs have the yellowest yolks I've ever seen!

*   *   *   *   *

Recently in a church gathering, someone asked, "Are all the gifts of the Spirit operable today?"

One person replied, "Of course not! During biblical times they were signs to prove that the Holy Spirit existed. We have the Bible today, so we don't need them."

Green eggs? "Of course not," I told my son.

Gifts of the Holy Spirit? "Of course not," some claim.

Jesus told Thomas, "Have you believed because you have seen me? Blessed are those who have not seen and yet believe."

I don't need to see someone healed with my own eyes to believe that God heals today. I don't need to prophesy to believe that another has a gift of prophecy. Nor do I need to speak in a language I've never learned to believe that others have this gift and are edified by it.

My Lord hasn't changed. He is the same yesterday, today, and forever (Hebrews 13:8). I am the one who is changing as my limited understanding of his greatness grows.

MAY 25   KNOWN BUT TO GOD!*

"You must visit the American cemetery," our bed and breakfast hosts told us.

We hadn't known about this cemetery three miles from Cambridge, site of one of England's most famous universities.

Upon our arrival, we were surprised to see the American and British flags at half-mast. Special Memorial Day services were scheduled to honor those buried there who had died in wars.

A large proportion were crew members of British-based American aircraft. Others died in the invasion of North Africa and France, at sea, or in training areas within the United Kingdom.

As we walked reverently around the beautiful grounds, we paused at the foot of a grave. It was one of twenty-four decorated with red and white carnations tied with a blue ribbon, and flanked by a tiny American and British flag. The words etched in the headstone read: "Here rests in honored glory a comrade in arms known but to God."

Tears came to my eyes as we stood in an attitude of worship. Known but to God! These service people were once known intimately by parents, siblings, friends, perhaps a spouse and children. Young men and women who fought for freedom and the dignity of humankind! Yet in death—known but to God!

Relatives and friends may forsake us. We may feel all alone in a world that offers many only poverty, cruelty, and apathy. But God knows each of us intimately. He is a husband to the widow—"for your Maker is your husband, the Lord of hosts is

---

*This piece first appeared in revised form in *Decision Magazine* in May, 1986. It then appeared as printed here in *Pentecostal Evangel* in May 17, 1987.

his name" (Isaiah 54:5). He is a Father to the orphan—"Father of the fatherless . . . is God in his holy habitation" (Psalm 68:5). He is Father to us all!

Known but to God! Isn't that the most important relationship of any? Thank God, we are known to him not just in life, not just in death, but for eternity!

MAY 26   UNWANTED BUSH*

Each spring my husband threatened to cut the little bush down. It was growing so close to the house.

"We don't even know what it is," he argued.

"But the leaves are shaped like lilac leaves," I countered.

"Then why haven't we seen any blossoms in all these years?" He logically replied.

After several seasons, we no longer discussed the bush. It had reached a height of about seven feet, and I was beginning to agree with my husband. When the wind blew, it rubbed against our bedroom window. It had long since blocked our view.

Then one May day I was washing the windows. I couldn't believe what I saw—purple flowers on our unwanted bush! It was covered with fragrant blossoms!

I wondered, "Do I also look at people as we did that unfruitful bush?" The shrub had within itself the capability to bloom, and given the right timing it did. How about my children? my friends? myself? What potential lies within each of us, perhaps not visible to others, yet exists?

It seems to me that's why patience is so important—patience to await the Creator's perfect timing. A plant, a bush, a person—when the timing and conditions are in his hands, who knows what beauty will emerge!

MAY 27   THE BATTLE HYMN OF THE REPUBLIC

Today marks the birthdate of one of America's most famous women. Most people remember her as the author of the beloved "Battle Hymn of the Republic." However, Julia Ward Howe

---

*This first appeared in *Decision Magazine*, April 1985.

garnered many other honors during her lifetime. Mrs. Howe gained popularity as a noted lecturer and writer, not only on women's rights but also on other social and literary topics as well.

Long before Anna Jarvis began a campaign for a nationwide observance of Mother's Day in 1907, Mrs. Howe made the first known suggestion for such a special day in 1872. She was responsible for annual mother's meetings in Boston for several years.

In 1861, Mrs. Howe and her husband watched a military review of federal troops outside the nation's capitol. Upon their return into the city, the road was congested with troops singing "John Brown's Body." The stirring melody inspired her to write "The Battle Hymn of the Republic" to encourage the Union forces.

In 1990, over four thousand attending a national *Aglow* Conference stood for two hours on the steps of our nation's capitol singing this hymn. It was their rallying call to tell the world about Christ. According to one delegate, "It was one of the most stirring experiences of my life. I felt a unity with women all over the United States, a special binding as we prayed for our country."

At one point in her illustrious career, Julia Ward Howe proposed that the women of the world unite to end war for all time. As I write this, our beloved country has just survived a time of war. Is it too late for women the world over to work toward this goal?

MAY 28   THE TENTH COMMANDMENT

> *You shall not set your desire on . . . anything that belongs to your neighbor.*
> —Deuteronomy 5:21 (NIV)

During the last days of May, the Royal Anne cherry tree across the street was heavy with blossoms. I eagerly watched the fruit grow. How ruthlessly I chased children who used the green cherries for pellets!

The tree was on church property, and its fruit always reached the picking stage during the annual conference. So the pastor's wife and I had an agreement. I picked and canned the cherries when they were out of town, then gave half to her.

Now a new family occupied the parsonage. With three pre-schoolers, this pastor's wife didn't plan to attend the conference. In fact, her family didn't like cherries, so she told me to help myself. My vigil began.

The cherries reached the peak of perfection during Vacation Bible School. Monday morning children swarmed all over the tree. Leaves began to fall, branches cracked, cherries flew through the air. I was about to dash across the street when I saw the pastor's wife. Thank heaven!

My relief was short-lived. She handed sacks to the children, and so the harvesting began. By the end of the morning, the cherries were gone.

I was filled with resentment and anger. How could she do this to "my" tree? There would be some changes next year, I vowed.

There were changes, all right. That fall the tree was cut down to make room for parking.

Lord, you know my covetous nature. Help me to replace each envious thought with praise and thanksgiving to you.

MAY 29   **PRIORITIES AND PATIENCE**

As I recall picking cherries, memories of my girlhood come to mind. All the kids in my neighborhood were Detroit Tiger fans; but, in those post-Depression days, most of us didn't get an allowance. So we picked cherries for two cents a quart to earn enough for streetcar fare into Detroit, admission into the bleachers (fifty cents) and, of course, for a hotdog!

Names still come back to me—Hank Greenberg, Mickey Cochrane, Dizzy Trout, Charley Gehringer, and especially Buck (Bo-Bo) Newsom. This winning pitcher was such a favorite that I skipped school to see him on the mound during a day game.

The only other time I skipped was to see Glenn Miller and his orchestra.

Baseball, big band music—they were my priorities then. My family did not attend church, and none of my friends were religious.

Then during college days a classmate invited me to a youth group. For the first time I became aware of God—One who actually loved me. Thus my spiritual awakening began; yet many years passed before I had a personal relationship with Jesus Christ.

So when I get discouraged about my kids and their mania for football and rock music, I remember God's patience. Like the "hound of heaven," he never gave up on me. I know he'll never give up on my loved ones, either.

MAY 30   PERPLEXITY

Are these my hands, Lord?
With veins so conspicuous they resemble roadmaps?

Are these my eyes, Lord?
Highlighted by dark and sunken circles?

Is this my hair, Lord?
Streaked with gray, so brittle it won't curl?

Are these my ankles, Lord?
Varicose-veined, turning as I walk in the pathway?

AH, LORD, THESE THINGS ARE DISCOURAGING!

BUT

Is this my mind, Lord?
Still eager to learn, to memorize Scripture?

Is this my will, Lord?
Determined to conquer the fear of old age?

Are these my emotions, Lord?
Capable of love, joy, patience, and peace?

Is this my spirit, Lord?
Communing with Thy Spirit, eternally young?

AH, LORD, THESE THINGS ARE ENCOURAGING!

MAY 31   **FRUIT IN THE VALLEY**

But the fruit of the Spirit is love, joy, peace, patience, kindness, goodness, faithfulness, gentleness and self-control.
—Galatians 5:22-23 (NIV)

Apples are a big crop in Washington state. In fact, we rank first in apple production for the nation. Recently an annual crop produced almost five billion pounds of apples, worth $282 million, with our Walla Walla Valley contributing $30 million of that amount. The Yakima and Wenatchee Valleys vie each year for the title of "Apple Capital of the World." Red and Golden Delicious, Rome Beauty, Jonathan, Granny Smith, Gala—the list could go on—Washington's *valleys* produce the best fruit.

I've found that to be true of my own valleys. The best growing conditions for spiritual fruit are often found there. As I rely upon the soil and sunshine of God's love in my "valley" times, he changes my

> hatred into *love*
> sorrow into *joy*
> worry into *peace*
> intolerance into *patience*
> rudeness into *kindness*
> envy into *goodness*
> unbelief into *faithfulness*
> grouchiness into *gentleness*
> temper into *self-control.*

Whatever circumstances await you in your valleys, let God transform them into the fruit of his Spirit.

Thank you, Master Gardener. Cultivate my soul that I may show forth your precious fruit.

JUNE

When Change Transforms Our Lives

BECKY DUROST FISH

JUNE 1	THE GOD WE CAN TRUST

(Read Proverbs 3:1-6.)

"I, Becky, take you, Bruce, to be my husband, to live with in love, regardless of circumstance. . . ." When I said those words one sunny afternoon in a little white church on the coast of Maine, I knew that I was starting out on an adventure where I had much to learn. But one thing I already understood: my life was changing.

Somehow it seemed appropriate to be facing yet another change in June. June was the month when I graduated from high school and began growing into adulthood. Four years later, I graduated from college and started my first full-time job.

Then there was the June when I drove from New York back to Maine to bury my grandmother. I saw my dad and his brothers and sisters wrestle with the knowledge that they were now the oldest generation in the family, that there was no longer a buffer of older relatives between them and death.

These changes face all of us at one time or another, and while they present the opportunity for spiritual growth, they can also bring pain and fear. When caught up in the unpredictable storms of life, it is essential that we are anchored by love, faithfulness, and trust in God.

Those three qualities have given hope to women throughout history. Like us, they made some wrong choices, but God always delivered what he promised. And today, as we acknowledge him, "he will make [our] paths straight" (Proverbs 3:6*b*, NIV).

JUNE 2   THE GOD WHO REDEEMS

(Read Genesis 3.)

Deceived! Betrayed! Eve had never felt anger like this. Life had been going along just fine until she was stupid enough to listen to that serpent.

Why had she craved that fruit in the first place? The other fruit in the garden was deliciously sweet. But somehow the forbidden fruit looked just a little plumper, just a little juicier. Could her life be complete without experiencing everything this new world had to offer? She *had* to taste it. The serpent agreed, even encouraged her.

So Eve had reached out, and the succulent fruit had dropped into the palm of her hand. Eve bit into the fruit, piercing its firm, cool skin, and the juices slid down her throat, quenching a thirst she hadn't recognized. She felt ecstasy, joy, and then an emotion she'd never known: fear.

Even as she joined Adam and hid from God, Eve knew that her life had irrevocably changed. And she was right. Never again would she and Adam play tag in the meadow with the deer or ride on the back of a cougar. The animals felt fear too.

But the change was worse than that. God found Eve and Adam. Eve hung her head in shame as God told her how her sin would change her friendship with Adam and bring pain to the world. Not only that, but they would have to leave the Garden.

Yet there was hope. As she heard God's words of justice, Eve also heard God's promise of redemption (Genesis 3:15). He would send a deliverer.

That promise of redemption stretches across time. Like Eve, we will face moments of despair when we realize that because of sin, our lives have been changed forever. We can't make the damaged relationships what they were before. But in our moment of brokenness, God offers hope. Through Christ, we can receive life and healing. He is the God who redeems.

(Read Genesis 18:1-15; 21:1-7.)

Sarah locked her teeth together. Pain was an old acquaintance of hers, but she had never felt anything quite like this. The contraction eased, and a servant girl wiped the sweat from Sarah's face. She hardly noticed. Instead, she stared with fierce concentration at the face of the midwife. How much more could she take? She was too old for this.

That, of course, was the point, Sarah admitted to herself ruefully, remembering the three men who had visited Abraham the year before. She had eavesdropped on their conversation, a skill she had perfected during her long marriage to Abraham. Usually, she managed to remain undetected, but when the one visitor had said that in a year's time Sarah would have a son. . . . Who could blame her for laughing to herself? The idea of having a child at her age was patently absurd. Men! What did they know about childbearing?

Sarah shuddered as another contraction gripped her body. "Push, push!" coaxed the midwife. As if I had any choice, Sarah thought.

"I see the head," exulted the midwife. "It's coming!"

Sarah felt her body tear and then heard the midwife's words, "It's a boy!" Suddenly, Sarah laughed. "God has brought me laughter, and everyone who hears about this will laugh with me," she said.

One part of Sarah's mind was dimly aware that the midwife was cleaning her up, but as she reached for her baby, Sarah thought of the future. Years earlier, Abraham's God had promised that she would be the mother of many nations. Sarah had thought the promise would be broken; the promise predicted the impossible. But the fulfillment of that promise was now lying here at her breast.

What was it that visitor had said? As she drifted off to sleep, Sarah remembered his words: "Is anything too hard for the Lord?"

(Read Genesis 27:1-13, 41-45.)

Rebekah watched as her son, Jacob, left home. The tears she had managed to hold back spilled unchecked down her dusty cheeks. When would she see him again? Would she see him again? She had thought she was doing so well at managing an impossible situation, and now, this. Her favorite son was fleeing for his life.

Rebekah knew she would never forget the morning she had overheard her husband, Isaac, telling Esau that he was ready to give him the blessing. The news had shocked her. It wasn't what God wanted. Hadn't he told her before the twins were born that the older would serve the younger? Jacob deserved that blessing.

Cautiously, Rebekah had watched Esau prepare to hunt game for his father. As soon as Esau was safely away, she had called for Jacob and told him her plan. They had disguised Jacob so that he smelled and felt like Esau, tricking blind Isaac into giving Jacob the blessing.

Rebekah sighed. Her plan had succeeded. It guaranteed that Esau, the older, would serve Jacob, the younger. But at what cost? Esau was so angry he was plotting to kill Jacob as soon as their father died. Would peace ever return to her family?

I've often wondered what would have happened if Rebekah had trusted God to fulfill his promise in his own way. But I can also sympathize with her. It's very tempting to manipulate people and then rationalize our behavior by saying we are trying to accomplish God's will in the situation.

Unfortunately, such actions usually bring unnecessary pain into our lives and the lives of others. Sometimes it's hard to trust God, but it's even more difficult to run things ourselves.

JUNE 5   I WILL PRAISE THE LORD

(Read Genesis 29:31-35.)

Glancing outside, Leah saw the sand shimmer in the sun. Her tent provided shade, but the air was motionless and the dry heat evaporated any energy she felt. Judah stirred in her arms. She looked down and sighed with relief. Finally, the baby was asleep. She'd enjoy this rest.

Leah smiled to herself. Rest! There certainly hadn't been much of that in her life when she met Jacob. What girl wouldn't have fallen for him with his firm, muscular body and piercing black eyes? And his laugh! Even now she could remember the shiver that had coursed down her spine the first time she had heard that unrestrained roar.

But of course, Jacob had never noticed her. His eyes were always for Rachel, the desert vixen who entranced everyone. Then her father had tricked Jacob into marrying Leah instead of Rachel—a form of justice if you could believe everything you heard about what Jacob had done to his brother.

Leah shook her head as she thought back to the early years of her marriage. How she had wanted Jacob to love her! That longing had colored everything else in her life. Even her sons names had grown out of her desperation.

Reuben meant "see, a son," and when he was born she had thought "Surely my husband will love me now." When her next son was born, she had said, "Because the Lord heard that I am not loved, he gave me this one too." She named him Simeon, "one who hears." And then there had been Levi, which means *attached*. "Now at last my husband will become attached to me, because I have borne him three sons," she had said.

Leah knew better. Some day, Jacob might honor her for being a good wife and mother, but he would never love her as she loved him. Some things in life cannot be changed; they must be accepted. But even then, there is a choice. So when her fourth son was born, Leah had said, "This time I will praise the Lord." And she named her son Judah, which sounds like the Hebrew word for praise.

JUNE 6   A PLACE OF SAFETY

(Read Joshua 2; 6:25.)

Rahab paced about like a caged animal. Would the waiting ever end? For six days, the city of Jericho had been closed. No one was allowed out, and certainly no one was allowed in. Day after day, they had heard the sounds of trumpets and marching feet, but no voices. Early that morning, it had started again.

She walked to the window and checked yet again that the red cord was hanging down. That was all she had between her family and certain death—that and the word of those two spies. Was the word of an Israelite more to be trusted than the promises of the noble citizens of Jericho? Rahab snorted, recalling the meaningless endearments of her esteemed customers sating their passion.

There was no doubt that the God of Israel was powerful. All Jericho had heard about the crossing of the Red Sea and the defeat of the Amorites. But did this God have any compassion? What happened to her and her family would answer that question. If the Israelites did not keep their word, then their God was no better than the gods of her own temple. They exploited the people, and no one but their priests ever benefited.

Rahab stopped her pacing and stared out her window. A loud war cry filled her ears. The floor shook. Suddenly, the walls of the city collapsed. Hoards of armed men swept into the city. The door burst open and two familiar men rushed in.

"Rahab? Is everyone here?" the older man asked. "Come quickly. We're taking you to a safe place."

God still offers safety. But for many women exploited by abuse, safety demands that they turn their backs on everything they've known. They must leave the comfort of familiar dangers and face the unknown. Will we show these women God's compassion by helping them make the journey?

JUNE 7   WHAT COULD HAVE BEEN

(Read Judges 4.)

Riding into battle with Barak, Deborah wondered what the day's end would bring. Israel was facing a crisis, and no one knew that better than she. For twenty years, her people had been cruelly oppressed by Sisera. Meanwhile, she had settled their internal disputes, wondering how long it would take them to realize they needed God's help to get rid of Sisera.

That day had finally come, and it was time to take action. God had promised Israel victory, but with a twist. Because Barak had resisted obeying God's command to take the troops into battle, Sisera was going to be destroyed by a woman.

Deborah glanced over at Barak and shook her head. Why was it that someone with so much natural ability would hesitate to take the lead in bringing freedom to Israel? To look at him, no one would guess that Barak was plagued by so much self-doubt. Oh well, regardless of individual performance, the battle was the Lord's.

By the end of the day, the battle was won and Sisera was dead. A woman killed him while he was sleeping. Barak arrived at the scene just in time to see the dead body and to wonder what might have been.

At the end of our day will we wonder what we might have done? Using our abilities in God's battle against sin can be a risky business, but the battle will be won. Deborah embraced the role God had designed for her; Barak held back. Which will we choose?

JUNE 8   THE RIGHT STUFF

(Read Ruth 1.)

As Ruth looked into the wrinkled face of Naomi, her eyes filled. How her mother-in-law had changed! When she first met Naomi ten years ago, Ruth had been struck by her sense of humor and her ability to put up with life's irritations. But then Naomi's husband had died. And just last month. . . . Ruth closed her eyes as the pain of losing Chilion swept over her.

Naomi hadn't recovered from the news that both her sons had been killed. "It is more bitter for me than for you," she repeatedly told Ruth. "The Lord's hand has gone out against me!"

And now Naomi was returning to her homeland and insisting that Ruth stay in Moab with her own mother. Ruth wasn't persuaded. Her own mother had other sons and daughters to keep her company, but Naomi had no one. And after being away from her homeland for ten years, she had no guarantee that friends would still be there to look out for her.

After the past four weeks, Ruth had no illusions about life with Naomi. Her mother-in-law had become bitter and self-absorbed. But Ruth determined she would love Naomi for who she had been and for the love she had shown Ruth on her wedding day.

"Don't urge me to leave you or to turn back from you," Ruth quietly said to Naomi. "Where you go I will go, and where you stay I will stay. Your people will be my people and your God my God."

Ruth did not know when she made that decision that it would lead to her joyful marriage to Boaz. All she knew was that loving an unlovable, needy person was the right thing to do. May we have the same courage.

JUNE 9   LETTING GO

(Read I Samuel 1:21-28.)

Hannah held Samuel's little hand firmly as they walked up the road to Shiloh. His toddler steps were unsteady, but he insisted on walking and would readily tell anyone who asked that he was no longer a baby. Hannah gripped Samuel's hand more tightly, trying to sear its shape in her mind.

"Ouch!" Samuel cried.

Hannah relaxed her grip. "Sorry, dear," she soothed.

Samuel's brown eyes, filled with concern, fixed on her face. "Are you all right?" he asked.

"Of course," Hannah replied. "I'm just a little unsteady."

Trying to distract her son, Hannah pointed. "Look ahead, Samuel. That's the house of the Lord. That's where you are going to live."

Samuel's face lit up with excitement as he strained to see as much as he could. Suddenly, he turned to his mother. "You can hold me," he said.

Hannah bent down and picked up her little boy. His legs hugged her waist and his arms wrapped around her neck. Hannah cuddled Samuel's head, resting against her shoulder. She felt the fine, dark hair cling to her fingers and smelled the dust and scented oil that coated his skin. She gave him one big hug and then put him back down. It was time.

Hannah brought Samuel to Eli, the priest, and said, "I prayed for this child, and the Lord has granted me what I asked of him. So now I give him to the Lord. For his whole life he will be given over to the Lord." Then she worshiped God and returned to her home.

Like Hannah, we must release our loved ones to God's care. We have no ownership claim on our husbands, children, parents, or friends. But the God who gave his Son knows the pain of letting go. He can be trusted with our lives and the lives of those we love.

JUNE 10   LIVING IN WISDOM

(Read I Samuel 25.)

Abigail swayed on the back of her donkey as they climbed back down the steep mountain ravine. Trust Nabal to stay true to character. He really had a gift for antagonizing people, that husband of hers. Sometimes—like today—she thought it would do him good to get his. If she had stayed home and done nothing, David would have come down and killed Nabal, thus solving a number of her problems.

Unfortunately, David would also have killed a lot of other people. Abigail sighed. Life would be so much easier if her husband weren't so surly and just plain mean. But he was. And she couldn't justify endangering their servants just to get back at him. But of all the stupid things she had seen Nabal do, offending David after he had protected their sheep took the prize.

At least she'd been able to talk sense to David. Now if only Nabal would be sober enough to listen to reason. Abigail looked toward their home. From the sounds of things, Nabal was enjoying another banquet. She'd tell him her news in the morning.

The next day, Nabal was sober and Abigail told him how close he had come to being killed by David. Immediately, Nabal had a seizure, and ten days later he died.

Abigail was known for her wisdom. Because of it, she didn't devote her energy to getting revenge on an impossible person.

Instead, she looked for ways to minimize the harm he did, and she confronted him with his foolishness. Some of us thrive on confrontation and forget about the harm it can cause when poorly timed. Others of us pour all our energy into damage control and run from confronting the cause of a problem. Like Abigail, may we have the wisdom to do both with discernment.

JUNE 11   HIS MERCY ENDURES

(Read I Kings 17:8-16.)

At the town gates, a woman bent over and picked up sticks for the fire, but her mind wasn't on her task. She was thinking of the meal she was about to prepare. There was just enough food for herself and her son to have one small meal, and then there would be nothing—no food, no money, nothing to sell. Inevitably, death would be their last visitor.

How could she explain death to her son? Since the drought had started, he'd seen people die, but that was different from seeing your mother die and feeling your own life ebb away. "Show mercy, God," she prayed. There had been little mercy in her life since her husband died.

The woman's thoughts were interrupted by a man's voice. "Would you bring me a little water in a jar so I may have a drink?"

She turned. The man stood near the gates. From his dusty clothes and weathered skin, it was obvious he was no native of her town. The woman nodded at him and moved to get him water.

"And bring me, please, a piece of bread," he called after her.

At his words, she froze. "As surely as the Lord your God lives," she replied, "I don't have any bread—only a handful of flour in a jar and a little oil in a jug."

Then the incredible happened. The man told her to make him some bread anyway because God was going to make her supplies last until the rains came. Was this God's answer to her prayer? It didn't make any sense, but to do nothing would only guarantee disaster. The widow obeyed, and God was merciful.

God still shows us mercy, but sometimes in ways we don't expect. When we set aside our own problems and extend ourselves to others in need, God is there. By giving, we are filled. By healing others, we are made whole ourselves.

JUNE 12   WHAT KIND OF INFLUENCE?

(Read I Kings 21:1-26.)

With a superior smile on her face, Jezebel watched Ahab leave. Her husband might be king of Israel, but he was a weak man. Fortunately for him, he had married a strong woman. Strong and beautiful, she amended, glancing at her reflection.

How many times had Ahab been ready to give in to circumstances? Without her, Israel would never have started worshiping Baal. Ahab simply didn't understand what it meant to be king.

Take this matter of the vineyard. Ahab had gone about it all wrong. To begin with, he had offered payment in land or cash for that strip of land. Ridiculous! What was a king for if not to take what he wanted in return for all the responsibilities of leadership? And then when that Naboth had had the temerity to refuse, Ahab had given up. Some king!

As usual, Jezebel had straightened things out. Naboth was dead. Now Ahab was on his way to claim his new vineyard. Jezebel doubted other subjects would be so unwilling to give up land in the future. A woman could accomplish anything if she understood the art of managing people. And Jezebel was nothing if not a master of arts.

While Jezebel herself did not do many of the evil deeds her husband Ahab was judged for, she did urge him on. God held her responsible for how she chose to use her influence, and her death is one of the most gruesome scenes in Scripture (II Kings 9:30-37).

We, too, have influence over people—probably more than we suspect. How do we use that power?

JUNE 13   TAKE ACTION

(Read II Kings 4:1-7.)

The woman strode toward Elisha with determination. She

was willing to live a simple life. How else could she have lived happily with her husband, one of Elijah's associates? But now her husband was dead, and what little money they had put aside was gone. Certainly God didn't expect her to stand idly by while her children were sold into slavery!

"Your servant my husband is dead," she cried out to Elisha, "and you know that he revered the Lord. But now his creditor is coming to take my two boys as his slaves."

Elisha replied to her, "How can I help you? Tell me, what do you have in your house?"

"Your servant has nothing there at all," she said, "except a little oil."

That's when the work began. Elisha told the woman to gather as many empty jars as she could from all her neighbors and to go into her house with her sons and pour her remaining oil into all the jars.

The woman and her sons worked eagerly, and when they had finished, they could hardly believe how much oil they had collected. Their problem was solved. The price of the oil would pay all their debts and give them enough to live on.

Just as God met the widow's need, he also will meet our needs. Usually, however, he asks us to take some part in the process he uses to solve our problems. What steps is he calling you to take today?

JUNE 14   GOD'S SURPRISES

(Read II Kings 4:8-17.)

The Shunammite woman placed her hand on her stomach and smiled to herself. What an event tonight would be! She could just picture the light in her husband's eyes when she let him know that at last, they were going to have a child. Who would have guessed that their friendship with Elisha would produce such a change in their lives?

It had seemed only proper to invite Elisha into their home for a meal when he visited Shunem. As they got to know him, they realized that Elisha was truly a holy man of God. That's when lightning struck. The woman suggested to her husband that they surprise Elisha by building a small room on the roof of their house. They could furnish it with a bed, table, chair, and lamp; and whenever Elisha was in Shunem, he'd have a place to call his own. Besides, what was money for if you didn't share it with other people?

The first time the Shunammite woman showed Elisha his room, she knew he was pleased. For once, her eloquent friend was speechless. But as usual, he had the last word.

She would never forget the prophecy Elisha had made during his visit just a few months ago: "About this time next year, you will hold a son in your arms."

How had he known that her childlessness was the one thing that caused her pain? She was afraid to believe him, but her bleeding had stopped. And today, for the first time, she had felt the baby move. She hugged her secret and danced to the door to greet her husband.

Elisha's next visit to the Shunammite couple must have been one long party, and with good reason. God's surprises deserve to be celebrated. Whether we've just been married, had a baby, received an unexpected bonus, or been healed, isn't it time to throw God a party?

JUNE 15   THE POWER TO FORGIVE

(Read II Kings 5:1-16.)

The young slave girl concentrated on her errand as she hurried past the men standing in the hall. She hadn't recovered from the terror that lodged in her heart the night the band of Aramites had dragged her away from her home in Israel. Being near men still frightened her, but she'd have to get used to it. She doubted she would ever see her parents again, much less her brothers and sisters.

Her mistress was a good woman, but her master was commander of the army. At first, the girl had been secretly glad that her master had leprosy. He was probably being punished for the misery he had brought to others. But lately, she had begun to wonder: Wouldn't the God of Israel want her to offer help?

The slave girl paused in the hallway, then entered her mistress's rooms.

"What is it?" Namaan's wife asked.

"If only my master would see the prophet who is in Samaria" the slave girl pleaded. "He would cure him of his leprosy!"

Immediately, Namaan's wife sent word to her husband about what the slave girl had said, and Namaan took steps to visit Elisha. Because a young girl was willing to forget the hurt Namaan's people had caused her, he not only was healed, but he also recognized God.

As we think of people who have hurt us, may God give us the strength to follow this young girl on the path of forgiveness.

JUNE 16   THE COURAGE TO BE INVOLVED

(Read II Chronicles 22:10-12.)

Princess Jehoshabeath thought quickly. Her father's mother, Athaliah, had been power hungry for years. Now that Jehoshabeath's father was dead, Athaliah was set on claiming the crown of Judah. To solidify her claim to the throne, Athaliah had ordered that all the royal princes be slaughtered. Jehoshabeath could hear the soldiers' feet coming closer and she knew that if she were going to act, now was the time.

She couldn't save all her brothers, so she grabbed the baby Joash and his nurse and hid them in a small, out-of-the-way bedroom. Then she returned to the scene of the carnage, hoping that the soldiers would not think to look for the infant prince. The men seemed to relish their bloody job. Finally, the massacre was over. The soldiers left, but the mangled bodies of the princes of Judah provided a grisly reminder of the afternoon's horror.

Jehoshabeath realized she couldn't indulge in her grief. Once she was certain that the way was safe, she returned to the bedroom. The nurse was cowering in a dark corner, covering Joash's body with her own.

"Come quickly," Jehoshabeath hissed.

The traumatized nurse followed Jehoshabeath through the back halls of the palace. Once outside, they raced down narrow alleys to reach the temple. There Joash would be safe. Whether Athaliah would eventually find Joash and kill him, Jehoshabeath didn't know. Nor could she predict what kind of person Joash would become. But for now, the line of David was preserved, and in the temple, Joash could learn about the God his nation had forgotten.

Like Jehoshabeath, we usually don't know what permanent good our actions will accomplish, especially in the face of great evil. Many of us are afraid to get involved. But as followers of Christ, let's not allow evil to go unopposed.

JUNE 17   THE MOMENT OF DECISION

(Read Esther 4.)

Esther could not believe what was happening. The king had been tricked into signing a decree ordering that all Jews be slaughtered, not realizing that his own wife was a Jew. No wonder her cousin Mordecai was in sackcloth!

Esther gazed down at the tiled floor of her royal apartments. What could she do? The king, with a houseful of concubines who could satisfy any appetite, had not called for her in thirty days. Unless Xerxes was feeling unusually merciful, an uninvited appearance before him resulted in death. The situation was hopeless.

The reappearance of the messenger she had sent to Mordecai interrupted Esther's thoughts. "What did he say?" she asked urgently.

Slowly, the messenger reported Mordecai's words: "Do not think that in the king's palace you will escape any more than all the other Jews. For if you keep silence at such a time as this, relief and deliverance will arise for the Jews from another quarter, but you and your father's family will perish. Who knows? Perhaps you have come to royal dignity for just such a time as this" (Esther 4:13-14 NRSV).

Esther stood motionless. In her mind, she heard the words of the great leader Joshua: "Choose for yourselves this day whom you will serve. . . . But as for me and my household, we will serve the Lord." Her mind was made up. She could not abandon her God and her people. She would see the king.

While our lives may not be as dramatic as Esther's, we too must choose whether to serve God and his people. In many areas of our country, religious freedoms are being curtailed. Maybe, like Esther, it is time for us to take a stand.

JUNE 18   OUR DEFENDER

(Read Luke 1:5-25.)

Elizabeth sat in her home, enjoying both her pregnancy and her seclusion. She still couldn't get over the change—not in her body (although that was drastic enough), but in her neighbors. Where once they had held her in contempt, now she was honored.

All her life, Elizabeth had scrupulously observed the Lord's commandments and regulations. She had been generous to everyone she met and encouraged her husband in his responsibilities as a priest. But all that hadn't mattered to her neighbors. They only noticed that she was childless. Because of that, they knew there was something wrong with her.

When she was younger, Elizabeth had tried to defend herself. But facts alone don't change people's attitudes. She had railed at her husband, Zechariah, about how unfair it was, but the only answer he could give was to hold her close and whisper that he loved her. Finally, Elizabeth had accepted her lot. She had learned to ignore the raised eyebrows and the sudden silences in conversations when she entered a room.

She and Zechariah had still prayed for a child, but because of their old age, they hadn't expected their prayer to be answered. So the message from the angel Gabriel had been quite a shock. Elizabeth smiled. At last her critics were silenced.

"The Lord has done this for me," she murmured to herself. "In these days he has shown his favor and taken away my disgrace among the people."

Have you been maligned? Have good friends been all too willing to believe false rumors about you? The psalmist said, "Commit your way to the Lord; trust in him and he will do this: He will make your righteousness shine like the dawn, the justice of your cause like the noonday sun" (Psalm 37:5-6 NIV). It may take years. We may not see it during our lifetime. But ultimately, good will win.

(Read Luke 2:15-19.)

Mary lay back on the hay, too tired to notice the stench of animal droppings anymore. Things certainly hadn't gone the way she had expected. When the angel told her that she would give birth to Messiah, Mary hadn't imagined that her pregnancy would include a hard trip to Bethlehem just before she was due. Nor had she considered that her newborn son would be placed in a filthy manger. The clean hay and swaddling helped some, but a manger wasn't anywhere close to her first choice for her baby's bed. Was God really in this?

Yet he must be, considering that story of the shepherds. (No one would describe shepherds as reliable witnesses, but even they couldn't have made up a tale about seeing angels who told them Messiah was born in a stable.) And Mary herself as well as Joseph had received messages from God.

Mary looked down at her helpless baby, her Messiah. It was more than she could understand, this mystery. But she knew what God had told her to do, and she would obey.

Mary's obedience can be difficult for our twentieth-century skeptical minds to swallow. We've been taught to doubt our leaders and question their decisions. We're encouraged to disregard rules and procedures that don't make sense. To obey God's commands, whether we understand them or not, goes against the independence and individualism our society prizes.

Does God value our intellect? Yes. It's a gift he wants us to develop and enjoy. But he also wants to know whom we are serving: our intellect or our God.

JUNE 20   THE RELEASE

(Read Mark 5:25-34.)

"Who touched my clothes?"

The woman started guiltily. While other people in the crowd wondered why Jesus had asked such a question, she knew. For twelve years, she had spent her money and energy trying to get well. But nothing had worked. Discouraged as she was, she had been determined to come to Jesus. Just by touching his clothing, she had been healed. Now all she wanted to do was leave before anyone noticed her.

The woman looked toward Jesus out of the corner of her eye. His dark eyes roved through the crowd, and she knew he was looking for her. Was he angry because she had used his healing power without asking? Would he take the healing away? Whatever he wanted, he would not stop looking until he had found her. She elbowed her way through the crowd and fell at his feet.

Trembling with fear, she said, "I knew that if I just touched your clothes, I would be healed."

Pulling her to her feet, Jesus said, "Daughter, your faith has healed you. Go in peace and be freed from your suffering."

Sometimes it's hard for us to believe that we can be released from pain. For several years, I've had a chronic illness. By definition, such illnesses cannot be cured except through divine intervention or a medical breakthrough. So far, this hasn't happened, and it's tempting to give up. But that only leads to a joyless existence. Pain controls my moods, my relationships, my life.

When instead, I submit my health to God, I am free to accept each day as a gift from him. Pain may still be my companion, but it no longer determines who I am. Regardless of when, if ever, I am physically healed, God has released me to live my life fully and in peace.

JUNE 21   **LOVING GOD**

(Read Luke 7:36-50.)

The woman walked briskly down the street, inured to the appraising looks cast her way. Her fingers tightened around the small jar of expensive perfume she carried. She hoped the Master would understand what she was about to do.

She turned into one of the houses and, ignoring the protests of shocked servants, went directly to the dinner table where Simon and his guests were reclining. Standing behind Jesus at his feet, she started to weep. Then the woman knelt down, wet

Jesus' feet with her tears, and wiped them with her long, dark hair. As she thought of the many sins she had committed during her short life and the compassion and forgiveness Jesus had offered her, she kissed his feet and poured her perfume on them.

The woman hadn't been paying attention to what the other guests were saying. She barely noticed Simon's indictment of her character. Then Jesus spoke directly to her. "Your faith has saved you; go in peace."

God's peace fills our lives as we love Jesus completely. We are no longer controlled by other people's expectations and opinions. All that matters to us is that we express our love for our Lord in everything we do. Then we long for his words of approval more than we seek the approbation of other people.

JUNE 22   CONFRONTING WHO WE REALLY ARE

(Read John 4:1-26.)

The Samaritan woman could not believe what she had just heard. Who was this man, this Jew who would speak to a woman from Samaria? And what he said!

For years, she had told people the half-truth that she had no husband. But now this total stranger had just said to her, "You are right when you say you have no husband. The fact is, you have had five husbands, and the man you now have is not your husband. What you have just said is quite true."

No one before had ever made her face up to the full truth of who she was. She tried changing the subject. Certainly she could get this Jew sidetracked into the perennial debate about where to worship. But no. Somehow he was managing to bring the subject back to truth: "God is spirit, and his worshipers must worship in spirit and in truth."

The woman said, "I know that Messiah is coming. When he comes, he will explain everything to us."

Then Jesus declared, "I who speak to you am he."

And Jesus wants to speak truth to us today. We all have facts about ourselves that we avoid facing. Some of us downplay our faults. Others of us devalue gifts God has given us. To the extent we deny who we are, we cannot worship God in truth. Are we willing to see ourselves as God sees us and let him bring us to wholeness?

JUNE 23   WHEN GOD DISAPPOINTS

(Read John 11:1-6.)

Mary sat at Lazarus's bedside, holding his hand. Her sister, Martha, pressed cool cloths on their brother's hot body to try to stem the fever. Nothing was working, and the doctor offered no hope.

A servant entered the room with fresh water.

"Is there any word?" Mary asked.

Avoiding Mary's eyes, the servant shook her head and left.

"Where can he be?" Mary asked, her voice tight with emotion. "With the political situation the way it is, I can understand him not wanting to get so close to Jerusalem. But I keep hoping he'll do something else, like when he healed that centurion's son without even seeing him."

Martha sighed. "If Jesus is going to help us," she said grimly, "he'll have to do something soon. Otherwise, I doubt Lazarus will last through the night."

Anxiously, the sisters hovered over their brother. They had done everything possible. As soon as Lazarus became ill, they had sent a messenger to Jesus with the news. They had called in their doctor and given Lazarus all the medicines and treatments that might possibly ease his pain. Nothing had worked. Now they could only wait.

The shadows in the room deepened as the sun lowered. Martha lit a lamp. The two girls picked at the food the servant brought for them. Then Mary noticed a change.

"No!" she cried.

Martha jumped up and felt for Lazarus's breathing. There was no air movement. His eyes were fixed. He was dead.

The pain Mary and Martha felt seems softened to us because we know that four days later Jesus arrived and brought Lazarus to life. But Mary and Martha didn't know what was going to happen. They knew only that Jesus had disappointed them.

We, too, face times of disappointment with God. And when

we raise our fists to heaven and ask why, there are no answers. In our despair, there are two things we can cling to: God exists and he loves us. We may experience seasons of grief, but because of the cross, we will also see the Resurrection.

JUNE 24   THE GIFT WORTH GIVING

(Read Mark 12:41-44.)

The woman hurried to the Temple, hoping no one would notice her. She realized her clothes were worn, but they were the only things she owned. At least they were clean. Her rough, swollen fingers rubbed the two coins they held.

She reached the Temple and walked to the place where the offerings were put. Quickly, she dropped her coins into the offering and returned to her home. How God could use her measly offering she had no idea, but what little she had would always go to him.

The widow hadn't noticed the group of men across from the offering place. If she had, she wouldn't have intruded on their conversation. Two thousand years later, however, the words of one of the men are still being quoted: "I tell you the truth, this poor widow has put more into the treasury than all the others. They all gave out of their wealth; but she, out of her poverty, put in everything—all she had to live on."

It's too easy for us to judge the importance of our lives by human standards. The big offerings are the most important. Famous people can do the most for God. The more people who are involved, the more significant is the occasion.

The God who created our world does not *need* anything we can produce, but he will use it. To God, all of us are poor, but we are also worth the life of his Son. Like the widow, may we give God everything and trust him with the results.

JUNE 25   SHARING HIS SUFFERING

(Read Matthew 27:55-56.)

The day was unusually cool. Storm clouds were gathering and the gentle breeze had become a stiff wind. The group of women huddled closer, but they would not leave. Afraid as they were of the Roman soldiers, they were not going to leave Jesus alone as he died.

The whole day seemed unreal. Late last night had come the news of Jesus' arrest, and this morning began with the procession to Golgotha. Why would God let the Messiah die?

Mary Magdalene gazed in horror at Jesus' tortured body. There hung the man who had given her the gift of forgiveness and self-respect. She could not save him, but she hoped her presence would ease his suffering.

Suddenly, Jesus cried out. Then he was dead. The stunned women grabbed each other for support as they felt a great earthquake move the ground. None of them had ever felt such pain.

The mother of James and John thought of the times she had asked Jesus to reward her sons with more power. Shame colored her face at the memory. How little she had understood what it meant to be a follower of Jesus.

Sharing in other people's suffering has always been part of following Jesus, but not many of us embrace it. A person in pain can be difficult, unreasonable, and unappreciative. They may be scorned and hated. When we choose to spend our time with them, we may find ourselves being ostracized as well.

Remember Jesus' words: "I tell you the truth, whatever you did for one of the least of these my brothers of mine, you did for me" (Matthew 25:40 NIV). Will we share in Jesus' suffering?

JUNE 26   SURPRISED BY JOY

(Read Luke 24:1-8.)

Mechanically, the women gathered the spices they had prepared for Jesus' body. The shock of his death had not yet worn off, but they knew they had to anoint his body.

The cool, early morning air enveloped them as they walked quietly to the tomb where they had seen Joseph of Arimathea place Jesus' body. They hoped they wouldn't meet many people and could get their job done quickly without much interference from the guards.

As they entered the darkened tomb, they stopped. Where was the body? Everyone agreed that it was the right tomb. What had happened?

Suddenly, light blinded their eyes. The women blinked and then fell on the ground in fear. Two men wearing clothes that gleamed like lightning were in the tomb with them.

"Why do you look for the living among the dead?" the men asked. "He is not here; he has risen!"

The women became the first believers to experience the power of the Resurrection. The grief at Christ's death had been transformed into the joy of his redemption.

Paul prayed, "I want to know Christ and the power of his resurrection and the fellowship of sharing in his sufferings, becoming like him in his death, and so, somehow, to attain to the resurrection from the dead" (Philippians 3:10-11 NIV).

We will face times when God asks us to sacrifice a dream, a relationship, a love. Sometimes sin will bring death and destruction. These are the crosses we are called to bear. But just as we face the pain of the cross, we will also experience resurrection power. Christ will restore what was lost, mend what was broken, and bring life where there was death.

JUNE 27   THE LIE

(Read Acts 5:1-11.)

Sapphira walked to the house where the apostles were staying. She kept her eyes lowered, trying to hide her elation. Finally, she and Ananias would get some respect. She had been almost sick, listening to what people said about Barnabas after he had donated the money he had made from selling one of his fields.

That's when Ananias had come up with his plan. He could sell a piece of property and tell the apostles that he was giving all the proceeds of the sale to the church. Of course he would keep some of the money for his family, but that didn't matter. It would be a win/win situation. The poor in the church would have more food, and Ananias and Sapphira would have more money and more respect.

As Sapphira walked into the house, she spotted Peter. She hadn't seen Ananias since he delivered the money to the apostles, so she wondered how Peter had reacted to the gift.

"Tell me, is this the price you and Ananias got for the land?" Peter asked.

"Yes," she said, "that is the price."

"How could you agree to test the Spirit of the Lord?" Peter said. "Look! The feet of the men who buried your husband are at the door, and they will carry you out also."

Those were the last words Sapphira heard. Instantly, she dropped to the floor and died.

The early church reacted to this incident with fear, and we shouldn't take it lightly either. Some women try to avoid personal responsibility for situations by hiding behind their husband, church leadership, employer, or other authority figure. This passage makes it clear that God holds us individually responsible for what we say and do. Let's commit to living our lives with integrity.

JUNE 28   ENCOURAGING YOUNG TALENT

(Read Acts 18:24-28.)

As Priscilla looked at the earnest young man eating the lamb she had prepared for dinner, she smiled—how he reminded her of herself and Aquila when they had first met Paul back in Corinth. They had been so eager to learn everything he knew about Jesus.

She sighed. That was some time ago. Now here they were in Ephesus, and at last report, Paul was traveling through Galatia and Phrygia. How the church needed good leadership! She had recognized that quality in Apollos the first time she had heard him at the synagogue. He preached with such passion and eloquence. But he didn't know the full story about Jesus.

That's why he was here today. She and Aquila would teach him in their home, just as Paul had taught them. And someday. . . . Who knew how God would use Apollos?

The New Testament tells us that Apollos became a great help to the church. "He vigorously refuted the Jews in public debate, proving from the Scriptures that Jesus was the Christ," we learn in Acts. First Corinthians chapter 3 makes it clear that Apollos also had a significant role in establishing the church at Corinth.

Priscilla and Aquila chose to open their home to a stranger. Instead of attacking him in public because of his incomplete knowledge, they offered him the gift of time, treated him with respect, and taught him to follow Jesus. It may not have been a service that received much public attention, but it had long-term significance for the church.

Do you know a modern Priscilla? Maybe she needs encouragement and appreciation for her faithfulness, love, and wisdom.

JUNE 29   WHAT'S A MOTHER TO DO?

(Read II Timothy 1:1-7.)

All we know about Lois and Eunice is that they were two women who had a sincere faith that they passed on to Timothy. We don't know if Timothy's father had died or if he didn't share the faith of his wife. He simply isn't mentioned.

All kinds of questions come to mind. How difficult was it to raise Timothy? When did he come to faith? If his father was not a Christian, how did Eunice handle the situation? And if she was a single parent, what resources were available to her as she raised her son?

Fascinating as it may be to speculate about their lives, the little we know about Lois and Eunice is encouragement enough. Through their actions and words, these two women were primarily responsible for developing a sincere faith in Timothy. That's the most important accomplishment any mother or grandmother can achieve, but the results are often long in coming and the process can be discouraging.

My own mother has half-jokingly told me that, more than any of her children, I drove her to her knees in prayer. While I'm sorry for the grief I caused her as I was growing up, I'm very thankful for a mother who not only prayed for me, but who also lived her faith every day in tangible ways.

Children often don't say anything, but they notice when their mothers and grandmothers live a sincere faith. The reward for such a life may not come immediately, but it will come.

JUNE 30   THE RACE

(Read Hebrews 12:1-3.)

I've never been a good athlete. It took me ten years to figure out how to ride a bike, and the only spins I've ever done while skating did not take place while I was on my feet. Maybe that's one reason I'm such an avid sports fan. I admire the control gifted athletes have over their bodies.

Being a product of New England, I dream that the Boston Red Sox will win one World Series before I die (something they haven't accomplished since well before my parents were born). I've rooted for my favorite team wherever I have lived. I even cheered for the Red Sox in Yankee Stadium!

The writer of Hebrews was thinking of sports fans when he wrote today's reading. The saints who have lived before us are pictured as fans in the stands, cheering us on. We are the athletes, involved in the long-distance race of life, an event that requires great endurance.

The choices and changes we confront in this race are not unique. As we've seen this month, women have been experiencing similar challenges for thousands of years. These women found God faithful to his Word, and so will we. During each day, each change, let's turn to Jesus and keep on running. Then one day, we'll finish our race and hear his words, "Well done."

Love One Another

REBECCA LAIRD

JULY 1   **LIVING PROOF**

(Read I John 1:1-4.)

My gentle grandfather had a hobby of visiting from house to house, inviting all he met to Sunday school. His witnessing to strangers embarrassed me, but I never told him. His actions flowed from an indisputable wellspring of kindness.

During my teen years my best friend and I drove around town after school, hoping to catch a glimpse of the older boys we secretly liked. Scott, a basketball player, practiced his jump shot for hours in front of his house. One afternoon, he motioned for us to stop. I silently watched him as if he were a movie star. My friend, who was tall and blonde, tried to beguile him, but he seemed preoccupied.

When Scott turned to me and asked, "You go to church, don't you?" I flushed, chagrined that my church attendance was the first thing he remembered about me. Scott went on, "An old man who sometimes stops by to talk just asked me if I wanted to go to Sunday school. What happens in Sunday school?" I knew immediately that Scott had unknowingly encountered my faithful grandfather. Dumbfounded, I answered, "Uh, we usually talk about how to live what we believe."

"That old guy sure does that," Scott replied. "I really like him." Then the conversation shifted back to matters of high school. The next time I saw my grandfather, I hugged him tight for being living proof of what he proclaimed.

JULY 2   **SOUL DUSTING**

(Read I John 1:5-7.)

When I was in college, the chaplain once said, "Paradise is a condition of transparency between God and us, where nothing is hid." Today, a decade later, I remembered those words as the mid-morning sunlight streamed through the window beside my desk. The purity of that beam exposed a cobweb formed alongside the desk organizer, full of files long untouched. I took a hasty swipe at the cobweb and returned to work. The sun continued to shine steadily, gradually becoming unbearably warm on the side of my face. I looked up again and saw the strings of the cobweb hanging loosely from the plastic organizer and shook my head, amazed at how consistent my outer life and inner life seem to be. Just as I swipe at the cobwebs that clutter my desk only when they are exposed to sunlight, so too I most readily take heed of the habits, fears, and unresolved conflicts in my soul when God illuminates them with intense clarity. Regular dusting of my desk and soul are what it will take to allow me to live more fully in God's light.

JULY 3   **TELLING OUR STORIES**

(Read I John 1:8-10.)

I recently talked to a minister of an activist inner city church about the dozens of recovery groups it offers for addicts of every kind. "What makes your approach different from any other program based on the twelve steps of Alcoholics Anonymous?" I asked.

His answer surprised me: "Most of our groups aren't anonymous here. We've seen that those who have turned to addictions after being abused, pushed down, and used in so many ways need to learn to stand up and tell their stories. They must find the courage to publicly admit their abuse, pain, and sin. When courage is combined with an experience of true

176

acceptance from God and a supportive community, healing happens."

His words confirmed my own belief that most of us are well aware of our hidden sins and wounds. We don't need to be told that something is wrong with us. What we need most is a safe place where we can admit and honestly face ourselves for the first time.

JULY 4   STEPPING INTO THE LIGHT

(Read I John 2:1-3.)

I first collided with the hard wall of injustice while I was a college sophomore. A summer assignment on three spectacular, yet squalid Caribbean islands made me question why a kind, compassionate God allowed faithful people to live in cardboard shacks and labor as human mules, carrying beastly loads for miles, just to make a few cents to buy meager portions of food. These people needed an advocate! When I returned to college I raged, I worked, and I spread the word that all was not well in the world.

Even months after my homecoming, my soul was distressed, but I didn't know why. I kept going to classes. Then one day I read a line in my philosophy textbook about the "existential predicament." That day I learned a term for my inner fears—I was alone, in a very real sense. No one would ever be able to walk inside my five-foot, four-inch frame or fully see through my eyes. Anew, I saw my own poverty and need for the companionship of God.

I did the only thing that any of us can do—I stepped into the light, admitting my anger, rage, inadequacies, and sin. The presence of aeons stood beside me and surrounded me with light.

JULY 5   WALKING AS JESUS WALKED

(Read I John 2:4-6.)

Walking as Jesus walked is not a summons to success, and that scares me. A gruesome cross stood on Christ's path before he rose in glory. Does walking as Jesus walked demand that I die, both in little ways daily and, perhaps, bodily?

On this date, one year while visiting my parents, I awoke after a fitful night to the sounds of my father's sobs. He stood in the hallway, holding the morning paper. My father told me that a troubled young man whom I had loved and prayed with for years had been arrested for the recent murder of a woman I knew and respected. I shook inside for months.

This man had confessed Christ as Savior and had grown in his ability to love. I'd spent hours alone with him. Did he do it? Could I have been the victim?

A year of spiritual struggle has taught me that God didn't promise physical protection to the first-century martyrs, nor are there such guarantees for me. Then and now, the greatest act of faith is to believe that God's presence will be enough at the hour of my greatest testing.

JULY 6   NO NEW COMMANDMENT

(Read I John 2:7-8.)

There is no new commandment to learn and no new course to take that will give me the upper hand on living. I once thought it was so.

I grew up in a professor's home, regularly filled with college students. From my childhood perspective, I thought they had learned the secrets of life.

I attended college, unconsciously expecting to be perfected, but I graduated with few answers.

Asking for the secrets to life is nothing new. In the Gospel of Mark, a scribe asked Jesus, "Which commandment is the first of all?" Jesus answered, "Love God completely, and love your neighbor as yourself."

Yesterday, I took a writing break and listened to my answering machine. A friend exclaimed that his wife had prematurely delivered their baby. I momentarily weighed my impending deadlines with the desire to visit my friends in their jubilation. The words "love your neighbor as yourself" popped into my mind. I can still remember those who interrupted their schedules to lovingly visit when my daughter was born. I grabbed my coat and pocketed bus fare. There is no greater secret to life than loving our neighbors.

JULY 7   HATRED IN THE BACK ROW

(Read I John 2:9-11.)

In my twenties, I helped start a faith community in an inner-city neighborhood. When a pastoral change was needed, we hired someone who silently began to replace the original leadership. Over time, I began to feel like a spectator, sitting on her hands in the back row of my church. My gifts were unwanted. Rage slowly overtook me until I realized that I was full of hatred. Going to church was worse than having weekly root canals. Finally I left, knowing my soul could not thrive in isolation and hatred.

For the next year, I waded through deep confusion. Why had God called and equipped me, then allowed me to be shoved out? How could I hate a fellow Christian so much? A wise spiritual companion walked with me through the hatred, anger, and despair. As my hatred dispersed, so did the clouds of confusion. Only then did I find a new church with a pastor who watched me take a seat in the back row, afraid of new commitment. She saw my gifts and called me forth. Timidly, with awe at God's graciousness, I walked back into the community of faith.

JULY 8   GOD PROVIDES

(Read I John 2:12-14.)

Santos Elizondo is one of my favorite mothers of the faith, for she knew God would provide. Santos, a Hispanic woman, came to faith in southern California in 1905 through the efforts of a woman holiness preacher in the Church of the Nazarene. Santos soon felt a call to the ministry, and despite protests from her husband, she began evangelistic work in Mexican border towns on the Rio Grande River.

For nearly thirty-five years, Santos almost single-handedly oversaw a church, day school, women's society, orphanage, and medical clinic, where she served as the midwife. Funds were scarce, and Santos financed much of the work out of her own meager salary.

The story is told of an early morning when Santos woke

about four o'clock and went to cover the orphan children. As she did, she realized there were not enough blankets. She first felt fear, for winter fast approached. She then prayed, "Lord, you have those blankets somewhere for me. Make the one who has them bring them in."

A few hours later, a knock came at the door. There stood the president of the Catholic societies with a dozen blankets.

JULY 9   LOVING GOD

(Read I John 2:15-17.)

Loving the world is like trying to attract an elusive lover. The chase of the fantasy offers excitement. Did I look good enough? Did I act impressive yet detached? Will he choose me? We know what it will take to love and lure the world. If we set our sights on winning the affection of the world at any cost, we probably can.

Loving God is riskier, for it is more like loving my husband. The constancy of intimacy, rather than the chase of elusive love, brings lasting fulfillment. After years of marriage, my task is to continue to love my dear husband even when he doesn't do things just as I wish he would. We've lived in this house for more than two years, yet he still forgets what day the garbage must be hauled to the curb. He too knows my foibles, and he can tell when I'm bluffing or feel insecure. I can't hide behind a well-made-up face or crisply pressed clothes.

Loving God, like loving my husband, requires that I be painfully honest with myself and live my life one day at a time. Loving the world requires only that I look good and learn to count my riches. Sometimes I give in to my lust for the world until I see the face of the God whom I love, and I realize that after all these years we have a good thing going.

JULY 10   THE GIFT OF DISCERNMENT

(Read I John 2:18-21.)

Here is a pearl of wisdom once given to me: Discernment is given to you for your protection rather than for your judgment.

For years I listened to my inner alarms when faced with

uncertain situations, and I labeled the people who set off my emotional caution signals as "bad" or "not to be trusted."

A few years ago a friend and I visited a prospective employer for several days. He promised a dream job and underlined his offer with eloquent promises and elaborate expense-account dinners. Everything sounded and looked good, but I felt uneasy. My friend didn't. At first I felt compelled to convince her, but the reminder that discernment was for my protection, rather than judgment, stopped me. I didn't pursue the employment opportunity, but my friend did. Her style of work made the job work for her. I would have been continually frustrated. The employer wasn't bad; the job just wasn't for me.

God, when my inner alarms sound, help me to remember that your spirit is guiding me into all truth and protecting me from what I am not able to handle. Help me to trust your gift of discernment for my protection while withholding judgment about others.

JULY 11   A SHARED GOSPEL FAITH

(Read I John 2:22-25.)
Several years ago during a retreat, the leader, a wise monk, told our group that one of the prerequisites for a true spiritual community is an adequate sharing of the same gospel faith.

Whether clearly articulated or not, a core set of beliefs holds together any faith community. One of the tasks of the spiritual community is to regularly reexamine its shared beliefs and mission in the world.

The retreat leader went on to say that community is formed to be a school of spirituality—a school of love. As a community learns to love Jesus together, each member learns to love and to warn one another of impending trouble.

In I John the loving and zealous defender of the faith calls for community members to reaffirm the core belief that Jesus is the Christ. Some in the community of faith believed that Jesus was a heavenly, supernatural messenger. John clearly encourages the faithful to confess the core belief that Jesus was the anointed, human child of God whose death atoned for human sin. As a wise leader, John knows that a shared gospel faith is essential for loving relationships in the community.

JULY 12   THE ONE WHO GUIDES

(Read I John 2:26-28.)

What a fearsome thing it is to trust that my own spirit will be able to discern truth from lies if I dwell in the nearness of God.

During seminary I took a workshop on the art of spiritual direction. I had greatly benefited from having a spiritual director. A pastor who regularly tuned her own spirit had graciously helped me to listen for the work of God in my own life. Could I ever learn to be of similar help to others? What if I misled someone?

One of the workshop exercises helped to lessen my fears. Participants were instructed to pair off and collect three chairs. My partner and I puzzled over the empty chair until the leader explained, "The Spirit of God sits in the third chair, guiding you both, as an active participant in your communication. The Spirit does the guiding as you seek to be honest and attentive to your lives."

What a relief that chair brought to me. Even if I had nothing wise to say, it wouldn't matter. The Spirit of God is the one who guides and inflames our spirits with truth.

JULY 13   GOD'S CHILDREN

(Read I John 3:1-3.)

Am I Irving's and Beverly's daughter? Michael's wife? Rachel's mother? How do the relationships in my life define me?

When I married, I did not change my surname. Taking a new name seemed to identify me primarily by my relationship to my husband. While he is the most important person in my life, he is not *me*.

My parents and my in-laws all thought I was silly. One relative even told me that a Christian speaker had said that a wife couldn't keep her name and be a Christian. Another friend asked with real concern, "What will the mailman think?" The mail carrier's opinion of me had never crossed my mind!

When our daughter was born, we gave her my last name as a middle name and my husband's last name as her surname. We wanted her to identify herself freely with both sides of the family.

Likewise, we are God's children. We must choose if we will be identified by our relationship with God, but nothing, not even a name, can change who it was that first gave us life.

JULY 14   A LACK OF LOVE

(Read I John 3:4-10.)

If obedience to the greatest law means that I love God wholeheartedly and love my neighbor as myself, doesn't that mean that sin always results from a lack of love?

Two weeks ago my next-door neighbor called me an hour before my party and began to tell me that her family would not be attending. While I honestly assured her that their absence would cause no problem, I silently wondered if she might be calling at the last moment out of vengeance. When she previously had invited us to a birthday party on short notice, I had telephoned our regrets the day before to explain that my husband had committed us elsewhere. She was nice enough, but I thought I detected frustration—perhaps she had purchased too much food or had several cancellations. Now, weeks later, I was assigning a negative motive to my neighbor's call.

When I thought about my response, I realized how unloving it was. One of the characteristics of love is that it believes the best in another. Today I must ask for forgiveness for my sin and find a way to show love to my neighbor.

JULY 15   LOVE BEGINS AT HOME

(Read I John 3:11-12.)

The first murderous act recorded in the Bible tells of family violence. Why is it that most violence is inflicted by the people who are closest to one another? Random violence is relatively rare, although terrifyingly real when it occurs.

I remember the shock I felt in 1991 when the television reported the murder of a soldier who had just returned from the Persian Gulf. There was public outcry because this man had survived war but had been randomly gunned down on an inner city street in his homeland. A few weeks later the news reported that it was suspected that the man's death had been planned by his wife, who wanted to use the insurance money to start a new life.

Appalling as this story is, it makes me think of the words of Mother Teresa: "Love begins at home." Unless I learn to love myself and those closest to me, I too could be one who lashes out from selfishness, cruelty, or jealousy at those closest at hand, those whom I have vowed to love the most.

JULY 16   EMOTIONAL MURDER

(Read I John 3:13-15.)

"We can murder a person's spirit by withholding love," writes Lloyd Ogilvie. Isn't murder an overt act of violence? These verses deal with emotional murder—the kind that kills when we close our hearts toward another.

A tender-hearted Christian woman I know became pregnant when she was young and unmarried. Terrified, she confided in an older, more sophisticated friend who said, "Several of my friends have had abortions, but not you. You are better than they were." Then the friend offered nothing but stony silence.

The young woman met with several ministers, searched her heart, and decided to end the pregnancy. Her friend broke her silence long enough to call her a murderer.

The young woman struggled with her friend's accusation for years. Her friend's accusation festered like an emotional bullet wound. Her friend, by withholding love, had essentially murdered her spirit. Is the one who chose an abortion or the one who withheld love the murderer?

Using the definition of I John, the judge's gavel would sound with a guilty verdict for us all. We all stand in need of God's mercy.

MY FRIEND DAVID

(Read I John 3:16-17.)

My friend David is back on the streets, living in a construction site downtown. After the crews go home, he and others of the silent homeless population climb the scaffolding and disappear into the hidden corners.

David rang my doorbell this morning. His unexpected visit irritated me. The last time he came over he wanted to take a shower. The time before, he hadn't eaten for a couple of days. What was it this time?

"David, what are you doing here?" I asked without even saying hello. My tone clearly communicated my testy attitude.

"I came to pick up the letter my social worker sent here."

I pointed him in the direction of the letter, but he stopped long enough to make my daughter laugh at the breakfast table.

David picked up the letter and told me that he and his buddy had found a dead man this morning. He must have fallen while trying to get in the building.

When David left, I hugged him and said, "Be careful, okay?" All he wanted was the use of my mailbox. Such a little inconvenience for this one I love.

ACTIONS SPEAK LOUDER THAN WORDS

(Read I John 3:18.)

The Reverend Cecil Williams, pastor of Glide Church in San Francisco, signs his letters with the salutation, "Walk that walk."

Cecil often incites controversy, but he gets things done. He once marshalled more than six hundred people who marched on a crime-filled public housing project.

The mass marched down a busy street, singing songs and carrying platters heaped with fried chicken and buckets full of paint. The marchers came to challenge the drug pushers, the users, and the residents afraid to stand up to the violence to make a choice for recovery.

Many residents responded to the call for change; some came for the chicken. Cecil walked up to the door of an apartment notorious for crack use and called to those inside, "Come join us." Amazingly, they did.

After the march, the crime rate at that project plummeted. Glide Church instituted long-range health, social service, and recovery programs that continue to make a difference at the project.

John Wesley once told his critics, "I like my way of doing things better than your way of not doing them." Actions speak loudly of the content of our faith.

JULY 19   BEYOND IMPERFECTIONS

(Read I John 3:19-22.)

This morning I reread my journal from a year that I remember most for its upheavals and setbacks. The entries surprised me. Many prayers for the people in my life and praises for God's presence are recorded in those pages. Time after time I acted out of love for my friends. Between the handwritten lines of daily happenings and hopes, there is a strength of faith that I didn't remember. Reading those pages that were written without censure infused my heart with confidence.

As one prone to believe that only excellent work counts, I tend to remember the times I failed more than the times I did my best to muddle faithfully through. How good God is to find ways to remind me that I am being molded and fashioned by love, even when I can't see beyond my imperfections.

JULY 20   WHAT DOES GOD REQUIRE?

(Read I John 3:23-24.)

Today I planted some bright poppies on my patio and indulged in an unproductive mental debate. I pondered for the umpteenth time what God wants me to do with my life. Should I continue working for myself so that I have time for my writing projects? Will I ever take another job in the publishing industry? What opportunities are there to utilize my seminary degree? When will my daughter be old enough to be in day care full time—and when will I be ready for that?

The sagacity in I John tells me that God views my questions through a broader lens than I do. God desires two things from my life: that I believe in the power and priorities of Jesus and that I love others.

What? God doesn't care what I do to make money? God doesn't have a perfect job waiting that will give me a deepened sense of purpose?

God's will for us all is changeless. Centuries ago the Old Testament prophet Micah declared, "What does God require of you? To do justice, to love kindness and to walk humbly with your God."

JULY 21   OUR FRIEND JESUS

(Read I John 4:1-3.)

San Francisco is notorious for spawning unconventional religious movements. The original site of the People's Temple is three blocks from my house. EST, the well-known human potential movement, still has its headquarters here, as do many other groups that might not be welcomed elsewhere.

There also are several openly gay churches scattered throughout the city. During a seminary class, I began talking to one of the pastors of these churches, and he invited the AIDS mission group to which I belonged to a healing service. We agreed to go. Our group had formed expressly to pray for and offer healing love to those who were suffering.

I approached the service with apprehension. I had been asked to serve Communion, and several leaders from my denomination would be attending. Yet it took only one song to put me at ease. Those present glorified and sought Christ. I offered the Communion blessing, saying, "When Jesus was with those he called his friends, he asked them to eat and drink with him. Tonight, Jesus bids us, his friends, to do likewise." Tears welled up in my eyes as an ailing man from the congregation ran sobbing into my arms. God's healing spirit was powerfully present.

DEEP CALLS TO DEEP

(Read I John 4:4-6.)

I John says that "whoever knows God listens to us." My first response to this claim was rueful. Many times I've felt unheard and unheeded by other people of faith. But then I realized that listening has little to do with agreement. Listening means offering respectful attention to another's experience and beliefs. When we take time to listen to the spirit of another, we can sense whether God is present.

The writer of Psalm 42 uses the lyric phrase "deep calls to deep" to describe how two bodies of fathomless waters beckon to each other when God's power is made manifest. The metaphor reassures me that God's presence in my life brings with it an ability to discern when others truly share a deep desire for God.

This happened to me this year! When engulfed in loneliness and fear, I sought a spiritual companion who helped me listen to the churning depths of my despair. Only as I learned to listen to myself could I recognize who were the kindred spirits in my life. Deep speaks to deep when I take the time to listen.

A MESSENGER OF LOVE

(Read I John 4:7-9.)

Teresa of Avila inspired the lyrics to a chorus I like to sing. The song explains that we are Christ's instruments in this world. We are his hands, his feet, and his eyes.

God, with such infinite, intimate wisdom, knew how much we need to show love for one another.

My friend Christine really knows how to love. She calls often to share a laugh or to leave a cheery message on my answering machine. When she visited yesterday, she brought a basket of bright toys and candy for my daughter. Last week she not only baby-sat while my husband and I celebrated our wedding anniversary, but also presented us with a bag full of homemade, heart-shaped scones before we left.

The tangible reminders of her love tell me that she has thought of me during her busy week. The knowledge that I am important to another makes me feel lovable and worthwhile. I'm grateful to God for Christine. She is one of God's messengers of love.

JULY 24   LOVE HEALS

(Read 1 John 4:10-12.)
I caught a glimpse of God today in a circle of recovering drug addicts. While gathering material for a story, I listened as twenty people opened up their lives to one another in the belief that together they could find strength to stay clean and sober for one more day.

The first man said, "I moved to a beautiful new room on Saturday. I'd been afraid to move, even though my roommates were all using drugs. I feared I'd end up in a roach-filled room somewhere, but God knew what I needed. Although I don't know where all the finances will come from, *I know* that God will provide for me. I've got a job interview at 3 P.M. Keep me in your prayers." His face glowed as he spoke.

"I'm so blessed," a homeless woman emphasized. "I don't even desire to take drugs today. Although I never thought I would have to live in a shelter, it's okay for now. I'm grateful to God because I'm free from crack."

After each one spoke honestly, the others applauded. Acceptance abounded in that circle. These people were loving one another to health.

JULY 25   LOVING OURSELVES

(Read 1 John 4:13-16.)
Love is God's address. It is where God lives. To abide in God means to dwell, inhabit, reside, and stay in love for God, for others, and for ourselves.

A woman told me a story today. She went to the bank and withdrew a large sum of money. Only when she went to purchase what she needed did she realize that she had been shortchanged.

She said, "My first reaction was to doubt myself. I tried to convince myself that I must have lost the money somewhere, but in my heart I knew better. I had no way of proving that the bank didn't give me all my money. Yet I knew that if someone else had lost $100, I would come to their aid. Why was it so hard to love myself enough to right a wrong done to me?"

The woman mustered her confidence and returned to the bank. The teller asked if she would stay after the bank closed when the tills were counted. There was $100 extra in the tills!

In a simple way, that woman chose to live in the love God has for her by believing in herself.

JULY 26   NO FEAR IN LOVE

(Read I John 4:17-21.)

Last night I kept the dog inside, even though it wasn't raining. I was afraid. With my husband away, the creaking floorboards of our old house and the late-night sound of voices from the street spooked me. I repeated the words "There is no fear in love" to myself, just as I did when I was afraid of the dark as a child. Those words have served as my talisman of safety many times when I have been filled with fear.

What am I afraid of? I'm afraid of intrusion and violence—the unknown things I can't control. I do my best to ensure my safety because, I guess, deep down I doubt that God will protect me. In fact, I know that God didn't keep safe my friend who was murdered. The way of Jesus led him to a violent death, and that scares me.

I read somewhere that fear comes from an unstable trust of God's grace. I do wonder sometimes if ultimately God's love is strong enough. Maybe I have to decide whether I want a long, safe life more than I want a life that is fully offered to God—whatever the cost.

JULY 27   WHO LOVES THE CHILD?

(Read I John 5:1-5.)

I John tells me that "everyone who loves the parent loves the child." Does love for God equal love for Jesus?

When I was little, my girlfriend's mother was not a Christian. My limited view of God made me worry about her fate. I remembered puzzling about how a loving God could send someone who was so compassionate and good-hearted to hell. She believed in God, but she wasn't clear about Jesus.

These thoughts came back to me years later when I received a Christmas card from her. Her note clearly told me that she was fully celebrating Christmas as the birth of Jesus, her Lord. She mentioned her faith and her church. From my enlarged view of God, I smiled. She had always loved God, loved other people, and sought the truth; it was only natural that in time, she too would come to love Jesus, the beloved child.

JULY 28   CALLED TO ADVENTURE

(Read I John 5:6-12.)

In Hebrew the word *spirit* means *wind,* and in Greek it means *breathe.* When God wants a third witness to testify that Jesus is the Son of God, God opens the windows of heavens and lets the Spirit blow.

The Spirit is an unpredictable witness: I can't anticipate the power or the direction in which it will blow. I can simply learn more accurately how to lick my fingers, hold them up in the air, and gauge the direction from whence it comes.

The spiritual life is not about orderliness, personal propriety, or respectable morals. It is about cultivating a life in which the witness of the Spirit can be sensed and followed.

British mathematician and philosopher Alfred North Whitehead once wrote, "The Worship of God is not a rule of safety, it is an adventure of the Spirit. . . . Without the high hope of adventure, religion degenerates into a mere appendage of a comfortable life." His words remind me that a commitment to live by the Spirit is to be called to adventure, to risk, and to the unexpected. Today, may I turn my face into the wind and trust what the Spirit is doing.

JULY 29   GOD HEARS US

(Read I John 5:13-15.)

During our first year of marriage, my husband and I lived in a dream house. The house sat high on a hill, overlooking the Golden Gate Bridge and the silhouette of San Francisco's shimmering skyscrapers. Deer tiptoed into the backyard from the nearby state park to nibble on the apple tree.

Each day my husband and I drove into the city where we worked, and at night we returned to this peaceful place. Unexpectedly, we learned that the house was being sold. We had only days to decide where to go.

One morning I woke up very early. I took my Bible, sat by the window, and watched San Francisco become bathed in a pink light as the darkness rolled back, giving way to the dawn.

I didn't know how to pray. Part of me wanted to beg God to let us stay in our home. Another part of me wanted to do God's will. But what did God want?

I read from my Bible and began to clearly sense that moving back into the inner city was God's desire. God wanted us to live among the people we served.

I prayed for the strength to divest myself of my home, and I knew that God heard me.

JULY 30   OBSESSED WITH FEAR

(Read I John 5:16-17.)

One of the men who came to the Wednesday night Bible studies for homeless people, which my husband taught, regularly took me aside. He was obsessed with fear that he had committed an unpardonable sin. Each time, I tried to ferret out the basis for his fear, but I found nothing. He was afraid that unknowingly he would offend God. He was like a man constantly checking his pulse to reassure himself that he was alive. He seemed to think God was unpredictably punitive. God would find some reason to flog him.

One night I told him that his earnest desire to honor God was in itself proof that he was unlikely to refuse the Holy Spirit. This man wanted life, but he so distrusted himself that he couldn't live in the freedom God offered.

The next week he came to Bible study and testified that he had sinned against a friend by getting angry and lashing out, but that he had confessed his sin and felt forgiven. At last this man was getting to know God as the just and kind friend of sinners, who would rather forgive and love than punish.

JULY 31 THE TRUE GOD

(Read I John 5:18-21.)

One summer, along with several friends, my husband and I traveled to Calcutta to volunteer with the Missionaries of Charity. We all got horribly sick.

On the day we were scheduled to be at the Home for the Dying, only two of us could get out of bed. We spent the morning emptying bedpans, clipping toenails, brushing hair, and hand-feeding some of the bone-thin patients. The work made me focus on the elemental nature of compassion. God calls us to show love in tangible ways.

When our work was done, my companion and I stopped next door to visit Kaligat, the Hindu Temple. Inside, a woman dressed in rags and carrying a scrawny, undernourished child bought a sweet tidbit. I looked in horror as she offered the treat to Ganesh, the elephant God who removes obstacles. I wanted to grab the morsel and hand it to the child, who eyed it longingly.

This woman, sincerely hoping for a better life, put her best before a cement elephant. How I wished this woman knew that what God really desires is that the little ones of God be fed.

AUGUST

Our Family

MARY RUTH HOWES

"There are many rooms in my Father's House. . . . I am coming again to welcome you into my own home."
—John 14:2 (Phillips)

In most of the places I've lived, August is a month of heat and humidity, when leaves hang dark and heavy, and we wait for the turning of the year for the freshening breezes and lightened colors of September. August is the end of summer, the last month of freedom from school for kids, and, for many families, the last chance to *get away from home* on vacation. But for me, August is the month in which I celebrate *coming home* in a fifty-year-old anniversary. (I'll say more about that on the appropriate day.)

Because that anniversary dates back to my childhood, I'd like to look this month at what we can learn from Scripture about home and family and being children and adults in both the literal and the spiritual senses. We'll be spending some time with the Sermon on the Mount, because there we see described so clearly what it means to be part of God's family.

Home. At some level it's what we all long for—a place where we belong, where we are loved, where we feel secure, at ease, "at home." A home is created by the people in it. Ultimately our sense of home comes from God, our Father, who not only has prepared our ultimate home for us, as Jesus told us, but wants to make his home with us now. God loves us so much he wants to be *at home* with us. Imagine! And as *we* love God, we create space for God to live with us (John 14:23).

Thank you, Father, for homes and vacations, but most of all that with you I can always be at home.

AUGUST 2   FATHER

> *"This then is how* you *should pray:*
> *Our Father in Heaven . . ."*
> —Matthew 5:48 (Rieu)

The Sermon on the Mount is perhaps the most daunting sermon ever preached. Yes, it's beautiful, full of vivid images, wonderful metaphors, and rhythmic language. But the standards it sets for us are so lofty, so immense, if we're honest, we know there's no way for us ordinary human beings to live up to them. This is probably the reason that some Bible students have relegated the Sermon on the Mount to a future age when all believers will have been perfected and the kingdom of God will have finally arrived!

But there is hope for us imperfect folk here and now. Have you noticed that the phrase "your Father in Heaven" runs all through the sermon? And that at its heart, Jesus tells us to pray to "our Father"? In this sermon, Jesus is showing us how children of his Father behave. In Aramaic, which was his language, Jesus called God *Abba*—Daddy (Mark 14:36)—an intimate, loving name. If God is our Daddy, then we are his children. Children not only can ask their Daddy for help but they also inherit their parents' characteristics. We have our Father's nature to help us live up to Jesus' standards. And we have Jesus, our elder Brother, to model those characteristics (Hebrews 2:10).

Thank you, Father, for making me a part of your family, sharing in your love with my sisters and brothers, and with Jesus your perfect Son.

196

Can a woman forget her sucking child, that she should not have compassion on the son of her womb? yea, they may forget, yet will I not forget thee.

—Isaiah 49:15 (KJV)

Every human family needs a mother as well as a father. What about our heavenly family?

Christianity has sometimes been accused of being a male religion. Certainly it has often been presented that way. It is true that Jesus only speaks of God as Father. But he pictures himself as a hen calling her chicks to come under her wings for protection, as he weeps over Jerusalem. And he likens God's kingdom—God's household—to a woman baking bread, a woman searching for a lost coin.

In human terms, we generally think of mothers as the nurturers, the caregivers, more tender-hearted and loving than fathers. But women don't have a patent on these qualities. In our family, my father was the one we went to when we had a sliver in our finger or a cut or a burn. He was a good nurse and always knew what to do. When my sister was tiny, Daddy was the one who could coax her to stand still while he combed the tangles out of her curly hair.

The God Jesus calls Father is not a *male* figure. The Old Testament is full of language that attributes feminine qualities to God. The prophets speak of God as comforting Israel, like a mother comforts a child (Isaiah 66:13). "O Lord, my heart is not lifted up," writes the psalmist. "I have calmed and quieted my soul, like a weaned child with its mother" (Psalm 131:1-2*a* NRSV). Like an eagle stirring up her nest to make her fledglings fly, and catching them on her outspread wings, so the Lord cared for and led Jacob in the wilderness (Deuteronomy 32:11-12).

God is neither male nor female, masculine nor feminine, but beyond both. I am grateful that both male and female are made in the image of God, who cares for us like a father and like a mother. And when our fathers and our mothers forsake us—emotionally or physically or through death—the Lord takes us up (Psalm 27:10).

Thank you, God, that when I need a mother, you are there.

One of the most amazing metaphors that recurs throughout the Old Testament in connection with God is that of the womb. The Hebrew word for womb is the root for words translated "compassion" or "mercy." God loves us with a mother's love, a womb-love. This is displayed in Phyllis Trible's paraphrase of Jeremiah 31:20:

Is Ephraim my dear son? my darling child?
For the more I speak of him,
   the more I do remember him.
Therefore, my womb trembles for him;
I will truly show motherly-compassion [mercy] upon him.*

As a young girl, I remember my mother talking about God's mother-love in her Bible classes. It was important to her, perhaps, because there was a time when her father rejected her. But I didn't know the basis for her statement. Then thirteen years ago, on the advice of two surgeons, I had to have a hysterectomy. The prospect caused me immense grief and constant tears, which no one seemed to understand, not even myself.

It wasn't until after the surgery, while reading Phyllis Trible's discussion of God's womb-love for us, that I found the basis for my mother's teaching, which helped me to make sense of my grief. A woman's womb is part of the image of God in her. My womb was not *just* a container for bearing children that I no longer needed (since I was past child-bearing age). It somehow connected me to God. I had lost a significant part of me. Listen to what Ms. Trible says about the womb as the Old Testament writers speak of it in connection with God:

God conceives in the womb; God fashions in the womb; God judges in the womb; God destines in the womb; God brings forth from the womb; God receives out of the womb; and God carries

---

*Phyllis Trible, *God and the Rhetoric of Sexuality* (Philadelphia: Fortress Press, 1978), p. 45. Chapters 2 and 3 in her book discuss many of the maternal images and metaphors used of God.

from the womb to gray hairs. From this uterine perspective, then, Yahweh molds life for individuals and for the nation Israel. Accordingly, in biblical traditions, an organ unique to the female becomes a vehicle pointing to the compassion of God (p. 38).

Yes, the womb is only a physical organ, and we are more than just physical people. But as individuals made in the image of God, our physical bodies are an integral part of our identity. It's okay to grieve over a loss.

O God who mothers me, thank you for your love. Help me to transcend my loss and to grow more like you in my ability to nurture others.

AUGUST 5   SEX

> *David was the father of Solomon by Uriah's wife.*
>   —Matthew 1:6 (Rieu)

Recently I heard a woman preacher discussing why some men have great difficulty accepting women in the pulpit. Women and sex go together. And if a woman preacher is pregnant—there is obvious proof that the preacher has had sex! (Somehow we have been able to forget that men and sex go together!)

Scripture acknowledges the reality of sex in all its aspects, including celebrating its ecstasies in the Song of Solomon. And the "problem" of women and sex is taken care of once and for all in the genealogy of Jesus. The four women mentioned in Matthew's genealogy all have some impure or sexual taint. Tamar seduced her father-in-law by pretending to be a prostitute, because he hadn't found another husband for her after his son died. Rahab was both a Canaanite—a foreigner— and a prostitute. Ruth was a foreigner from Moab whom Israelites were not supposed to marry. And Bathsheba (who is not named by Matthew but mentioned as "the wife of Uriah") committed adultery with King David. Here is blatant sex—seduction, prostitution, adultery—along with the normal sex that maintains the human race.

With sex, as in the rest of life, God overturns all our

199

categories. Mistakes become part of the plan, as does our obedience. God also uses what we tend to despise to do great things. Think of admitting to all those scandals in your family tree! Scripture makes clear that we should not deliberately or recklessly sin, but also that it is with our bodies, as well as our spirits, that we serve and glorify God. And, thankfully, sex—which causes so much heartache and trouble, along with pleasure and ecstasy—will be done away with in heaven, our final home. Our knowing of one another will be on a different and deeper level.

Thank you for the gift of sex. Help us to offer it back to you so that we may use it lovingly and in your plan.

AUGUST 6   BIRTH

"Very truly, I tell you, no one can enter the kingdom of God without being born of water and Spirit."
—John 3:5 (NRSV)

The Gospel of John uses the metaphor of birth to describe the way we come into God's family, but makes it very clear that this is not like a human birth, dependent on sex and passion. Those who become children of God are "born, not of blood or of the will of the flesh or of the will of man, but of God" (John 1:13, NRSV). These are the people who receive the true light, the Word who became flesh—Jesus Christ.

The part of the church I was brought up in emphasizes this image. We come into God's family by being "born again." But in reading the Gospels I have been fascinated to see that the only person who was told he needed to be born again was probably the most religiously moral person in Palestine. It was not the promiscuous woman at the well, not Zaccheus the tax swindler, but Nicodemus—a Pharisee who kept the law, a member of the Sanhedrin and probably the foremost religious teacher.

As a young person reading my Bible, I always skipped over Jesus' condemnation of the Pharisees, because it didn't apply to me! I congratulated myself that I wasn't one of *them*, an enemy of

Jesus! I was one of the good guys. I had accepted Christ as my Savior. I was keeping the rules.

But who was it that needed to be born again? Nicodemus did. I did. It's the "good" person, the religious person, the "superior" person, the person so caught in his or her standards that there is no way for the Spirit of God to penetrate that shell. It's the person who sees perfection as keeping all the right laws, doing the right things and not doing anything on the banned list.

Why did Nicodemus come to Jesus? According to John's chronology, he had seen and heard Jesus cleaning out the Temple. He had witnessed Jesus' passion for God and his fearless confrontation of set-in-its-ways authority that too often ignored God. To Nicodemus this must have seemed a breath from God. Jesus responded to his flattering greeting by answering his unspoken question: "Yes, if you want to see God at work, if you want to feel God's breath, you must open yourself to the wind of God's Spirit. Leave the old. Admit your poverty of spirit. Let God do new things for you and change you from the inside out. Be willing to let go of all you thought you knew about God and come into God's family like a baby, who has to learn everything from scratch. Let God's Spirit fill you and teach you."

Lord, keep me from pride and mere moralism. I want to be open to the fresh wind of your Spirit.

AUGUST 7   BEGINNING AGAIN

The way to life is by a narrow gate and a difficult road.
—Matthew 7:14 (Rieu)

I'm learning that I need to be reborn again and again.

When a baby is born, it is usually through a very narrow way out of the mother's body, a very constricting way. I suspect that babies do not enjoy the process of coming from the security and weightlessness of the mother's womb into the extraordinary different world that we are in now. Nonetheless, most of them manage and are little the worse for it.

Every new beginning involves the same kind of narrowing.

We chose to follow Christ, put our trust in him, and give up our trust in everything else. We narrow our job choices from several to one. We quit running from church to church and choose to stay with one. We quit dating several people and focus on our marriage partner.

Right now I'm resisting the passage to "old age"! (I know both *old* and *age* are relative terms.) This year I turn sixty. I keep saying to myself, *How could this ever have happened? I'm not sixty inside! I don't think I even look sixty!* Yet more and more of my mentors, and even my friends, have died. College kids look like babies to me; what I experienced first-hand is only history to them. And people are giving me their seats on buses!

The result is that I want to hold on to youth, to the past, to mementos that reach back to my mother and grandmother and the history I have no other connection with. I want to stay in the comfortable present, where I have lots of treasures.

But to feel God's Spirit blowing, to let God's wind blow through my life, I need to leave the past behind and go gladly through the narrow way of aging into the new life of being a senior citizen. Technically I still have five and a half years to go, but I don't want to be dragged through kicking and screaming!

Some years ago at a contemplative retreat, we were asked to describe the images of God we held at various ages, and then project how we might picture God when we are seventy-five. The revelation that came to me then, and that comes back to me now, is that at seventy-five I want to worship God with flags and firecrackers, with joy and verve!

I'm on my way! Come join me!

Thank you, God, that you are my God, into old age and beyond.

AUGUST 8   THE FATHER WHO LOVES BEAUTY

"Let your light so shine upon the world that it may see the beauty of your life and give glory to your Father in Heaven."
—Matthew 5:16 (Rieu)

What kind of a family have we come into? In the next few days we'll look at what Jesus tells us about our Father in the

Sermon on the Mount and what implications that might have for our lives.

I came home tonight at dusk from meeting a friend for an early dinner to find I'd inadvertently left my blinds up and the lights on, so that my living room was clearly in view of passersby. My thoughts tumbled after each other—*oops, I'm wasting electricity—guess the neighborhood kids enjoyed seeing the cats—oh dear, everyone can see my mess!*

With these devotionals on my mind, I had to smile ruefully. I had certainly let my light shine—but it wasn't revealing much beauty, mostly an untidy room. With a small house, four cats, two newspapers, reams of junk mail, two hours of commuting each day and forty years' accumulation of books to contend with, untidiness is hardly surprising. But then, neither am I neat!

I know that it is the quality of our character Jesus is talking about that will cause people to be drawn to God when they see its beauty. And I know, too, that inner beauty isn't dependent on outer circumstances.

But sometimes I wish I lived in such beautiful surroundings that creating a beautiful life would be automatic!

No such luck! Nothing is automatic. Creation is a matter of choice, deliberate preference of one way over another. The beautiful life or the good life (the Greek word is the same) is the life Jesus describes in the Sermon—the life we choose to live, the actions we choose to perform.

Creating a beautiful home is a matter of choice too, beginning with neatness: keeping papers out of cats' ways, picking up newspapers, deciding to do chores instead of reading, putting things away—doing whatever it takes to create a pleasing environment, beauty.

"Your good works," is the way both KJV and NRSV put it. The good things we do. Morally good, beautifully good. Why do we do them? Because our Father who lives in us and with us loves beauty.

I forget too often that you live with me in what I call my house. Abba, I do want your home in and with me to be beautiful.

AUGUST 9   THE FATHER WHO SEES IN SECRET

"Your Father who sees in secret will reward you."
—Matthew 6:4 (NRSV)

"Were you naughty today?" Did you ever get that question put to you when you came home from play on an afternoon and found a parent waiting for you? Of course you'd been naughty. I mean, you weren't grown up, so obviously you weren't perfect, and therefore you were naughty, right? So of course you said yes, even though you might not have been sure what specific naughtiness you were being asked about. And whatever you thought, it wasn't what you ended up being punished for.

God was like that, I grew up thinking. Only, of course, he *knew* without asking when and how I was naughty, even when I hid it, and was always there waiting to punish me.

In reading through the Sermon on the Mount this time, I've made a startling discovery. Jesus tells us that what God sees in secret are our *good* deeds! What a switch! And he is waiting to reward us, not punish us. He is looking for the good deeds even we aren't aware of. Don't "let your left hand know what your right hand is doing," Jesus tells us. We are to be good, to do good deeds, to create beauty—without fanfare, not to get admiration or applause. The fanfare and the applause are their own rewards, so no others will come. God is looking in the secret places of our lives for our hidden prayers, for our generous acts that aren't front page news, for our kindnesses that go unnoticed by others. Jesus assumes that they will be part of our fabric of living. "Practise charity," he tells us (Matthew 6:3, Rieu). Keep at it. I still have those "secret faults" the psalmist talks about (Psalm 19:12). But I don't have to be afraid to bring them to my Abba Father. He's not waiting to punish me but to help me discover what I did today that was good.

Thank you, God, for noticing the good things about me, the evidence that you are part of my life.

AUGUST 10   **THE FATHER WHO LOVES THE GOOD AND THE BAD**

"Love your enemies . . . become children of your Father in Heaven, who causes his sun to rise on the wicked and the good, and rains on the just and the unjust alike."
—Matthew 5:44, 45 (Rieu)

I also grew up thinking that we Christians had a special "in" with God. Because we had believed in Jesus Christ, accepted him as our Savior, we were on God's side, and therefore God was on ours—which meant that he wasn't on the side of those who hadn't believed in Jesus. It meant, too, that our "in" entitled us to special favors from God.

The New Testament certainly tells us that God is on our side (see Romans 8:31). But if you keep reading, you find that God's blessings don't depend on us or our performance. God, out of "the great love with which he loved us, *even when we were dead through our trespasses,* made us alive together with Christ" (Ephesians 2:4-5, NRSV, italics mine). That is, God doesn't wait for us to measure up or to get on his side before he loves us. God's goodness and love come to us with his sun and his rain, regardless of our performance.

This kind of even-handed generosity and unconditional love is the standard we're to aim for—loving even our enemies. In his book *Creation Continues,** Fritz Kunkel suggests the possibility that the enemy we're asked to love is that "shadow" side of ourselves that we can't stand, the things in us that we hate and tend to project onto others. Facing that possibility, we begin to realize that there is no "us" versus "them." We're all "them"—people whom God loves and for whom Christ died.

Thank you for your unconditional and transforming love.

---

*Revised edition (Waco, Tex: Word Books, 1973), pp. 80-82.

AUGUST 11   THE FATHER WHO KNOWS
WHAT YOU NEED

"Your heavenly Father knows that you need all these things."
—Matthew 6:32 (NRSV)

In going through my ninety-two-year-old father's papers recently, before his move to a retirement home, my sister and I came across a 1939 leaflet from a Shanghai company about a piano built to look like a desk. This special piano was discounted to $750 Mexican (silver) dollars, because it was pre-owned. The leaflet tells a tale.

My parents had been married for almost ten years before they got their first settled home—an apartment in the mission headquarters compound in Shanghai. During the year previous, the family had been separated. My father was doing evangelistic work in Chekiang Province, just south of the Yangtze River, and Mother was the housekeeper for the Boys School on the north China coast, filling in for an ailing co-worker, while I started prep school and my sister recovered from bronchitis.

For Mother, the prospect of our own apartment was both welcome and daunting. She longed to be settled, but how would they furnish the four rooms plus kitchen and bath? As she and Daddy discussed it, by mail at first, they prayed for wisdom and help—and for three specific necessities.

The first was a refrigerator. In 1939 Shanghai, refrigerators were not all that common. But without one, food would spoil quickly in the hot summer, necessitating daily trips to the market and leaving little time for missionary work. The refrigerator was clearly a necessity.

The second was good beds. This was Daddy's necessity. You could stand a lot of other inconvenience or difficulty if you'd had a good night's sleep.

The third was a piano. Yes, this was a necessity! For the past ten years, Mother had been without her music. Being able to play the piano would be like a long drink of water.

The Father who knew what our family needed supplied the

206

funds for four rooms of lovely furniture—including the good beds, the refrigerator, and the special piano that could be used as a desk. My sister and I both started music lessons on that piano. And when the Japanese began the internment process and impounded all our furniture, the only pieces we were able to save or sell were the beds, the refrigerator, and the piano!

Thank you, Father, that you not only know what we need but love us enough to meet those needs.

AUGUST 12   A LONGING FOR HOME

"I am coming again to welcome you into my own home, so that you may be where I am."
—John 14:3 (Phillips)
I long to leave this world and live with Christ.
—Philippians 1:23 (Phillips)

Today's devotional interrupts the discussion of our family characteristics to celebrate the anniversary of a homecoming.

August 12, 1942. A ten-year-old girl stands on the deck of a small steamship moving slowly into the muddy waters of the Whangpo River. As the buildings of the Shanghai Bund come into view, she vows, "I will always remember this day, the day I came home.*"*

For almost a year and a half I had been in boarding school on the north China coast, unable to leave because of the Japanese fighting in China. For months I had had fiery nightmares of living on the edge of a volcano and of Japanese troops parachuting into our compound and invading our buildings. Then in December of 1941, it happened. Japan attacked Pearl Harbor, armed guards were stationed at our school gates, and our headmaster was imprisoned for a while as a political prisoner. All foreigners had to wear identifying armbands, and trips outside our compound were severely curtailed and monitored. It was the first Christmas I had spent away from home.

Finally, it was possible for several of us students with one or two teachers, to get passage on a coastal liner for the two-day, three-night trip to Shanghai, a familiar trip, except this one was different. The war now involved us foreigners as well as the Chinese, and there were the threats of Japanese planes or warships or mines. I couldn't know that barely a month after we left, the Japanese would seize the school compound for their own use and cram all the students and faculty into a few small buildings about a mile away in another part of Chefoo. Most of those students wouldn't see their families until after the war was over.

What would it be like in Shanghai? Were the Japanese there? I didn't know for sure. I also did not know that seven months later my family and I would join a thousand other foreigners in crowded conditions in a "Civilian Assembly Center" on the edge of Shanghai and spend two and a half years in the same room with nine other people.

Even if I had known, it wouldn't have mattered because I was going *home*. Home was where my family was. It was the events and activities of the week faithfully transcribed in the letters that came regularly, that let me know I was missed, I was loved, I belonged.

Finally the wharf came into view—and there they were! Mummy and Daddy and Flora Nell. The tears I hadn't shed when I left sixteen months ago, now came freely. I was home!

Abba, I'm not always homesick for you and heaven, except when I remember that the only time I'll ever really be at home is with you. Thank you for my homes—my childhood home, my present home, the ideal home I've never found—and the Home I have with you here and now and forever.

AUGUST 13   BECOMING PERFECT

"You then must be perfect, as your Father in Heaven is perfect."
                                        —Matthew 5:48 (Rieu)

To be part of God's family, we must be perfect! What does that mean? Most of the time we ignore the context of Jesus' command, God's love for both the good and the bad, which we looked at two days ago. Instead, we do what I did in the most miserable week of my life, which occurred one November.

A friend had been urging me to join her health spa. I knew I *ought* to exercise more, so that week on Tuesday, I signed up for a year's membership.

I hadn't been at my job long and wanted to improve my performance. My company had offered to pay for a motivational seminar designed, according to the advertisement, to increase productivity and efficiency on the job. That sounded good, so I signed up—for Wednesday afternoon.

Some time previous to this week, I had written for information about an organization called Sidetracked Home Executives (S.H.E.), designed to help harried homemakers cope more efficiently with their housework. I certainly needed help there. I was—am—a lousy housekeeper. They wrote that they were offering a seminar in my town for just two evenings— Wednesday and Thursday. I signed up to attend.

I had been feeling low spiritually and so called my minister to talk about spiritual direction. Without thinking I accepted an appointment for Friday afternoon. At the end of the hour we agreed to meet once a week. I left his office expecting to feel a sense of fitness and peace, but by the time I got home Friday evening I was gasping and sobbing in an anxiety attack.

When a friend came over, I tried to account for my tears and began to describe my week, going backward from Friday night. By the time I got to Tuesday, I was laughing—even if a bit shakily. *I had spent the week trying to get perfect!* And on all fronts at once! No wonder I was miserable! And there was more. All my efforts were negating one another.

I had joined the spa even though I much prefer "natural" exercising like gardening and walking over indoor programmed exercise. The motivational meeting turned out to be what I call an "enthusiasm rally," and I dislike whipped-up enthusiasm. In the S.H.E. workshops I discovered that I also dislike being organized within an inch of my life.

The last crazy thing about that week, I finally discovered, was that I was trying to live up to imagined parental standards. That was the week before my mother's birthday. Though she'd been dead three years, I was making the supreme effort to present her with a perfect child!

This is not the way Jesus calls us to become perfect. But how crazily human this is, to want to whip ourselves into shape overnight, to get rid of all our human imperfections so that we will be really lovable. We don't really believe that we're as dear to our Father as we are.

So how does Jesus call us to be perfect? We'll look at some answers in the next few days.

Dear Lord, help me to accept your love for me just as I am.

AUGUST 14   ON BEING IMPERFECT

"Unless your righteousness exceeds that of the scribes and Pharisees, you will never enter the kingdom of heaven."
—Matthew 5:20 (NRSV)

Jesus leads up to his direction to us to be perfect by talking about five areas in which we need to be more righteous, more perfect than the Pharisees of his day who prided themselves on keeping the law perfectly.

But is it possible to be more perfect than perfect? I certainly haven't committed any *murder,* but I have cheerfully called drivers in front of me at various times a stupid fool. And I have gotten furious at many people. So I deserve to be condemned to hell fire, Jesus tells me, as though I were a murderer (Matthew 5:22). Jesus has taken perfection a step further away from me. He does the same thing with *adultery*—moving sex from the act to the desire, so touching all of us, and throwing divorce into the pot as forcing adultery on those who remarry. Then there's *swearing*—that is, calling on God to witness our veracity. Not only are we not to go back on what we have sworn, but we shouldn't swear at all—we should be truthful and live up to our words without having to swear. I certainly don't keep all my promises, nor do my words always represent the truth. And *revenge*—how often we can taste the desire for it. We should not seek revenge, but should offer the hated person a further opportunity to take advantage of us! Don't our fists curl on that one! And to add insult to injury, we shouldn't *hate* at all but should love our enemies who have so mistreated us.

This kind of perfection is humanly impossible. By these examples, Jesus is showing us that none of us has ever perfectly kept the law. And that's good news! Because Jesus came for sinners, for those of us who've fallen short of the standard. We don't have to be perfect for God to love us. So why does Jesus tell us to be perfect as our Father is perfect and warn us to be more righteous than the Pharisees? Righteousness is our right relationship with God, involving our heart and spirit, not an outward keeping of laws. Perfection is growing toward maturity. The Greek word translated as "perfect" also means mature, full-grown, complete. That is, we are to become what we were meant to be, fully adult members of our family. We'll look at how to do that two days from now.

Father, I see so many areas where I'd like to be able to cope in a truly adult way and where I fail. Thank you for still being my Father, no matter what.

AUGUST 15   FREEDOM

> *So Jesus said again, "I am the door of the sheep. . . . Whoever enters through me will be saved, and will pass in and out and find pasture."*
> —John 10:8-9 (Goodspeed)

Today is a significant anniversary for us all—V-J Day, the day in 1945 when the Japanese stopped fighting and sued for peace, bringing World War II to an end. It's a date I remember well.

Saturday, August 11, a man on a motorcycle had shouted "victory" over the barbed-wire fence of Chapei Civil Assembly Center (read, internment camp), on the edge of Shanghai, causing tremendous excitement. Sunday, coming out of church services in the community shed which served as school, church, meeting hall, and library, we had seen a smoke-written *V* high in the sky. From American planes? But Monday and Tuesday we'd

211

had no word, and life went on in our camp of about one thousand "enemy aliens" as usual. Was it just another rumor?

Now, Wednesday, August 15, our Japanese commandant and our internee chairman were called out of camp to the office of the Swiss Consul in Shanghai proper. Was it really the end of the war?

And then the word swept around the camp, "Meet in front of the West Building." All of us gathered that afternoon, to hear our chairman say the words we had given up hope of hearing: "The war is over. As of noon today, we are free."

Two and a half years earlier, we had been ordered to consider this place our home and love it. We had tried to keep our place neat and ourselves in order. We had not loved the barbed wire fences around us or the crowded conditions or the attempt to limit our outlook and our viewpoint. We refused to be confined in spirit. We had followed the fortunes of the war as best we could through secret radios, hidden maps, and Japanese rhetoric in the local press. We had prayed for our friends and families around the world. Our spirits had remained free.

But a place can only truly be a home when you are free to be yourself and to come and go.

On August 15, 1945, at our chairman's signal, we turned around—and there were our Allied flags flying free in the August sunshine for the first time in four years. For the first time behind barbed wire fences we sang our national anthems, choking back the sobs. We were free to make a place our home, again.

Thank you that in your family you promise us protection and safety but also leave us free to roam and find nourishment in our freedom.

AUGUST 16   BEING ADULTS

> *"O the bliss of those who realize*
> *the destitution of their own lives."*
> —Matthew 5:3 (Barclay)

How do we grow into truly adult members of God's family? We keep trying to whip ourselves into shape and to shame ourselves into doing better. But still we fail, we lapse into immaturity, always aware of our many faults.

It seems to me that Jesus gives us the key to the kind of perfection he is looking for in the very first sentence of this Sermon. "Blessed are the poor in spirit, for theirs is the kingdom of heaven" (Matthew 5:3, NRSV). The truly adult in God's family are always honest about their failures and their lacks. "Blessed are those who feel their spiritual need," is Goodspeed's translation. To be perfect means to realize that we aren't perfect, that we don't have it made, that we haven't arrived, that we're always falling short of God's glory. We are always coming to God with our hands out, like beggars, which is the original meaning of the word translated "poor." We're always saying, "I need your help, God. I'm not able to love like you, be truthful, cope with anger. I need more of your Spirit."

Being a beggar in our society is something to be despised. Today on the streets of New York, there are always homeless people asking for handouts. And the same people! One woman is always by the main library. A giant of a man for over a year always waited for homebound commuters going into Grand Central Station, standing motionless with his cupped hands extended and his eyes down.

Why the same people all the time? I ask myself. I find it frustrating that their situations don't improve. And I don't want to give them anything because they are still at their begging. But now I see in their very persistence what my Father wants from me. I'm always in need of God's Spirit. As long as I realize that and keep my hands out, I'm not only part of God's family, but, as Barclay puts it, "the blessings of the Kingdom of Heaven" are mine "here and now." My Father loves me and always gives me access to the family wealth, to the Spirit who helps me grow like him. God is more generous than I am.

Father, I keep wanting to have arrived at perfection, and you keep asking me to keep admitting my imperfections, so I can receive more of your Spirit. Thank you that I don't have to whip myself into shape to be your daughter.

"Happy those that mourn; for they shall be comforted."
—Matthew 5:4 (Rieu)

We women tend to cry a lot. And that's a problem. Both from what psychologists tell us and from our own experience, we know that tears are generally frowned on by most men, especially in the business world. Tears are called a woman's weapon— might it be because men feel so uncomfortable with them?

Parents also tend to resent children's tears. How often were you told as a child, "Stop crying," after you'd been punished or reprimanded? But how could you? We learn to cry as babies, because that's the only way we can communicate our needs and problems and that's not a lesson we easily unlearn. For us adults as well, tears often say what we can't put into words.

Instead of telling us to "stop crying," Jesus tells us that it's good to cry. As full-grown members of God's family, we are happy when we "know what sorrow means" (Phillips), when we mourn. Mourn and feel sorrow for what? Jesus lets us fill in the blank space after that benediction. Mourn for ourselves, for our lacks, our imperfections, our failures, the pains of our childhoods? Yes, all of that, and more. To mourn implies that we think about and remember that for which we are crying. We mourn our departed loved ones, remembering them as fully as we can, grieving over our loss. We weep over our loss of innocence, the child we once were. We mourn the perfection that eludes us, the relationship with God that keeps going awry, the pain we cause ourselves and others.

To deny our tears, our sadness, is not maturity. It is to deny our humanness. Only when we admit our sadness, feel our pain, let the tears fall, can we receive the comfort and strength we need.

If you're ever tempted to kick yourself for crying, remember this benediction and count yourself blessed and happy.

Mothering God, the next time I cry I will think about why I'm crying and let myself feel my pain. I will remember Jesus' promise that mourning is blessed work through which I'll receive strength to cope and continue.

AUGUST 18   GENTLE STRENGTH

"Blessed are the meek, for they will inherit the earth."
— Matthew 5:5 (NRSV)

Sometime today read through the Beatitudes in Matthew 5 at one sitting. How would you describe the characteristics Jesus calls happy? Aren't most of them usually labeled "feminine"?* And therefore too often despised? Women, the generalization goes, cry too much. They're perfectionists. They're not aggressive. They tend not to like confrontation, wanting peace at any price. They're too sympathetic. And they're doormats, just taking anything the man in their life dishes out, because they're aware of their failures.

Interesting, isn't it, that Jesus takes these despised characteristics and makes them descriptive of God's family members.

But we need to be clear about what these "despised" characteristics really are. What does it mean to be meek? In *The Gospel of Matthew,*** William Barclay describes the Greek word translated as "meek" as meaning tameable or trainable. A show horse and a seeing-eye dog, for instance, have allowed their strengths to be harnessed and controlled. Moses was called the meekest man on the face of the earth (Numbers 12:3), but he certainly was no doormat. In the meek person, assertiveness is under control, aggressive impulses are handled wisely. The meek woman is sure of herself but is willing to wait for results. The aggressive person often ends up being destructive as well.

I saw negative aggression on the job a few years ago. A young, aggressive department manager started his job determined to make his presence felt, to clean up all the lackadaisical performance and poor workmanship he thought he saw, to change the cumbersome system of decision making, and to make

---

*I am endebted to my sister Flora Nell Duke, a lay preacher in the Methodist Church in England, for this insight.
**William Barclay, *The Gospel of Matthew,* vol. 1, The Daily Study Bible Series, revised edition (Philadelphia: The Westminster Press, 1975), pp. 96-97.

215

sure every other department head knew he was a force to be reckoned with. He immediately butted heads with almost everyone, not only making them angry, but infuriating himself. At the end of six weeks, he went to the hospital with chest pains, and died within a few hours of massive heart failure!

"O the bliss of those whose strength is in their gentleness," is how Barclay puts this Beatitude in his translation, "for they shall enter into possession of the earth." The meek person wins in the long run.

Help me to believe that I am strong because I am your daughter, Abba. Help me learn to use my strength with gentleness.

AUGUST 19   DISSATISFACTION WITH
                             OURSELVES

"Happy those that hunger and thirst for righteousness; for they shall be satisfied."
                                   —Matthew 5:6 (Rieu)

Here it is again, the paradox that to be perfect means to admit that you're not perfect. The only way to be satisfied is to admit that you're hungry and thirsty, that you haven't gotten filled up yet, that you're dissatisfied.

What are we hungering and thirsting for? Much of the time, I suspect, we're hungering and thirsting for things like money or love or sex or position or achievement. Or perhaps as women, for intimacy and understanding. But if we're honest, we find that having those things still leaves us hungry and thirsty. What Jesus says will really make us happy is to have an insatiable thirst for righteousness. Not the amoral perfection that never strays from a straitjacket. Righteousness is right relationship with God. "Happy are those who are hungry and thirsty for true goodness" is how Phillips translates it. This has often been considered a feminine characteristic—the desire for spiritual things, the involvement in church activities, the time spent in daily devotions with prayer and Bible reading. (That's one of the reasons for this book!)

I attend a small urban church, and usually 90 percent of the

216

congregation present on Sunday mornings are women. The women, some of them in their eighties, also do the work of running the church. I suspect that's true of most small inner-city churches.

I tend to get tired of this constant responsibility and wish that more men would take part in the church. But reading this Beatitude again, I am stopped from resenting the responsibility. It is a happy thing to keep on being hungry and thirsty for God's goodness and our relationship with him—to keep on meeting together where we worship God and celebrate the love and blessings that come to us in Jesus Christ. It is a happy thing not to be satisfied with ourselves and our surroundings, to want more of God's goodness to prevail. Why? Because Jesus promises that we "will be fully satisfied!" (Phillips).

Father, I realize that I'm hungry and thirsty for a lot of things that don't satisfy. Thank you that you promise full satisfaction when I focus on you and my relationship with you.

AUGUST 20   DISSATISFACTION WITH OUR WORLD

> *"How happy those who hunger and thirst to see right prevail."*
> —Matthew 5:6 (NEB)

We can't hunger and thirst for our own right relationship with God without wanting to see right prevail on the earth. To know that things are not right in our own lives, in society, in our families, with our friends, and to long with all our hearts that they should be—that is to find complete satisfaction. Why? Because it drives us to action. And how often this is the characteristic of women.

Think of all the causes that have been championed in this century, or even in your lifetime. How often was a woman or women in the forefront of the cause, in a leadership position, or the instigator? Two women in Northern Ireland received the Nobel Peace Prize for bringing Protestants and Catholics together. The battle for civil rights was begun by Rosa Parks on a bus in Alabama. The cause of women's rights, of course, has been championed for centuries by women, sometimes seconded by men. It was mothers and homemakers in England who chained themselves to airbase fences to oppose the deployment of nuclear weapons. Mothers Against Drunk Driving was started by a woman whose son was killed by an intoxicated driver. The battle against toxic waste was brought to national attention by a housewife at Love Canal. You can think of more.

Championship of rights is not limited to women, of course. Plenty of men have done the same, from Ralph Nader to Father Berrigan of the Ploughshares Eight in our generation. But I know of instances when a man discovers a wrong and starts a committee to investigate it. (How many committees are going in Congress now, costing us how many millions of dollars?) And I know of many times when God's daughter has discovered a cause, discovered that she could do something about it, and so discovered her own strength. A strength that acts with gentleness.

Father, help me to see what I can do about my dissatisfactions, and most of all to share them with you, so that I can get your point of view and your standards and receive the strength to act.

AUGUST 21   SEEING THE OTHER PERSON'S
                                        POINT OF VIEW

"Happy those that show mercy; for mercy shall be shown to them."
—Matthew 5:7 (Rieu)

I once helped drive a group of junior high students from Minnesota to a Christian camp on an island in Lake of the Woods, Ontario. When we first crossed the border into Canada, I was both amused and irritated at the kids. They compared everything unfavorably to the way things were back home. Canadian hamburgers, highways, gas stations, grocery stores, and especially vocabulary—all were really stupid because they were unfamiliar.

My hope was that by the time they'd spent two weeks with young people from other states and all over Canada, they'd have matured a little and would have learned that other ways of doing things were equally as valid as their own familiar customs.

The maturity that refuses to judge everyone else by my point of view is part of what Jesus is calling for in this Beatitude. As God's children we don't set ourselves up as judges and our way of doing things as the only way—a point made by Jesus later in the Sermon (Matthew 7:1). We don't say about another person, "Boy, are they stupid," because they don't do things the way we do or see things like we do. We show mercy by trying to understand them.

And we can do that because we know *we* aren't perfect but are still begging for more of God's Spirit. We know sorrow and have cried over our failures. We're learning to handle our aggressive impulses creatively—to be gentle, not pushy.

How happy we are when we live like this, Jesus says. Because when we show mercy, we are most like our nurturing, mothering God, who has mercy on us with motherly compassion. (See meditation for August 4.) God is rich in mercy (Ephesians 2:4), an attitude that never changes, but endures forever (Psalm 136). And the promise is that we will receive mercy in return. We too will be loved and understood—not always or by everyone, but certainly by our loving, mothering God.

Keep me open to other people, able to understand, empathize, and sympathize with them, so that I can share with them your nurturing love.

AUGUST 22   SINGLE-MINDED

"Happy the pure in heart; for they shall see God."
                                    —Matthew 5:8 (Rieu)

We tend to read this Beatitude as saying that we must be so morally unblemished that we're sinless. But we've already seen that we can't reach that kind of perfection. The word translated "pure" comes from a root which means to wash, to make clean. It's used for the Jews' ceremonial washing or "purifying" of hands before meals. It's also used to describe Jesus' washing of the disciples' feet at the Last Supper (John 13). That was not just a ceremonial cleansing. Their feet really needed washing. They'd been out in the dusty roads and dirty streets of Jerusalem, wearing only sandals.

Later Jesus explained that the disciples had already been cleansed through the message he'd given them (John 15:3). By their listening to and following Jesus' teaching, their lives had been purified, made clean. But he had washed their feet to show them that they still needed the day's dirt washed away. In other words, we don't have to achieve sinlessness to be in God's family, we just have to keep getting washed clean.

But there's another facet to this Beatitude. Søren Kierkegaard, the Danish philosopher/theologian, tells us that "purity of heart is to will one thing," which is the title of one of his books. To be pure in heart is to be single-minded in our focus on God. But what does that mean? That we must shut ourselves away in a convent and spend all our time in prayer and meditation? That we shouldn't fall in love or study literature or enjoy great music?

For the biblical writers, the heart stands for the whole person—mind, will, emotions, the whole way we live. If we are cleansed, if we are pure, if we are single-minded, we will be looking for God's purpose in all the events of our lives and in all the people that we meet. By focusing on God's presence and God's righteousness, we'll avoid being duped or conned. And we'll refuse to stay frustrated, to get angry at others or depressed about ourselves. We will go beyond those emotions and ask, "Lord, what can I learn out of this? What is your purpose here? How and where can I see you in this part of my life, in this person?"

The woman who is pure in heart keeps coming back for fine tuning of her focus. Because she wants to see God more than anything else in her life. The promise is that you will.

Forgive the frustration level that rises high in me at times. I want to see you, my loving Father, my nurturing Mother, in all my life.

> *"Happy the peace-makers; for they shall be called sons of God."*
>
> —Matthew 5:8 (Rieu)

The woman who can see God in all aspects of her world and in all the people she meets is the woman who can reconcile differences, who can make peace.

But first of all, we have to be at peace in ourselves. To do that we have to acknowledge that we are at war in ourselves! A good many of us, I suspect, have hidden agendas in our dealings with other people that we don't acknowledge—unconscious motives, buried desires. The truly adult person in God's family knows this. It's not that we no longer have unconscious motives, but we are aware that we are never as honest as we claim to be! And we are working on becoming at peace in ourselves.

Only when I am making peace in myself can I make peace between quarreling neighbors or warring factions in society. To be a peace-maker is not just to say, "Quit fighting." It is to find a creative way to reduce differences, to help each party see God in the other person, the other side. It is to be the mother who wants each one of her children to flourish and grow.

And what do we women make of the promise that we will be called God's *sons*? In Jesus' time, it was the sons who inherited not only their fathers' property and wealth but also his blessing, the spiritual wealth of the family. (Remember the story of Jacob and Esau fighting over the birthright and blessing.) To be called a son was to be acknowledged as having all the rights and privileges of the family. But even more than that, the Jewish idiom "son of—" implied that you had all the characteristics of the "father." "Son of peace" (Luke 10:6) implies that the person was a peaceful person. "Sons of this age" (Luke 20:34), "sons of light" (Luke 16:8), "sons of thunder" (Mark 3:17), and Jesus' name for himself "son of Man" all focus on the "parent" quality demonstrated by the child.

This Beatitude gives each of us our birthright. When we act

for God in the world, we will be called God's fully adult, fully invested children. And if Jesus were here in the flesh today, I think he would call us women God's *daughters,* equal heirs of God's grace and wealth (see I Peter 3:7), just as he reinstated two sick women into their Jewish heritage (Luke 8:42-48; 10:10-16). And if challenged, he would point back to the daughters of Zelophehad of the tribe of Manasseh, who inherited their father's apportioned land on the same basis as their uncles and male cousins (Joshua 17:3-4).

I want to be your daughter, mothering God, a daughter of peace, and a daughter who makes *peace.*

AUGUST 24   BEING MISUNDERSTOOD

"Happy those that have been persecuted for righteousness; for theirs is the Kingdom of Heaven. Count yourselves happy . . ."
—Matthew 5:9 (Rieu)

Do you ever feel as though you're completely misunderstood because you're a woman in a man's world? That misunderstood feeling isn't going to change, Jesus tells us.

The person who lives as if she is a member of God's family, who acknowledges her own poverty, her inability to measure up, who tries to see the other person's point of view and to find God in every circumstance, who is strong yet gentle, and who longs for God's goodness and righteousness to be in her life and her world, is not going to be understood by everyone. But Jesus tells us, that's a happy thing! Why? Because she has the kingdom of heaven. She's a full-fledged family member. And now we've come full circle, back to the first Beatitude. To be poor in spirit *and* misunderstood is to possess the kingdom of heaven.

Up to this point, Jesus has been talking in general terms. "Blessed are the . . . ," "Happy those that . . . ," "Blessed are they . . . ," but now he points it right to the disciples, to us, and says "Blessed are you." "Count yourselves happy when the time comes for people to revile you and maltreat you . . . on account of me. Rejoice and glory in these things, since your reward is

222

great in Heaven" (Matthew 5:10-12, Rieu). It's become not a matter of the general Christian, but a personal matter. If I really live like this, using my feminine, mothering family qualities to the fullest, I'm not going to find it easy, and not everyone is going to love me. Some, in fact, will hate me.

The misunderstanding and suffering that come with this quality of life are unavoidable. We're like salt and light. You can't hide the nature of salt. When you put it on food, you can taste it. If you put it on a wound, it stings. If you rub it on meat, it preserves it. Salt is always salt. (It can, however, be adulterated. And if it gets mixed with dirt, it becomes worthless.)

You also cannot hide light. The littlest hole in the bushel basket, the least carelessness in the blackout, and it escapes! As mature daughters in this family, modeling God's characteristics, our quality of life will shine out. We may not be understood, but as we've already seen, other people will recognize that beauty as coming from God, whose daughters we are, and to whose kingdom we belong.

Just as your grandeur that fills the world cannot be hidden, Abba, but "will flame out, like shining from shook foil,"* so may beauty shine from my life, even when I am not understood.

AUGUST 25   HOME IS WHERE THE HEART IS

"Wherever your treasure is, your heart will be there too!"
—Matthew 6:21 (Phillips)

Some years ago when I took a new job in another city, I spent my first month living in rented quarters, so I could look for a house. The apartment was small and sparsely furnished. I had the barest amount of cookware and tableware, and nothing for entertainment. Living involved few choices. There was almost nothing to the housework, and nothing to tie me to the place. For those four weeks I had no investments in the place where I lived. I found it a most freeing experience.

---

*"God's Grandeur," Gerard Manley Hopkins

But then I bought a house and moved my five rooms of furniture, plus kitchen, bath, and garage stuff. And I was caught again with a big house of earthly treasures—to which I have kept adding more.

Still, I keep hearing Jesus' words. Don't keep adding to your earthly treasures. Don't tie yourself to your possessions. They don't last. Your cloisonné will dent, your soapstone will shatter, your lovely china will break, the movers will steal your jewelry. When I'm honest with myself, I know that my possessions possess me and my emotions, not so much out of fear that I'll lose them but rather tying me into a kind of cocoon that I keep winding around me. I'm not yet pure of heart in this realm of my life.

Our real home isn't here. Our real possessions are those we give away—the gifts we give in secret, the disciplines we practice quietly to connect us to our Father in heaven. And so I have to ask myself, "What have I given my heart to? Do I want to be free?"

Help me to see you beyond my possessions, and so to possess them lightly as belonging ultimately to you.

AUGUST 26   CAREFREE

"Don't worry about living. . . . Look at the birds in the sky. They never sow nor reap nor store away in barns, and yet your Heavenly Father feeds them. Aren't you much more valuable to him than they are?"
—Matthew 6:25-26 (Phillips)

Do you remember when you were a child and took your food and clothing pretty much for granted most of the time? Children know that Mom and Dad are there to meet their needs, that meals appear on the table, that periodically they go shopping for clothes.

Such childlike confidence in our heavenly Father is what Jesus asks of us. It's based, Jesus tells us, on the kind of Parent we have. God loves us, rewards us, and gives us what we need. We can't earn or work for that care, any more than the birds or flowers do, but if they're taken care of, how much more we, who are worth far more in God's sight, are cared for.

But sometimes that confidence is hard to maintain. There was a period of months during our two and a half years in the internment camp when the Japanese supplied only one tiny meal per day. Many of us in the camp were sick and almost every person lost weight, including Mother, who lost over forty pounds. My sister almost died of dysentery. At probably our lowest point, we received a shipment of American Red Cross parcels, enough for one ten-pound box for every person in camp. Each box looked so little—12″ × 12″ × 8″—yet what treasure we found: a pound of raisins or prunes, a pound of powdered milk, half a pound of cheese, a tin of spam or corned beef, a tin of jam, a tin of butter, a tin of liver paté, half a pound of chocolate, a bar of soap, at least two packs of gum, several packs of cigarettes—which became the medium of exchange—and more that I've forgotten.

How delicious it all tasted. How we savored the chocolate, one tiny half square each per day after lunch. How we parceled out the raisins, one small handful at a time for snacks. How we enjoyed the Spam fried over our own tiny biscuit-tin stove, one slice each for supper to eke out the two tiny spoonsful of watery vegetables from the community kitchen. And butter! Never has anything tasted so rich. Mother swore she could see the energy level of the whole camp pick up.

And clothing? Well, it may not have had the beauty of Solomon's robes, but the winter when we had to close down school because it was too cold to hold a pencil or to sit for even half an hour, Red Cross blankets came into camp somehow. And out of ours, Mother made two pairs of dull gray-blue overalls for me and my sister. When it was 45 degrees in our room, we took warmth over beauty any day.

I know Mother in particular worried—for herself, for us. But she also prayed and trusted, and the food supply never ran out. At the beginning of 1945, we received a second allotment of Red

Cross parcels, this time *four* boxes apiece! By careful use, we still had food left when we left camp in September 1945.

After seeing how wonderfully you have supplied my needs all through my life, forgive me for worrying about the future.

AUGUST 27   LIVING LIKE A MILLIONAIRE

"Consider the lilies of the field . . . they neither toil nor spin, yet I tell you, even Solomon in all his glory was not clothed like one of these."
—Matthew 6:28-29 (NRSV)

Many voices on radio, TV, and tape today promise you that if you'll do what they say, practice faithfully the exercises they give you, or send in the seed money asked for, you'll reap abundantly, and certainly become a millionaire, particularly if that's your goal.

Well, let me tell you how our family became millionaires—without any exercises, or seed money, or even asking. And in the process, my sister and I were clothed, at least in our eyes, as brilliantly as any royalty.

When the Japanese surrendered on August 15, 1945, the Nationalist government began to take back control of China. As a gesture of good will to all foreigners interned by the Japanese, the government gave each adult a gift of $500,000 and each child $200,000. So our family of four became instant millionaires! We'd done nothing to "deserve" or earn it—just lived through two and a half years as "guests" of the Japanese government.

Unfortunately, that one million, four hundred thousand dollars didn't last long. Yet even though its purchasing power was limited, we really did feel like millionaires while we had it. Because for the preceding two and a half years we'd had no money of our own—we'd had to turn in all our monies to the Japanese forces over us.

What did we spend $1,400,000 on? Four sundresses, made by a Chinese tailor in Shanghai, for my sister and me to wear on the boat going back to the States. We'd gone into camp aged seven and eleven, and were going home almost ten and fourteen, so we literally had nothing to wear.

How royally God clothed us! We even got to pick our own material. And though we soon grew out of them from eating good healthy American food, nothing ever quite equalled our million-dollar dresses.

Thank you that you love to provide for us royally, spending lavishly on us even when those gorgeous robes only last a day.

(P.S. How much really was that $1,400,000 CRB worth? About $14.00 U.S.! But an infinite amount in demonstrating God's care for us.)

AUGUST 28   ASKING

"If you, bad as you are, know how to give good things to your children, how much more will your heavenly Father give good things to those who ask him!"
—Matthew 7:11 (Barclay)

Jesus not only calls us to be mature adults in God's family, but he reminds us that we're also children. In fact, unless we become like children, we can't get into the family (Matthew 18:3). That's another way of saying that we need to start over without preconceived ideas, to experience God's Spirit moving in the present as something entirely new. Living without worry and enjoying the richness of life are characteristics of healthy children. For the next few days I'd like to look at some other qualities children have.

When I was about ten or eleven, I had a desperate longing to own a pair of stilts. Several of my schoolmates had them, and occasionally I could borrow theirs, but I wanted my own set. I remember one day sitting in the dentist's chair and wishing hard for them at the dentist's direction, as I blew one of my eyelashes off his finger. I'd get my wish, the dentist told me. But I didn't. (And I've never trusted wishes since!) Why? I never said my wish out loud. I never talked about stilts in my parents' hearing. I never asked.

Would I have gotten my stilts if I had asked for them? Would my parents have considered stilts frivolous? I don't know. But I never gave them an opportunity to give them, or explain why they wouldn't, or to offer me something better. Because they didn't know I wanted them.

In this family that we belong to, God's family, our Father wants to give us good things—when we ask him. That means that as a child in God's family, I feel free enough and confident enough to tell my Daddy what I want, knowing he'll give me something good. Perhaps it won't be the thing I ask for. But then it will be something better.

And if my heavenly Father makes things as frivolous as a butterfly and as crazy as a giraffe, I think he likes for me to have fun, even on a pair of stilts.

Thank you for all the good things you have given me, even when I haven't asked. And thank you that you want me to come to you, not only with my needs but also with my wants.

AUGUST 29   RHYTHM AND BLUES

"They are like children sitting in the market-place, calling to each other:
'When we played you a happy tune,
you did not dance;
when we wailed you a sad lament,
you did not weep.' "
—Luke 7:32 (Barclay)

I stopped tonight at Burger King, hoping to get a 99-cent hamburger meal, but those specials were only for breakfast. Nonetheless I ordered a hamburger, fries, and cola.

While I was getting catsup on my fries, my fingers, and my face, I watched a little boy wander around the condiment islands while his mother was ordering. She spoke Spanish, but the boy had obviously learned English from his playmates, because I heard him chanting to himself, "Did not. Did too. Did not. Did too!" And his feet kept time to the chant.

Was he replaying a quarrel with a friend or merely echoing words he'd heard, repeating them for the rhythm? He made me think of the children Jesus heard in the marketplace who couldn't decide what they wanted to play, but who enjoyed the rhythm of their song.

That one little voice proclaiming both sides of the argument made me smile wryly. It seemed prophetic of the split in ourselves we, as adults, know too well, the arguments we have with ourselves, our inability to decide, our inconsistent expectations, our failure to act—all of which end up making us argue with our sisters and brothers.

I hoped, though, for his sake, that he was just responding to the rhythm of the words, enjoying the chant.

And what about us? What rhythm do we march to? As children in God's family, Jesus calls us to live not by the childish rhythm of inconsistency but by a different rhythm—the rhythm of focused persistence. "Ask and you shall receive," he tells us in a bold rhythm. "Seek and you will find."

Thank you, Jesus, for the rhythms of your words. Help us to keep time to their beat as we put them into practice.

AUGUST 30   PERSISTENCE

> *"Keep on asking,*
>   *and you will get;*
> *keep on seeking,*
>   *and you will find;*
> *keep on knocking,*
>   *and the door will be opened for you."*
>   —Matthew 7:7 (Barclay)

Here is the rhythm Jesus wants to put into our lives, a persistent beat that underlies everything we do and never stops. We are to keep on asking.

In human families, children can drive adults crazy with their persistent questions and insistent demands. When we were babies we loudly demanded our bottles or our meals, and to keep the noise down, as well as to satisfy us, we were promptly fed.

But the older we got, the less those loud demands were met. If we were too insistent, our parents told us to be quiet! And sometimes, if we asked too many questions—or the same question too many times—we got really crazy answers from desperate adults.

Jesus tells us, though, that in his family, insistence pays off. We won't be told to shut up! What are we to be insistent about? Jesus doesn't tell us here. He just makes the promise six times that we will succeed; we will receive, find, and have the door opened when we keep on asking, seeking, knocking. (The present tense in Greek implies a continuing action.)

Jesus states these as universal truths. "Everyone who keeps on asking/gets what he asks for" (Matthew 7:8, Barclay). Whatever we keep seeking we'll find. The door we continue to knock on will be opened. That's a bit scary, isn't it? Is it possible that we might be so insistent for a stone or a snake that we'll get them—instead of the things we need like bread and fish? That we'll knock on the wrong door and end up going through it?

It's possible. But Jesus has just told us to put God's family first in our lives (Matthew 6:33). "Make the Kingdom of God, and life in loyalty to him, the object of all your endeavour," is how Barclay translates it. Just as your heart keeps up its insistent beating in your chest that keeps you alive, so these words can become the persistent beat of our lives: ask, seek, knock—for God.

Help me to put my mind and heart to becoming fully adult, as I let the rhythm of your words fill my mind and heart. Thank you for the promise of fulfillment.

AUGUST 31   THE BEST GIFT

"How much more will the heavenly Father give the Holy Spirit to those who ask him!"
—Luke 11:13 (NRSV)

In my first year of graduate school, my parents moved into their own apartment in Philadelphia, after six years of living in the Mission Home, a big double house that served as American headquarters as well as a hostel for missionaries on furlough.

By the time I got home for the summer, the apartment was completely furnished, including the pictures on the walls in the bedroom that my sister and I would share. And I hated them. They were old-fashioned prints of two girls playing with cherries and birds in a style I disliked and in ugly, carved frames. *Why in the world did Mother put these things in here?* I thought. I can't remember if I said as much to Mother or just went to take the pictures down. (I know I hurt her by other remarks I made about the old-fashioned furniture.) Then I discovered a hand-written note on the back of one of them: "Given to me by my favorite teacher when I was nine years old in Levant, Maine. Nellie Lord Fickett." These were not just old, they were family heirlooms! Because Grandma Fickett was born in 1865.

It took me quite a few years before my opinion of those prints and their frames changed. But when I bought my first house many years later, those "ugly" prints were cherished possessions that I was proud to display.

I've had somewhat the same reaction to Luke's version of Jesus' promise to give us good gifts when we ask. What God thinks are good gifts and what I think haven't always coincided. Matthew's version (7:11) is much more my style. Imperfect parents give their children good gifts; God will even more certainly give us good things, particularly when we ask for them. That means that I can decide what I want—certainly not anything old-fashioned!

Luke's version, though, specifies what gifts God wants to give us children. There is really only one—the Holy Spirit. That used to seem to me *too* spiritual, too limiting, too old-fashioned. (I thought the excesses of the charismatic movement ugly.) But as I'm growing up, I'm realizing that with the gift of the Spirit, God makes me part of his family. I remember, too, that the most mature thing I can do is admit that I need God's Spirit. And when I do, I possess the kingdom—I have everything I need.

Thank you for the best gift you have for me, your Spirit, your very self, who connects me with you and with all your family, and makes me at home with you. I'm asking now for that best gift.

SEPTEMBER

Invitations to Wisdom and Rest

ANNE WILCOX

SEPTEMBER 1   **INVITATIONS TO SPIRITUAL WISDOM**

(Read Proverbs 9.)

What a wonderful invitation! I had been asked to join a Bible study group, and, as a young adult, I was thrilled with the idea of good fellowship and stimulating teaching. The people who extended the invitation were very kind and seemed sincere about growing spiritually. What more could I ask for?

I finally asked for more after three weeks into our studies. I made the mistake of asking when we were going to talk about Jesus Christ. I was told we would "get to him eventually." When I expressed that I thought he was the central reason we were all here, the room fell silent. I soon learned that this group believed Jesus Christ was only one of many routes to God. They also believed the Bible was an important book, but that other books were needed to interpret it.

The invitation had seemed so right. The people had been so nice. But their invitation to spiritual wisdom led only to a dead end.

There have always been rival invitations to wisdom—one authentic and many counterfeit. Proverbs 9 explores these opposing invitations by using the figurative tool of personification (a figure of speech in which a thing, quality, or idea is represented as a person). In this chapter, Wisdom (9:1-12) and

Folly (9:13-18) are portrayed as hostesses inviting the simple to their banquets. Enjoy comparing their invitations in Proverbs 9:1-18.

SEPTEMBER 2   RIVAL HOSTESSES

(Read Proverbs 9.)

Today the invitations to spiritual wisdom come from everywhere. Gone are the sneers of a high-tech age that once belittled spiritual interest. It is again in vogue to address the religious needs of society. There is no lack of invitations. The lack is not even of sincerity. The famine concerns truth.

Often it takes fine-tuned discernment to recognize the discord between Wisdom and Folly. At first these voices appear to be in unison. Both serenade the simple from the highest point of the city—the place of power and prestige heard by the entire community (9:3, 14). Both use similar lyrics (9:4, 16). However, closer scrutiny reveals a crucial difference. Wisdom calls her guests to the Lord (9:10). Folly calls hers to deception (9:17).

Many are calling us to spiritual oneness today. What could be more biblically sound than spiritual unity? But with further investigation, we discover they really mean that the universe is one. A world view of monism is not only different from but also is opposed to the biblical revelation of a personal Creator distinct from his creation. This paraphrase of Colossians 1:17 says it well: "Creation is not a homogeneous soup of undifferentiated unity but a created plurality. Creation is not unified in itself but in the plan and purpose of God—in Christ 'all things hold together' " (Douglas R. Groothuis, *Unmasking the New Age*). Spiritual oneness can sound like an invitation to spiritual unity, but often two very different banquets are being offered.

SEPTEMBER 3   WISDOM'S SINGULAR
                                   ENTRYWAY

(Read Proverbs 9.)

Wisdom has only one gate to her banquet table; Folly has many. For the latter, any door will do; but the door to Wisdom's feast is singular. Proverbs 9:10 says, "The fear of the LORD is the

234

beginning of wisdom. . . ." There is no other door, no other passageway, no other channel to true spiritual wisdom than this one. Hebrew scholar Bruce Waltke has said, "What the alphabet is to reading, what notes are to music, what numerals are to mathematics, the fear of the LORD is to wisdom."

If someone says to you, "Come. Gain clarity for your spiritual path. Access your inner self. Enjoy the divine oneness we share. Come join us in the discovery of spiritual wisdom," be sure to check the invitation twice. Through the door of revering the one true Lord is a banquet alive with promise for the future (9:6-12). This is the authentic invitation that results in wisdom and life and the knowledge of God. The other doors yield counterfeit banquets that promise wisdom but deliver only destruction (9:18).

As you receive invitations to gain spiritual wisdom, test them carefully. Do they confirm that only one door opens to the banquet hall, or is the way to their feast eclectic? A banquet with many entrances may seem generous and tolerant at first, but Folly is always promising sweetness (9:17) and delivering food laced with poison (9:18).

SEPTEMBER 4   VALIANT LADY WISDOM

(Read Proverbs 8 and 9.)

Some of the contemporary invitations for spiritual renewal include spirit contact through channeling and harmonious body/spirit alignment through crystal consciousness. These methods make no mention of holiness, but they speak at length about experience. These methods also make no moral or ethical demands on their subjects. It is almost as if these intense, immediate excursions into a spirit realm provide a counterfeit resolution to human alienation from God. These techniques take no discipline, and their promises of spiritual renewal only dull the real need for rebirth and redemption.

The contrasts between the characters of Wisdom and Folly provide helpful ways to evaluate new invitations that may come your way. Folly is undisciplined (9:13) and speaks deceitfully (9:17). Wisdom is prepared (9:1-2) and speaks with insight (9:7-9). Proverbs 8 gives further descriptions of Wisdom: she speaks truth and hates evil (8:6-7, 13); what she has to offer is of greater worth than anything on earth (8:10-11, 19); prudence, knowledge, and discretion are synonymous with her (8:12, 14-16); she treats with goodness those who seek her (8:17-21); she is not the same as God, but was appointed by him to steward his world (8:22-29); she finds delight in her position and in the world God has made (8:30-31). Most important of all is that finding Folly means finding "the depths of the grave" (9:18), but finding Wisdom means "finding life and receiving favor from the Lord" (8:32-36).

SEPTEMBER 5   THE PURSUIT OF WISDOM

(Read Proverbs 4:5-7.)

Some things we have are easily discerned. When the flu hits our household, achy, feverish symptoms provide unquestionable confirmation. Some things are also easy to pursue. When dashing after a truant toddler, it's possible to know the chase is over by the feel of a wriggling little body in one's arms. When chasing butterflies, the evidence of success or failure can always be seen in the net.

But how do we chase something like wisdom? How do we ever know if we have it or discern if someone else has it? How do we pursue this elusive resource, and, even more difficult, how do we know when we've captured it? Wisdom is never found fluttering within our grasp. In fact, the minute we think we possess it is usually the moment we've lost it. It seems that the only certainty is the passion with which we are to pursue wisdom.

Proverbs 4:5-7 instructs us to sacrifice for this precious commodity. We are taught with the words "do not forsake wisdom," "love her," "esteem her," and "embrace her." This passage says that though it cost us all we have, wisdom and knowledge must be gained.

With such strong, passionate words underscoring the pursuit of wisdom, there must be a way to check our nets.

SEPTEMBER 6   WHO IS WISE?

(Read James 3:13.)

The book of James is masterful in pulling intangible, spiritual concepts out of the theoretical clouds and translating them into touchable, concrete daily life. As with all the topics in his letter, James helps to remove some of wisdom's elusiveness.

In James 3:13, James first says that wisdom and understanding will be discernible by a good life. I was expecting something a little more breathtaking, or at least a little more awe-inspiring. A good life sounds so daily and so practical.

Next, James says that wisdom will be touchable through its deeds. Those who have wisdom don't just become discerning; they act. But their actions are flavored with something unique. All they do is done "in the humility that comes from wisdom" (James 3:13*b*). There is an aura about the wise, but not the kind I assumed. This humility or meekness is nothing that floats at all. It is the absence of selfish ambition. Competing, struggling, and contending do not exist with this humility. The wise are not easily irritated, and their anger is directed toward issues of justice, not personal gain. There is a sense of being strongly submitted—not resigned, but willing to be shaped even by things that hurt.

With the evidences of a good life and of actions done in genuine humility, James has given us nets to examine as we pursue wisdom.

SEPTEMBER 7   HOW DOES WISDOM ACT?

(Read James 3:14-16.)

After giving us the evidence of wisdom, James uses contrast to teach us further. In 3:14-16, he shows the evidence of a lack of wisdom. Wisdom deficiency is characterized by bitter envy and selfish ambition. He exposes the source of these characteristics as the evil one. He goes on to say that their fruits are disorder and evil practices. When wisdom is absent from a life, a family, a church, a nation, or a world, the results are tragic.

Asking ourselves a few questions is often a helpful way to "check the nets" and see if we've captured wisdom:

1. Which is operating most frequently in my family, or church, or community: a spirit of competition with the accompanying power struggles or a gentle strength that is not competitive?

2. Is there ordered faithfulness in my family and church, or is

there a disquieting sense of a lot going on but nothing of substance occurring?

3. Am I primarily concerned with *my* comfort and the promotion of *my* ideas, or am I committed to serve those I live among with a strong gentleness?

James would never claim that wisdom could truly be captured and turned over in our hands to be examined. But he has shown that it becomes touchable as we live effectively in community.

SEPTEMBER 8   MISUNDERSTANDING THE
                               WISDOM FROM ABOVE

(Read James 1:5.)

It was so unexpected. With heartbreaking thievery, infertility had stolen our hopes for children. But we refused to let it have the last word. After six determined years, we had a daughter of our own through adoption. As more years passed, we began wanting to enlarge our family once again. Finally, after many long months of working with specialists, I became pregnant. Our world was filled with celebration—and nausea. Our daughter would have a sibling, and we would be entrusted with another child! Every night a faithful preschool prayer warrior brought her favorite petition before the Lord: "God, help the baby grow strong in Mommy's womb." We were too excited to suspect what was ahead.

The baby did not grow strong. At ten weeks, ultrasound technology revealed a heart that had stopped beating. In the days ahead, we were numb as we tried to absorb the shock that this child had died and would not be carried to term. So soon after rejoicing in new life, it was necessary to give this little one back to the Lord, untouched and uncuddled.

I wanted to know why. Well-meaning people kept saying that something had probably been very wrong and the Lord mercifully took the child home. How hard we try to find answers for the unanswerable. Finally the lab reports came back. Everything had been "fine." There would be no explanation.

If ever I needed James 1:5, it was in those days following our loss. But I soon began to see that the wisdom from above was something entirely different from what I was pleading for.

SEPTEMBER 9   WHAT IS THIS GIFT?

(Read James 1:5; 3:17.)

We've all heard James 1:5. In fact, many of us have memorized it, but do we understand it? We have needed wisdom desperately but have found it eclipsed during heartbreaking circumstances. If we dare evaluate our experiences, we must frankly assume that this promise doesn't always work. We hesitate to be that honest, because perhaps the problem is with us, as the next verse describes: "But when he asks, he must believe and not doubt, because he who doubts is like a wave of the sea, blown and tossed by the wind" (James 1:6). We might even be accused of being "double-minded" and "unstable in all our ways" (James 1:7-8). We are left confused because we know God's promises are trustworthy, but we have no idea how to ask or believe any more sincerely. Though faith is a critical ingredient required for receiving this gift, I propose that the belief issue is not the one that trips us as much as does our misunderstanding of the gift.

When I read that I will receive a generous portion of wisdom, I assume that this obligates God to give me specific guidance for my decisions and detailed explanations of my hurts. In James 3:17, however, the definition of wisdom has nothing to do with clairvoyance but everything to do with godly character. Guidance for the future and explanations of losses aren't even mentioned. What is mentioned has to do with who I am. It appears that the process of living through unanswered whys is how purity—wisdom's hallmark—is worked into us (James 3:17*a*).

SEPTEMBER 10   DOES WISDOM KEEP?

(Read I Kings 11:9; Proverbs 4:6.)

We had all ignored the usual Saturday activities and had gathered to hear Old Testament professor Dr. Bruce Waltke teach from Proverbs. The crowded chapel was evidence that the practical wisdom of Solomon is timeless and still greatly desired. As the lectures progressed, we wished for a year, not just a day, to be taught the wisdom of Solomon. When the time came to ask questions, queries concerning textual structure and interpretation droned on and on, until a young man strode to the microphone. He asked the question none of us will forget: "How could Solomon be so wise, but die such a fool?"

Indeed, how had this happened? How had a man with such insight become one who eventually lived contrary to his own words of wisdom? Throughout the lectures, each of us had formed strong resolutions to saturate ourselves with the Proverbs. But now those determined plans were shaken by this disquieting observation. If this wisdom had not worked for Solomon, what hope was there for us? We could memorize the entire book of Proverbs and still be like Solomon who started so well but ended like this: "The LORD became angry with Solomon, because His heart had turned away from the LORD, the God of Israel, who had appeared to him twice" (I Kings 11:9).

Dr. Waltke answered the question deliberately and simply. "If you stop listening, you will stray. The spiritual life must be attended to daily. Neglect it and you will forget the revelation of God and become a fool—even as Solomon did."

SEPTEMBER 11   WISDOM IN NUMBERING
                                          OUR DAYS

(Read Psalm 90.)

Dr. Waltke's answer echoed for me the words of another Hebrew scholar who had long ago instructed a generation of wisdom seekers. In Psalm 90:12 Moses said it this way: "Teach us to number our days aright, that we may gain a heart of wisdom." This daily attention to our spiritual life or this numbering of our days must be the key. Maybe Psalm 90 will unveil not only how to gain a heart of wisdom, but also how to keep it.

As you glance through the entire psalm, you will immediately see the brevity of human life contrasted with the eternalness of

God. The psalmist is attempting to discover how a person's brief life-span can be meaningful in the overwhelming context of eternity. As you look at the psalm in depth, it may be helpful to note these elements: verses 1-2 affirm an everlasting God; 3-6 expose the brevity of human life; 7-10 groan under the results of humanity's fallen nature; 11-12 reveal God's holiness and the resulting human plea; 13-16 are a prayer for mercy and joy; and verse 17 ends with a plea for human endeavors to endure.

Throughout the psalm, Moses repeats again and again the words *years, days,* and *morning* in an attempt to find for his generation—and ours—a means to gain wisdom in the confines of time, even as God is working out his infinite plans.

<table>
<tr><td>SEPTEMBER 12</td><td>LEARNING THROUGH
PARADOX</td></tr>
</table>

(Read Psalm 90.)

This psalm expresses so clearly that God's perceptions supersede time. In contrast, we humans understand nothing outside the context of time. What do we do before a God who views an entire millennium with the same ease as he views one day? What is the point of living wisely if our debut in history is as brief as new grass that grows in the dewy morning and withers by evening? Why number our short days?

How insignificant this perspective makes us feel until its truth is amplified by the aging apostle Peter: "With the Lord a day is like a thousand years, and a thousand years are like a day" (II Peter 3:8*b*). If the converse is true—that a day is like a thousand years—then each moment of our lives is vitally significant. Maybe the balanced tension of this paradox gives us a new way to count our days. Maybe our attempts at gaining equilibrium between today and eternity cause us to gain—and keep—a heart of wisdom.

Verses 9 and 14 of Psalm 90 expose another paradox. Verse 9 describes the groaning of our years; verse 14 portrays the gladness of our years. Here Moses explores the weariness and sinfulness of our lives in one strophe of the psalm and then reveals the joy of fellowship with a merciful God in another stanza. Again, through paradox we are shown that in order to gain and keep a heart of wisdom we must expect that life will hold both requiems and songs of celebration.

SEPTEMBER 13   KEEPING OUR BALANCE

(Read Psalm 90.)

In Psalm 90, verses 10 and 17 reveal yet another tension of truth. Verse 10 agonizes over the fact that our days "quickly pass, and we fly away." These words give us a sense of hopelessness. Not only is our life-span short, but also nothing of influence or consequence remains once it's over. If we fly away like a bird, what is the point of ever having lived?

In verse 17 the psalmist reconciles this frustration by calling on God to "establish the work of his hands." In other words, Moses asks God to preserve the efforts attempted during his brief life-span so that there might be a legacy to pass on to the coming generation. God obviously honored his prayer because we, who are many generations from Moses, can read this Hebrew poem and still be moved to number our days and gain a heart of wisdom. Paradox again has taught us what nothing else could: our lives and our efforts are fleeting, but, by the mercy of God, we will provide something useful for those who come after us.

Numbering our days is an intricate process of living with paradoxes. In this psalm we have seen an unbelievable set of mathematics: 1,000 years = 1 day, and 1 day = 1,000 years. We have explored contradictory emotions—the groans and the gladness of our days. And we have tried to reconcile transience and permanence. By understanding these paradoxes, and thereby maintaining an equilibrium between them, we gain, and keep, a heart of wisdom. We must walk carefully between these parallel truths. Solomon is proof of how easy it is to lose our balance.

SEPTEMBER 14   GREATER THAN WISDOM

(Read Jeremiah 9:23.)

In this study of wisdom, one last voice from the Old Testament must not be forgotten. The prophet Jeremiah warns, "Let not the wise man boast of his wisdom . . ." (Jeremiah

9:23*a*). I must admit my first response to this passage is, "Why not?" Wisdom is so rare these days that anyone who has even a little of it ought to celebrate. I can understand the rest of the verse which says that the strong man shouldn't boast in his strength nor the rich man in his wealth. We all know that might and riches are often capricious. But shouldn't wisdom be a valid reason to exult?

As usual, my questioning came before the author's crucial point. The word of the Lord through Jeremiah continued to reveal that something greater than wisdom should be our reason to boast. In verse 24 he says, "Let him who boasts boast about this: that he understands and knows me, that I am the Lord." God values our relationship over our insight.

If Jeremiah 9 is the poetic expression of this precept, then Philippians 3 is its autobiographical counterpart. Paul, of all devout Israelites, had every reason to boast. But through the evaluation of his life in Philippians 3:4-11, he makes this concluding statement: "I consider everything a loss compared to the surpassing greatness of knowing Christ Jesus my Lord" (Philippians 3:8).

Wisdom has come full circle. Wisdom's beginning will always be the fear of the Lord, and its full maturity will bring us humbly back to its relational starting place.

SEPTEMBER 15   A RESOLUTION TO REST

(Read Proverbs 6:9-11.)

"My favorite holiday is not Christmas, it's New Year's Day."

I was intrigued by my friend's preference and immediately asked for his reasons.

"New Year's Day is my favorite because I use it as a day to start over. I try to lay aside the guilt from my lack of accomplishment the previous year, and I begin making new goals for the year ahead."

I winced as I listened to this high achiever's view of New Year's and wondered what he'd think of the resolution I had made for this year. This year I had only one item on my list, just one resolution. This year I wanted to learn to rest.

243

So far, however, I am living more like my friend. No matter how resolved I am to learn restfulness, my strong work and achievement ethic seem to get the best of me. Maybe I could lay aside this overemphasis on achievement and work more easily if it were imposed on me only by my culture. But I struggle because it appears to be echoed in Scripture and often seems the godly way to live.

Proverbs 6:9-11 says it all: "How long will you lie there, you sluggard? When will you get up from your sleep? A little sleep, a little slumber, a little folding of the hands to rest and poverty will come on you like a bandit and scarcity like an armed man." Is it okay to rest? Is my resolution to rest appropriate?

SEPTEMBER 16   LOOK TO THE ANT

(Read Proverbs 6:6-8.)

After reading Proverbs 6:9-11, I certainly get motivated. I don't want to be considered a sluggard, and I would like to avoid poverty, if possible. But this dilemma of work versus rest is much deeper than these issues for those who are serious about living as Christians. We are afraid to stop because so much of what we do is intended to minister to a needy world. We are here to serve—and serve diligently.

If this passage isn't enough to get us charging, all we need to do is look to a previous section in Proverbs 6. "Go to the ant, you sluggard; consider its ways and be wise! It has no commander, no overseer or ruler, yet it stores its provisions in summer and gathers its food at harvest" (Proverbs 6:6-8 NIV). Every time I hear these verses I vividly remember one picnic. The ants were everywhere, and once we realized that we couldn't get rid of them, we decided to watch them. One ant in particular was fascinating. She carried a piece of hamburger bun three times her size up a small mound of sand. It took several attempts, but she finally achieved her objective. For the first time in her life, picnickers were applauding her instead of trying to squash her. I couldn't believe the diligence and determination of one tiny insect. This extraordinary ant made me impose on Proverbs 6 the idea that, if I am truly spiritual, I should be learning to carry bigger loads farther and faster as I mature in life.

But do we have these Proverbs in balance with the rest of Scripture, and are we seeing them accurately?

SEPTEMBER 17   THE JOURNEY IS TOO MUCH FOR YOU

(Read I Kings 19:7.)

The same God who gave Solomon the wisdom and inspiration for the Proverbs has also revealed a very important moment in the life of Elijah. In I Kings 18 this prophet of the Lord had his famous encounter with the prophets of Baal. In a dramatic duel on Mount Carmel, Baal was exposed as a false god and the God of Israel was proven powerful and real. In many ways it was the pinnacle of Elijah's ministry. But it is the events after the duel that give us insight into the importance of rest.

Beginning with I Kings 19, Elijah is in serious danger. Queen Jezebel is furious about the death of her Baal prophets and takes an oath to kill Elijah by the next day. Exhausted by the contest on Mount Carmel and filled with terror by the wicked queen's plans, Elijah runs away. It's not long before Elijah quits and simply wishes for one thing—for God to take his life. In complete exhaustion he falls asleep.

It is here that our God, who has deep compassion for human limitations, makes provision for Elijah. Despite Elijah's fear and despair—which is almost comical, coming from a man who has just watched God bring fire down from heaven to ignite a water-soaked altar—God still gently provides. In one of the most tender scenes between God and man, Elijah is refreshed and renewed by the angel of the Lord, who says, "Get up and eat, for the journey is too much for you" (I Kings 19:7).

SEPTEMBER 18   A QUIET PLACE

(Read Mark 6:31.)

The scene from I Kings seems to have its counterpart in Mark 6. In this New Testament episode, the disciples had just returned from ministering in the name of Christ. They had experienced the power of God working through them in miraculous ways.

Because of this amazing ministry, people were engulfing them to the point of making it impossible for them to eat. At this point Christ says to his disciples, "Come with me by yourselves to a quiet place and get some rest" (Mark 6:31). Once again our Lord gave his people permission to rest. In a sense, he said it is wise and good to be renewed.

In all of life, there must be alternate periods of exertion and recuperation. We modern-day servants of the Lord continually err on the side of constant exertion. We have not balanced our Proverbs with Mark and Elijah.

Not only is our balance off, but so is some of our interpretation of the Proverbs. The Proverbs 6 passage that speaks of a little folding of the hands does not instruct us to remove rest from our lives. In its wise, pithy form, it warns us against doing nothing. It pushes us away from laziness toward faithfulness, not workaholism. Wise faithfulness makes provision for the need to recuperate, recreate, and rest.

SEPTEMBER 19   ANOTHER LOOK AT THE ANTS

(Read Proverbs 6:6-8.)

While trying to understand how rest could ever fit with Proverbs 6:6-8, I uncovered some interesting facts about ants. Ants are not the independent overachievers my picnic experience led me to assume; ants are very social. According to a renowned zoologist, ants have a complex system of cooperation and labor division. If we were to look to the ways of the ant and be wise, the results would not be the proliferation of supermen and superwomen. Instead of individual striving, we would be providing and receiving support from a caring community. Ants divide labor and cooperate for the good of the community. We try to do it all ourselves and end up exhausted and irritable. Once again, a more discerning look at Proverbs pushes us toward faithful foresight and cooperative community, rather than isolated workaholism.

I think my resolution at the beginning of the year was appropriate. With about three months left before another New Year's Day, maybe there is still time for renewal and refreshment to become an important part of each week.

Starting today, I'll enjoy a few moments like those Cheryl

Forbes describes in *Imagination: Embracing a Theology of Wonder*. She tells the story of a little boy who intuitively understood the potential that rest holds for us. She writes, "He sat for hours one day on his grandmother's porch, cat beside him, teddy bear in his lap. Finally his grandmother had to ask what he was doing. 'I'm loving, Grandma. Jus' loving.'"

SEPTEMBER 20   THE DANGERS OF REST

(Read Deuteronomy 8:12, 17.)

Though rest is wise and necessary, it also can create the danger of misplaced confidence or the danger of forgetfulness. Moses illustrates the first danger in Deuteronomy 8:12 and 17: "When you eat and are satisfied, . . . and all you have is multiplied then . . . you may say to yourself, 'My power and the strength of my hands have produced this wealth for me.'" Nehemiah, one of Israel's leaders after the exile, illustrates the second danger as he recounts Israel's history in a prayer of confession: "But as soon as they were at rest, they again did what was evil in your sight" (Nehemiah 9:28 NIV). In places of prosperity and rest, we humans often congratulate ourselves and turn a deaf ear toward God.

How, then, will we ever rest? If we are to be constantly on guard, we'll only become more neurotic in our already fearful, fast-paced world. How can I take a much-needed rest without incurring the dangers of rest?

Maybe the key is to be certain I do not take forgetfulness along on my vacations. There is a difference between *carefree* and *careless*. One is the absence of stress; the other is disregard for those things we should honor. When I come to pleasant places, instead of congratulating myself or growing spiritually deaf, I must remember to give thanks. Maybe resting without danger is letting down our guard without letting down our gratitude.

SEPTEMBER 21   REST THROUGH FRIENDSHIP

(Read II Corinthians 7:5-7.)

After reading of his relentless zeal, I had always assumed the apostle Paul was above needing human encouragement. He seemed almost like a New Testament Ulysses—severely tried but always invincible. Certainly he was one who would never let a few shipwrecks, snakebites, and imprisonments stop him. He may have had a thorn in the flesh, but when God said, "My grace is sufficient for you," he carried on courageously. One of his letters even says, "I delight in weaknesses, in insults, in hardships, in persecutions, in difficulties. For when I am weak, then I am strong" (II Corinthians 12:10 NIV). But II Corinthians 7 candidly brings the crucial balance to all this heavenly mindedness. In verse 6 we discover that even Paul the apostle needed rest and comfort through tangible human friendship.

Few would write as honest a missionary letter as II Corinthians. In this letter Paul transparently reveals the stinging criticism he has incurred in the ministry (II Corinthians 10:1-18). He also details the sufferings he has endured on his travels (II Corinthians 11:16-33). Paul even lets us glimpse his most private moments by sharing the ecstasy of his visions and the agony of his thorn in the flesh (II Corinthians 12:1-10). Through this unique letter, Paul has sketched the ideas of comfort in affliction and strength from weakness. Then, as every good teacher must, he has illustrated these precepts with the rich, unforgettable hues of his own experience. And most fascinating among these experiences is the rest that friendship brought to Paul.

SEPTEMBER 22   THE COMING OF A FRIEND

(Read II Corinthians 1:3-4.)

Through his theme of comfort during affliction Paul reveals an important perspective on rest. In II Corinthians 2:12-13, he tells of a situation that causes him great restlessness. He has gone to Troas (a city located on the western coast of modern-day Turkey) and has discovered great opportunities for ministry. But the apostle has no peace of mind because Titus, his friend, cannot be found. It is so crucial to be rejoined with him that Paul leaves the opportunities in Troas and continues north to Macedonia. We hear nothing more about this situation until II Corinthians 7:5.

Apparently Paul's trip to Macedonia is a time when this

passionate missionary loses his zeal. He and his companions are discouraged—even depressed. The influences that press upon them are not only outward but also inward (7:5). Paul describes it as a tense time of restlessness and harassment and fear. But then something happens to change it all: Titus appears (7:6-7).

Paul seems to say that rest and renewal come not from Ulysses-like invincibility but from the mutual giving and receiving of comfort forged through friendship. Titus himself has been strengthened by the friendship and obedience of the Corinthians (II Corinthians 7:13-15). Therefore, he can minister to Paul and faithfully perform the principle of II Corinthians 1:3-4: "Praise be to God . . . who comforts us in all our troubles, so that we can comfort those in any trouble with the comfort we ourselves have received from God" (NIV).

SEPTEMBER 23   MIRROR, MIRROR, ON THE WALL

I couldn't help noticing how lovely her scarf looked—the perfect color enhanced by the perfect drape. After hours of working with my scarves, they always end up looking as if I've slept in them. Let's face it, I'll never get it right. But why do I feel pressure to keep trying? Why must I look as dressed for success as she does?

Some days I feel as if I'm acting out that familiar fairytale line, "Mirror, mirror, on the wall, who's the fairest of them all?" We women of the nineties would never ask that exact question, of course; we nobly deemphasize physical beauty. But I suspect we still stand in front of our mirrors asking, "Mirror, mirror on the wall, who's the most capable of them all?"

Of course, we don't literally talk to mirrors, but aren't we constantly checking our competence in one way or another? Do we faithfully parent our children, or must we be the best mom of all? Do we conscientiously perform the duties of our careers, or must we always be the best in our field? Is our service in the church motivated by love for Christ, or do we want to be a renowned parishioner? With this attitude of comparing, we dash through a life of high expectations and relentless competition. Is it any wonder we're so tired? Maintaining our position and importance requires exhausting vigilance. We haven't time to be rested or to consider living a life gently shaped with mercy.

SEPTEMBER 24   LONGER PRAYER SHAWLS

(Read Matthew 11:28-30.)

The "comparing attitude" is found not only in fairytales and in our competitive age, but also is revealed through the pages of the Gospels. The people were jockeying for the position of most important in all the land. Ironically, those competing for the top were the religious leaders of the day. Instead of modeling God's refreshing mercy, they were concerned with impressing others. They made "their phylacteries wide and the tassels of their prayer shawls long; they [loved] the place of honor at banquets and the most important seats in the synagogues; they [loved] to be greeted in the marketplaces and to have men call them 'Rabbi' " (Matthew 23:5-7 NIV). In many ways they were saying, "Mirror, mirror on the wall, who's the greatest of them all?"

As these teachers of the law fussed and preened, another Teacher wearing the simple robes of a peasant spoke:

Come to me, all you who are weary and burdened, and I will give you rest. Take my yoke upon you and learn from me, for I am gentle and humble in heart, and you will find rest for your souls. For my yoke is easy and my burden is light. (Matthew 11:28-30 NIV)

This gracious invitation to the weary and the burdened, though addressed to another generation, extends to us. In fact, the attitudes and influences that caused weariness so long ago are still the reasons for our weariness today.

SEPTEMBER 25   EXHAUSTING EXTERNALS

(Read Matthew 23.)

One of the chief causes of exhaustion is pretense. Maybe that is why Christ's gentle tone in Matthew 11 changes drastically in

Matthew 23, where his sharp words slash through the prayer shawls of the Pharisees to expose hypocrisy.

First he accuses these leaders of preaching one thing and living another (23:3). They were master models of deceit, and they discipled the people in the burden of duplicity. Christ also addressed their practice of tithing (23:23-24). Though tithing was commanded, these misguided leaders did it to the exclusion of more important matters of the Law. They went so far as to tithe their spices. Determining a tenth of a head of dill gave them little time to accomplish justice, express mercy, and model faithfulness.

Christ's sharp words were accompanied by vivid images to illustrate the Pharisees' hypocrisy. He accused them of being "like white-washed tombs, which look beautiful on the outside but on the inside are full of dead men's bones and everything unclean" (23:27-28). He attacked their meticulous practice of washing eating utensils. How ridiculous to wash so carefully when the hearts of those doing the washing were greedy and self-indulgent (23:25). How tiring are external rules and regulations. How much better is the honest fatigue from cultivating a pure heart.

SEPTEMBER 26   AN EASIER YOKE

(Read Hosea 11.)

Christ's invitation to rest is filled with Old Testament images. When Christ used the metaphor of a yoke, his Hebrew audience would have remembered Hosea's use of it. In Hosea 11, the prophet draws an unforgettable image from the cumbersome yokes used in his day. Animals yoked together were so constricted they were unable to bend their heads to eat. Therefore, Hosea uses the image to speak of a God who loved his people so tenderly he would "lift the yoke from their neck and [bend] down to feed them" (Hosea 11:4*b*). The image holds such compassion; no wonder Christ used it to call the people away from the pretense imposed by the Pharisees.

Through hindsight we know that many in Christ's generation rejected the invitation, just as their forefathers did in

Hosea's era. It makes me wonder what our generation will do. Will we accept his invitation to be rescued from pretense to a refreshing, honest walk with him and others? Will we begin to rest from asking who's the most capable of them all?

Tomorrow, as I stand in front of the mirror tying my scarf, I'll remember the prayer shawls. First, I must understand that the one in the mirror is accepted as she is—crumpled scarf and all. Then I'll need to see others not as ones to compete with but as ones to affirm and enjoy. Already the yoke feels lighter. Already I feel more rested.

SEPTEMBER 27   SABBATH REST OR SUNDAY MARATHON?

There's never enough time in one week to do it all, and, frankly, by Sunday morning what I really need is extra rest. But all too often our Sunday starts rudely with a 6:45 A.M. alarm. We dress at top speed, forget breakfast, and dash to church to run in myriad directions to teach, lead service, rehearse, make announcements, and pray (of *all* things to rush!). After the 11 A.M. service, we bolt down dinner in order to be ready for any number of activities—from carpooling kids to children's choir practice, to making a quick dash to the store for a weekend special, to attending a Sunday night Bible study. No wonder Sunday feels more like a marathon than a sabbath!

What is this day set apart supposed to be? If it is to be a day of rest, then I'm violating it completely. If it is a refuge of joy and holiness, then I'm missing it entirely. If the sabbath was a day when Israel remembered her Divine Lover, and if Sunday is now the day Christ's Bride celebrates her Bridegroom, then I'm in desperate need of a second honeymoon!

Subtly, my spark of sabbath celebration has been replaced by conscientious commitment. Instead of expressing spontaneous adoration, I merely keep an appointment. If these replacements were *additions* to celebration and adoration, they could be acts of mature love. But when commitment becomes a *substitute* for passion, duty shrivels into performance by rote.

Maybe the way to recapture the essence of the sabbath is to see it as a sanctuary in time.

SEPTEMBER 28   THE FOURTH COMMANDMENT

Each reference in the Old Testament that admonishes Israel to keep the Sabbath helps to unveil the essence of this day set apart. When the Ten Commandments were given in Exodus 20, the fourth commandment was tied to God's rest on the seventh day. Because God is not human, this rest was not from weariness (Isaiah 40:28) nor was it the result of completing his work forever (John 5:17). It seems more probable that this resting and blessing was an expression of satisfaction. Maybe the sabbath is the pinnacle of creation, rather than male and female, because it provides the invitation to enjoy all that has been created. According to Exodus 23:12, the sabbath is also the agent of refreshment and renewal that sustains creation.

Deuteronomy 5 also lists the Ten Commandments. In this passage, the fourth commandment includes remembering God as redeemer and liberator. After years of slavery in Egypt, this day of rest, worship, and community gathering would have been a treasured refuge.

Through the prophet Ezekiel, God said, "I gave them my Sabbaths as a sign between us, so they would know that I the Lord made them holy" (Ezekiel 20:12). Instead of a ring or a document, God chose a living, active sign of covenant. Instead of a *symbol* of loyalty, the Sabbath was a *response* of loyalty. It was not something merely to be looked at; it was something to be enacted.

SEPTEMBER 29   THE RABBI'S ASSISTANT

(Read Isaiah 58:13-14.)
I had just discovered she was a rabbi's assistant and had eagerly asked her the essence of the sabbath. She chuckled at the idea of stating the sabbath's essence succinctly, and kindly explained that its effect reaches through the Jewish community with unceasing implications. But she did have something to

show me as we both gazed out her office window at the freeway below us.

"See—this never, ever stops. On Friday evening in Israel, everything stops—cars, people, animals. It even feels as if the land rests. Yes, it all stops except the sun, which we watch setting with joyous hearts. . . ."

As she paused, I interjected a question only an overachieving Protestant Gentile would ask: "But what do you *do* when you stop?"

"We stop in honor of the Creator, who on his seventh day ceased creating. So we too must stop the works of creating and respond to the Creator by enjoying what has already been created. The sabbath is a time for holy assembly. It is also a time to remember and renew the interwoven vows to God, to community, and to family. On that day, all are bathed and dressed in white as if to celebrate a wedding feast."

As she continued speaking, she seemed to echo Isaiah 58:13-14. The word translated *delight* in verse 13 really should be translated *exquisite delight* to more closely capture its Hebrew meaning. The sabbath is a sanctuary of worship that is to be anticipated with the deepest joy.

SEPTEMBER 30   SABBATH SUNDAY

(Read John 20:19-21.)

For Christians, this day set apart has become the first day of the week—that day when the resurrected Christ first showed himself to the believers (John 20:19-21). But somehow our contemporary Sundays hardly resemble a sanctuary in time.

Our family finally decided to prepare a sabbath meal and discover through its rituals what we've lost in our bustling Sundays. So I prepared the challah (sabbath bread) and lit the candles of redemption and creation. My husband prayed over the wine and our seven-year-old watched with wide eyes. I must admit we Gentiles fumbled a bit, but we discovered something invaluable. The sabbath prayers resonate with humble worship for God, with sincere honor between husband and wife, and with tender blessing from parent to child. They are a powerful mode of refreshment and rest.

But this sanctuary is not just for the family unit; the sabbath is also a day of holy assembly. What would Christ say about our present-day Sunday worship? Could we—our families and our churches—really stop achieving and acquiring for just one day? It seems that we, of all generations, need time to rest, to worship, to strengthen family bonds, and to recapture community. If we could stop, maybe we would discover rest and recreation in the deepest sense. Maybe through this sanctuary in time we would regain the exquisite delight that comes through communion with the Lord of the sabbath.

OCTOBER

On Terms of Care and Prayer

PHYLLIS A. TICKLE

OCTOBER 1   **A POINT OF VIEW**

Meditations are intended as honing tools for the mind, as attainable disciplines for the soul, and, upon many occasions, as comfort for the discouraged heart. Because of this, they are subtly dangerous things.

Going, like monks and hermits, in the guise and gowns of the religious, meditations all too frequently enter our sacred space unquestioned. We admit them readily from off the printed page, opening to them all the prayer chapels and private confessionals and individual oratories of our own separate experiences.

As one who, from time to time, is grateful to write meditations as part of my own vocation, I have over the years become increasingly occupied by a kind of fearful awareness of what it is I am doing; but never more so than now.

October is one of nature's most active months of the year's twelve. It is also and variously a point of view, a changing season, a stage in life, a pivotal point for vegetation, a housing place for angels and demons and all the citizens of Narnia. Meditations about and during October are like the month itself—things to be entered into carefully. I also enter them prayerfully, inviting you to do so with me . . . inviting you, in fact, not to come on any terms other than those of care and prayer, for beyond this page there be . . . But enough! I have already said that once. Shall we go in?

*October devotions © 1992 by Tickle, Inc., Memphis, TN.

More than twenty years ago, Sam and I lost to pneumonia our fifth child and second-born son. His death was, and remains, an experience that informs every part of our life.

Just as irrevocably as the heated iron sears into flesh the identity of the branded creature and becomes, if not predictive, then certainly diagnostic of the creature's future course, so that death was for us. I have written of it often, drawing from it solace and agony and poignancy and maudlin self-pity, faith, wonder, perhaps compassion, common ground with other pain, a false impunity, surety of Resurrection. Like a drawer filled with an inexhaustible supply of scarves and ribbons and ties, that one single event has decorated our life and furnished the weather flags by which we have dressed our masts and trimmed our sails.

But even such a grief as bonds its victims by its magnitude must also be privately endured. Lying, as it does, too interior to be rationally known, it shapes unobserved and does the work of God unspoken—but not unseen.

Sam's prayer book, unlike mine, has almost no notation or marginalia in it. He is far too careful of possessions for that. Yet on the fly leaf there is writing. It is dated the day of Wade's interment and says simply: "Take heed that ye despise not one of these little ones; for I say unto you, That in heaven their angels do always behold the face of my Father which is in heaven" (Matthew 18:10).

If Sam and I were Roman Catholics, which we are not, today, October 2, would be for us the Feast Day of Guardian Angels. Our Lord certainly spoke frequently and freely of angels, and it is his words which Sam has re-copied into the fly leaf of his prayer book. But because I am Protestant and this is the twentieth century, it is hard for me to take all those words at face value—as serious, as meaning what they say, as bringing to me something which I am afraid to admit into my world.

But if Jesus of Nazareth were really being truthful and really knew, as he claimed he did, that there are guardian angels in God's face talking constantly about every human child living in reality right now. . . . if he were, then, my sisters, I ask you to think today with me about what kind of women we should be and must become, what kind of mothers, what kind of believers.

OCTOBER 3 REMEMBERING THE EDGEWATER

It was October 3, 1990. I do not usually remember so particularly (or record so specifically) the events of life, since for most of us—and especially for me—life is more a series of impressions organized by impact and vividness rather than a matter of dates and historicity. But this was October 3, 1990.

We were in Florida, and "we" were Nora and Laura and I. The occasion was a trade show—the Southeastern Booksellers Association book show in Orlando, in fact. I was there in my professional role as director of trade publishing for a large southern publisher. Nora, our oldest daughter, had grown up, like all of our children, in the publishing business and had, at the end of law school and a judicial clerkship, entered practice in the field of intellectual property and copyright law. She was there for the same trade show, representing her firm and meeting with several clients as well. Laura, likewise to the manor born, was attending the Orlando meeting as director of distribution for the country's oldest distributor of community cookbooks.

Although the three of us had come from separate cities, we had shared the same pleasing problem. The book show did not begin until Thursday, but the cheapest accommodations required our arriving on Tuesday; so we arrived. We met at the Orlando airport as we had agreed to do. Nora's plane came in last. We rented a car, threw our briefcases and garment bags into the trunk, and beat the 5:30 P.M. traffic out of town headed northeast for Daytona and the beach.

We were not heading for any piece of beach, however. We were heading for 400 North Atlantic Avenue, Daytona Beach (where now a Holiday Inn high-rise commands the oceanfront), but where for all the years of my girlhood and theirs a much humbler structure named The Edgewater had stood. The old Edgewater, a 1920s collection of twelve by-the-week-or-month apartments, had seen three generations of us through sabbaticals and family holidays and various recuperations.

When the old building was sold to make room for a more lucrative enterprise like the Holiday Inn high-rise, we mourned its memory; but, as a family, we had become too scattered and two occupied to miss its reality. The Edgewater was immutably etched in our lives, and its actuality was no longer a question of personal concern . . . until Nora stood at the desk of the Holiday Inn that Tuesday night and explained to an annoyed clerk why we *were* going to check in with him and with no one else in Daytona Beach; until we, my daughters and I, walked in the Atlantic ocean barefoot that night, just as we had used to do; until we sat in a boardwalk honky-tonk and drank the midnight into the post-midnight the way I would never have dreamed we might; until I lay down in rooms I had not felt before except in space and over earth my father had taught the three of us to trust and be free in; until I awoke refreshed on that morning of October 3 and, walking out onto a balcony that I had never enjoyed before, looked down upon my two grown daughters frolicking like children, throwing sand and sea water at each other.

"Do you see them, Daddy?" I asked his ghost. "Do you see what you began when you taught them to toss low and light like that?" And in that small moment I understood October, for my father was closer to me than my two daughters were and his presence nearer to God than to memory.

OCTOBER 4   A DIFFERENT ECOLOGY

Today is October 4 and the Feast Day of Saint Francis of Assisi, a monastic who, among other things, has since 1979 been the patron saint of ecologists, as well as the favorite subject for a great deal of expensive and bad garden sculpture. None of us has to have been born a Roman to know this one!

It is, in fact, the easiness of our familiarity with Francis that always troubles me on October 4 . . . that and the garden sculpture and our emotional sloppiness (one woman's opinion) in parading animals into our church yards and blessing them as if Francis of Assisi had been no more than a devout Walt Disney.

There is danger in domesticating one's saints—even greater

danger in tipping the hat cavalierly to something one doesn't really respect. It's ironic that Francis, that most self-impoverished, charismatic, and particular of the monastic founders, should be the one whose feast day would trigger such a comment, or the celebration of whose acquired gentleness should elicit it.

Now, the practice of ecology is undoubtedly a moral positive in addition to being a matter of current political vogue. It is good for our common life and for our predictable future as creatures. The practice of humility and perhaps even the joyful discipline of respect are likewise learned exercises open to men and women of good faith and divine intention everywhere. Francis, of all men, knew that well and acknowledged it as a useful truth, saying "Sanctify yourself and you will sanctify society" (which is not exactly the same as what we imply when we exhort each other to be ecological in the name of Christianity, but it's close enough to encourage us in that direction).

The difference is that Francis thought that all human phenomena and all creatures are possessed, as we ourselves are, of spirits—spirits which he acknowledged in conversation; to whom he preached; from whom he sought expiation and consolation. That is a different ecology and one most unlikely to hold contemporary vogue anywhere, for it recognizes the discarnate as well as the carnate world and asserts a seamless existence emanating from them. It is Francis's ecology. It is Christian ecology. It is not, I fear, the ecology of the churchyard children this afternoon, nor of the average recycler. In fact, as ecology grows in secular appeal, it seems to me that our political rectitude and moral self-congratulations come ever closer to obscuring the divine passion which afflicted Francis of Assisi and which drove him to the sparrows and the chickadees.

OCTOBER 5   THE MIRACULOUS ORDINARY

The Park's Seed Company catalog arrives about this time every year. Park's is probably not the world's largest seed company, or for all I know, even one of the better known ones. It does happen, to be, at our house anyway, a respected one. Every year when the Park's catalog comes, I am struck once again by that respect, or by what I perceive to be the reasons for it.

The claims made by Park's—both the visual ones contained in its photographs and the written ones folded into its descriptive paragraphs—are actual and reproducible, which, I think, is why Sam so favors Park's. As a marketer and as a company, Park's has somehow managed to remain respectful of the process that lies beyond itself, of the result that it is the province of earth and water and seasons and human skill alone to provide for. By its corporate submission to the actual over the easy, Park's persuades Sam to accept the possible and the ordinary as the most sufficient and most worthy. So, like his mother before him, Sam refers to the company's catalog as his bible, and he orders.

He will order, tonight or one night soon, the two or three envelopes of infinitesimal seeds which, under his tutelage, will make our lettuce in January; the narcissus bulbs for my Easter bowls; the malabar that will garnish our salads and complete our quiches; the onion sets that may or may not survive to a life beyond their first initial, delicious greenness; and the twenty or twenty-five other dormant things that Park's faith will ship and Sam's reverence will assume.

By the time the transactions have all been completed, it will no longer be October, of course, nor will either of us still be concerned with old catalogs—save that in that dark time of December I trust we will be even more mindful than we now are of the ineluctable power that rests in the hands of those who speak only truth about the miraculous ordinary.

OCTOBER 6   THE POWER OF WORDS

My family is Episcopalian, a condition of religious preference which, more than any other, seems susceptible to jest.

We crack them all in our family, from the celebratory jokes about being "whiskepalians" to the old saw about being the Republican Party at prayer. (Better to poke fun at oneself, after all, and control the flow of humor than to let the other fellow go first and get out of hand with it.) We even occasionally permit ourselves—especially on Sundays when we are standing up with all those lectionaries, hymnals, service leaflets, and prayerbooks in our hands—to mutter the acid quip about being God's most literate communion . . . but not today. Never on October 6.

October 6 is the commemoration of William Tyndale, and Anglicans around the world stop to pay him homage. On this day in 1536, William Tyndale suffered martyrdom in order that we might have our jest.

Born in England only two years after Columbus arrived on these shores, Tyndale was a child of the early Reformation and a militant (if self-effacing) soldier in its final army. And his was a simple thesis: Equal access to holy words is the right of all believers.

Driven by his radical idea, in 1523 Tyndale set about translating the New Testament into English. Because of persecution, he fled England in 1525, making his way safely that winter to Germany where he met Martin Luther and finally began the actual publication of his translations.

For another ten years, William Tyndale was to both print his New Testament and expand his translations into the rest of Scripture. Although Tyndale himself was captured in Antwerp in 1535, tried, and then executed in 1536, his work endured, becoming finally the basis for the Authorized (King James) Bible.

Even knowing this story (and we all more or less know it at some vague level of rote history) and even having a commemorative day each year on my calendar to call me to remember and honor, it is hard for me to lay hold upon Tyndale's passion.

A time when words were forbidden is a time beyond my ken. It lies outside the range of my imagination. And for that reason, so too the power of words lies beyond my reverence. I throw them and toss them and jot them and sometimes even curse them, but all too rarely do I recall myself to the potency of them and, once they are spoken or written, to the indestructible and indissoluble life of them. William Tyndale may be the great benefactor of literate and English-speaking Christianity, but for those of us who practice it, he must stand as one of October's dark and haunting memories. His autumn death was born out of that which we, to our peril, have ceased to fear.

There is a directness to October, an attitude within its populousness, that intrudes into the senses and renders October into a time of unselfconscious patterns. Especially in the country, where we live and where all things contrive to remind us of the brief respite which is autumn, do I feel the consolation of systems.

I would view my observation as an idiosyncratic whim or as a romantic indulgence were it not that so many of our city friends and all of our city children manage to find their way to us in October . . . and were it not for the fact that most of them, having found their way, want not us at all but each other and the farm.

Our crows, too, always come home in October. In March they restore their heavy wooden nests in the pine treetops and in April lay their eggs. In May and June they teach and train. In July they leave, taking the fledglings with them. But they begin that regenerative process each October when they come home again to winter. Always, without fail, by mid-month they have re-established their guard posts in the trees bounding our pastures and have re-asserted their right to the airways of the farm as their territory.

I suspect, as I sit here now watching their guards change in the upper meadow just beyond the fence line, that somewhere there is a process or a wisdom that acknowledges no difference between us, our children, our friends, and our crows. What will be generated in the spring must inevitably begin by wintering in what has been.

That is hardly a deep observation; it is certainly not a religious one. What troubles me in October, however, is that in our concrete society we are so easily seduced into thinking it is. Yet, Christianity actually instructs us to presume that the presence of natural constancy in order that we may spend ourselves in seeking a spiritual one. "Behold the fowls of the air: for they sow not, neither do they reap, nor gather into barns; yet your heavenly Father feedeth them. Are you not much better than they? . . . But seek ye first the kingdom of God, and his righteousness; and all these things shall be added unto you. Take therefore no thought for the morrow: for the morrow shall take thought for the things of itself. Sufficient unto the day *is* the evil thereof" (Matthew 6:26 passim KJV).

Hard words. I would greatly prefer to pass my fall in maudlin homage to the visible and intricate wonders of natural process than in commitment to a God who has no need of seasons, of beginnings and endings—I would rather, that is, except for the fact that the only God I, in the October of my life, am persuaded of is One without seasons, beginnings, or endings.

OCTOBER 8   HOW GOD MUST LOVE

Georgia O'Keeffe sits watching me as I write this.

It would not matter greatly where in my house or even in my office I was sitting; I could still make that statement. It is probably a vanity of mine that it should be so, but at least it is familial rather than individual.

On my office bulletin board, right by my desk chair, is pinned a delicate and potent sepia of O'Keeffe in a 1920s, dust-bowl housedress, sitting on the brick steps outside her house and looking up at the camera. Her hands, however, and not her face, are the subject—long-fingered, slender, and worshiped, they seem almost to glow in the natural light.

In my writing room, O'Keeffe and Anita Pollitzer stare at each other from my tack board, their marcelled hauteur speaking a thousand words about the potency of friendship and the darkness of its interruption.

Above Sam's desk hangs the more usual O'Keeffe, the botanical and bulbous and, by deft exposure, the erotic O'Keeffe on canvas. In a house of seven children it would seem both appropriate and inevitable that the painter O'Keeffe should find some affinity between the householders and her own work, but it is not for that reason that I keep her, nor for the fragile hands from which she drew such gifts. I keep O'Keeffe about me because she, more then any other artist, instructs me in how God must love.

In our secularized culture where artists are consulted as if they were priests and denizens of some arcane but vital truth, such a statement is subject to misinterpretation. (Sometimes I think that maybe even my action in housing so much O'Keeffe is subject to misinterpretation.) But O'Keeffe loves.

O'Keeffe loves, not as all artists must with infinite attention to the objects of their attention, although she certainly does do that. Rather, Georgia O'Keeffe loves with a kind of profligate abandon. She invests herself totally in what is here today and gone tomorrow, asking no more of any single object or canvas than that it be while it is.

What O'Keeffe is really painting, of course, is not on any of her canvases. It can't be. Had she been able to incarnate that consuming affection she would indeed have been a god. It is rather her stark recognition of her own failure that exposes for me first the miracle of God made man, and then the unutterable passion which lay behind the gesture. So, too weak to sustain such comprehension long for myself, I keep the failed beauty of Georgia O'Keeffe as talismans.

OCTOBER 9   OF CATS AND PUMPKINS

October is the month of pumpkins, or at least of the beginning of pumpkins. One of the atrocities of contemporary America that is most likely to elicit my contempt is our inappropriate treatment of the pumpkin, especially its relegation to tin-can pies and shopping-mall displays.

Being a poor historian at best, I am still respectful of the pumpkin's culinary past. Being an even poorer cook, I have, until recently, also been its grateful defender; I truly can contrive more superb dishes from pumpkin than from any other vegetable: pumpkin souffle, pumpkin and apple muffins, pumpkin and cinnamon rolls, pumpkin custard, pumpkin bread. You name it, and I—given a good, proper pumpkin and time—can accomplish it. Gustatorially speaking, October's harvest traditionally was the beginning of my time in the hearts and affections of my children . . . that is, it was—until Sam's discovery about the cats.

Our patio, like our barn and our old hen house, is full of cats. I am fond of them, but Sam is pathological about them—a cat on both shoulders when he's working, a kitten in every pocket . . . you get the picture. And they are a constant source of concern to his powers as a physician, especially to his interest in preventive medicine. Accordingly, every October as the field mice begin to leave the outside in order to move in with us where it's warm, Sam begins to compensate the cats for the loss of their natural food supply and to prepare them for the hard cold ahead. He dutifully buys a case of lard (I myself don't love cats, my kids, or anything else *that* much, but that's beside the point) and begins each day to mix a healthy hunk of the stuff into the food in all the feeding dishes. By Christmas, every cat we own and a number that we don't will be as glossy and insulated as they are round and laconic, but that's not the point either.

The point is Sam's passionate concern with winterizing the cats and the way I deal with preparing pumpkin for cooking. To do the latter, I select fairly small pumpkins, break off their stems, plunge a knife in their sides somewhere and then pop the whole into the microwave for however long it takes them to begin to smell like pumpkin. Once that is done, I let my lovelies cool to handling temperature before I cut them in half, discard their seeds, and spoon their meat into my mixing bowls. Now, I'm not pathological about much of anything, being morally lazy as well as somewhat overworked, so my scooping out of the pumpkin's flesh inevitably leaves some small traces of itself—whole hunks, Sam says—but it also results in rather elegant orange "bowls" of halved pumpkins.

It was the bowls that got Sam last year. He took two or three sets outside one afternoon in order to have more dishes for serving his cat mix. The next morning, to our amazement, not only was the mix all gone, but so were my "whole hunks" of unscooped pumpkin meat. He tried it again with two more pumpkin halves. This time we watched. To my consternation and his enormous amusement, our cats plowed right through lard and pellets and made for just plain pumpkin with real fervor. So much for culinary skills and rare spices and the ego investment of secret recipes.

It was a deflation that, while it continues to rankle, has almost been worth its own weight in the amusement it has given the family . . . and perhaps the grain of humility it has granted me. It is scarcely mid-month and already the patio beds are awink with licked-clean and bleached-white pumpkin halves, reminding me of the therapeutic surgery of the soul our near-and-dear do on us all the time, and perhaps of what a gift it is to be simple.

OCTOBER 10   INDESCRIBABLE LIGHT

Once, years ago, Sam went to Arizona without us for a meeting and came home two weeks later with cactuses for the children and stories for me about the light. He talked for weeks about that light, about how I must someday see it to understand the shafting of it, the drama of its clarity, and the uninterrupted sharpness of its descent. Eventually I did make it to Arizona, and Sam was right. One has to stand at three o'clock on a clear day in the open land of Arizona. There is no vehicle of expression that can say more than that; none that can contain and transport the light of Arizona.

But that light that is caught in a single geography has an analog that is caught in time. The light of October, which comes after the dust and pollen of crops are done and before the winter rains begin, that light, too, is a given thing requiring presence. I am watching it now as it bathes across our fields, blueing the sky above them and vibrating every blade and leaf upon them. The glow of it emanates as if the light has pierced every living thing about me and shines from them rather than from itself or from the sun that gave it.

Years ago, after I had been to Arizona and seen for myself, I fell into the habit of referring to Arizona's light as "Sam's light." Lacking any other means of description, I did as people always do: I named the indescribable. And last year I named the light I am watching now. It is Charlotte's light.

Charlotte, a fellow-writer whose work I am humbled by and whose friendship I trust, visited us early last October. It was a clear day with a light breeze and no humidity. By mid-morning the glow had begun and by mid-afternoon even our conversations were stabbed by its wonder. Finally, unable to express what we were seeing and unable to tolerate the burden of our own inarticulateness, we drew away from the fields and even, once indoors, from the windows, until the dusk had fallen.

The two of us have spoken several times of that day, of the phenomenon which it represented, of the ineffable quality of its autumn light, but we have never assuaged the anguish of not being able to capture and hold it. It was when I had finally accepted our failure that I began to call it "Charlotte's light."

But when I am, as now, watching the transient play of Charlotte's light or recalling the drama of Sam's light, I am arrested always by how few there are among us for whom a light could be so named, and by how great a grace it is to have known one or two of them.

OCTOBER 11   NO WORSHIP WITHOUT
                                SACRIFICE

A year ago last night Sam and I attended a banquet in the cafeteria of one of the larger Roman Catholic schools in Memphis. The affair was being sponsored by the local chapter of the National Council of Christians and Jews and was a fundraiser for a proposed Gandhi Institute at a nearby university. The speaker was Arun Gandhi, grandson and political heir of the Mahatma.

At that time, Sam and I were working with Arun and his wife Sonanda rather closely on the biography of Arun's grandmother, Kasturba, wife to the Mahatma and revered across their homeland as "the mother of India." We were attending, therefore, more in support of Arun than in support of, or interest in, anything else. The place was packed, quite literally. And what I had attended out of friendly obligation was becoming a delight, at least in sensual pleasures. I had foreseen neither that most of the Hindu population in Memphis would wish to attend for reasons similar to ours, nor that they would elect to heighten their show of respect by coming in native dress. The result was brilliant as well as opulent. Additionally, because the National Council is broadly supported, many of the city's concerned and involved synagogues were represented, as were a Muslim communion or two, also in ethnic attire.

Arun rose to speak, which he does so often and so easily that I scarcely was aware of his beginning or of the fact that I was listening to him. I was awash in a banquet hall of perfumes that were exotic, of dyes that were unfamiliar, of whispers that were unintelligible, and of skins that were glorious. And Arun, I realized vaguely, was bothering me, interrupting my pleasures by droning away.

He was speaking about his grandfather's teaching of the Seven Blunders, seven perceptions or principles which humanity continues to violate and to whose immutability we must constantly return. I have no idea what the Seven Blunders are; I heard only the sixth one. And the sixth one, which I shall know for the rest of my life, says: There can be no worship without sacrifice.

Around me the puzzle of the unintelligible whispers faded, along with the gloriousness of the sarongs and the muskiness of the perfumes. I saw and heard and took in only Arun's words: There can be no worship without sacrifice.

I am not a universalist. Because I am a hedonist, I rejoice in the variousness of mankind and in our elaborations upon ourselves, but I am not persuaded that all roads lead to heaven or that all spirituality is salutary beyond this life. In fact, I am very much persuaded that it is not. Yet the girders and pilings of truth underlie all experience, needing only our sharing to expose themselves to us. The Mahatma knew that when he listed his Seven Blunders, just as he reverenced the accuracy of all of them without judgment.

What I had never realized until that moment was that while I can recognize accuracy as well as the next woman, I am guilty of judgment. I had always found the Mahatma's sixth principle to be pagan and repugnant. In that instant, however, when his grandson so respectfully read the words of the great man, I heard not only the accuracy but also Gandhi's acceptance. I understood (in a kind of distorted ten seconds of comprehension) that one has to sacrifice, be sacrificed, and receive sacrifice if one is to completely worship. One must, in other words, accept his or her own part of the guilt.

It was not until later when I had left that cafeteria of many colors and scents and what I had thought was my moment of amazement—not until much later, in fact—that I also suddenly received, like a click in my head, the second amazement. In that room of many faiths only one God, historically, has ever proposed to enter into all three requisite parts of sacrifice. Inappropriately perhaps, or therapeutically, I laughed at that understanding, and I have continued to laugh in the intervening months since.

OCTOBER 12   A CHANGED POINT OF VIEW

Columbus Day! I am startled by how different a thing it is for me now than it was more than fifty years ago when I was a school girl.

In those days of handmade, construction-paper flags and bathrobe Indians (they were Indians to me then; today I think of them as Native Americans), we envied the conquistador posted on the bulletin board with his radiant face looking heavenward, his sword pointed downward, and his men, along with his chaplains and the conquered Indians, gathered in a circle of homage around him. We knew that this man had achieved the good as God defines it. That plainly was the message not only of the bulletin board Columbus, but also of the whole day itself.

Nowadays, of course, very few of us, including ten-year-old school girls, would be so quick to assign God's total sanction to colonialism or its conquests. But it has taken us five hundred years to arrive at that changed point of view—five hundred years to even discern the dark as well as the glory of the shining faces and priestly blessings depicted on that bulletin board; five hundred years of suppression and anguish for thousands of us because in 1492 *church* and *blessing* and *God-is-with-you* were words of the mind and tongue, not of the heart. Is this still partially true today?

Now isn't that an arresting question?

OCTOBER 13   APPLES AND OLD AGE

The bowl on our kitchen counter always grows in October from the small one that holds peaches and apricots in the summer to a cafeteria tray that holds, as now, a little of everything: fat pine cones too perfect for wasting; guinea feathers, bizarre in their polka dots and ideal because of their contrasts; tiny pumpkins too ornamental to bake, and Indian corn, because Sam couldn't resist it at the store; a few early pecans, some still in their hulls, and a walnut or two; the first of the fall squashes, drying out a bit before I cook them, and the last of the eggplants; here and there a small tomato, its green still refusing to blush; and apples. Everywhere on the tray, around the tray, spilling off of the tray . . . apples.

They are my favorite fruit now, in my old age. For almost fifty years, although Sam flatly refuses to believe me, I could not eat an apple without suffering the pangs of the damned twenty minutes later. My stomach would rebel so viciously that I finally gave up even trying; but I never gave up my envy of Sam's ability to bolt three of them in a row without so much as a fare-thee-well to any of them. Now one of the many joys of my aging is the fact that I can and do eat uncalculated quantities of apples without even so much as a rumble. (One of the ironies of that same process is that Sam no longer can, but that's another matter!)

I always thought that apples got rather a bum rap in Judeo-Christian myth, what with the Garden of Eden and all. I also think they got rather a bad break in our Scriptures, insofar as the one book that really celebrates them is the one book of Holy Writ which seems universally to make us all nervous: The Song of Solomon.

Like apples, King Solomon and his Song have become a lot more digestible for me in my old age. What one desires in one's youth and then lasts long enough to partake of is, after all, in many ways a confirmation of things not seen, a proof of changes neither apprehended nor planned. It is, in short, the fruit and glory of having lived to see October.

OCTOBER 14   THE DINING ROOM TABLE

Mary Gammon, our second-born, was thirty-three last night, and we stayed up late, sitting around the dining room table drinking coffee and picking at the remains of her birthday dinner—so late, in fact, that the remains are still waiting for me this morning.

It always surprises me, just faintly and very pleasurably, that they come home, these adult children, to mark the commemorative events of life at this table. Even with spouses and children and careers, they come back here.

Here will not be "here," of course, for many more years. Last Christmas, for instance, we went to Nora's new house for the weekend after Thanksgiving. It was the first time any of our children has owned a home large enough to bed and board all of us for forty-eight hours.

Nora and Devereaux have named it Rosehill, and it is as handsome as it is commanding on its rolling hilltop near the Kentucky border in middle Tennessee. We were there to decorate it, to make Christmas, even though Nora and Devereaux and their child, Dunlap, would be with us on the farm for Christmas itself. All of Saturday Sam wove pine roping and trailed red ribbon around columns and created wreaths from grapevines and magnolia leaves. And all of Saturday night we sat around the dining-room table at Rosehill, drinking wine and picking at the remains of dinner. Sam, no longer at the head of this table but beside me at its center, slipped his hand under the cloth and patted my knee.

Three weeks later, when everyone was finally home for the holidays, it was not at the farm that we began but at Laura and Lee's apartment in Memphis. Gathered in their living room and around their dining table, we ate and then lingered late (far too late, Sam said) drinking sherry, but it too was "here." The rubrics of family and the familiar vocabulary of a common beginning and a frequently shared diversity saw to that.

Now, sitting at my breakfast table and looking through the kitchen door to last night's birthday mess still waiting for me to clean, I am completely grateful—grateful for that messy table and for all it has seen and served and made possible; grateful for the kind of blind grace that has made Sam and me honor it as well as fill it; grateful for the fertile field it has been; and, most of all, grateful that its harvest has begun to come in.

Ah, October 15 and the first serious chill in the air this morning! I welcome it as one welcomes an old friend after many months of absence . . . and I begin the ritual of fall.

In the sitting room, on the wall just beyond the kitchen door and between it and the back door, is the family coat rack, a massive wooden goose from whose base protrude half a dozen very substantial pegs. The rack was a gift from dear friends and is therefore twice valued. Certainly no one ever discovered or gave a coat rack any better suited to a big family than this one is.

In the summer the rack is filled with baseball caps, bright scarves, leashes, always a pair of sandals or two—though I have never figured out why—and my straw fedora. But in the fall—in October when the first chill sets in and there is the first whitening of the grasses in our morning fields—I take down the scarves and caps and return them to the rooms and closets where they belong. I take my fedora to its wintering place on my bookcase upstairs. And I get out the wool shawl, brown and tan and white with traces of gray, which was my mother's, and I hang it on my hook.

The shawl is growing older with me, of course, but each October its authority seems to stretch farther behind me. With each new October I find myself slipping more completely into its folds. I accept more readily the natural restrictions of the shawl's form upon my doing, and their insistence on my being. I discover and assume new postures or stances remembered in my bones (if not in my mind) and learned from all the women who have ever wrapped themselves in shawls before me. And every October I find that the tales I tell and the observations I share when the shawl is wrapped around me are nearer to those women's tales, truer to their lives, and simpler, like their truths.

OCTOBER 16   WORTHY OF THEIR FIRE

Today is a strange day for me, the strangest in the calendar of the Anglican communion. In our *Book of Common Prayer,* the first section of any length is "The Calendar of the Church Year" which, in its listing for October, contains these words: "October 16—Hugh Latimer and Nicholas Ridley, Bishops, 1555, and Thomas Cranmer, Archbishop of Canterbury, 1556."

I have always been terrified of fire. Even as a little girl I can remember shrinking from it unreasonably, dreading equally the winter ones my father built for warmth and the picnic ones he built for fun, lest they mysteriously should escape their bounds and destroy us. That primal fear is, without question, a part of the primal awe that afflicts this day. Latimer, Ridley, and Cranmer all died by fire. They were burned by Mary the First for their refusal to abandon the new communion of Anglicanism and return to the communion of Rome.

Established by Henry the Eighth, Mary's deceased father, for reasons more political than faithful, English catholicism had had scarcely thirty years to persuade the minds and affections of the British public when Cranmer, Latimer, and Ridley elected to die for it rather than to recant it. Their example was to be followed by hundreds of others, less prominent and therefore less celebrated, before the end of the sixteenth century.

So one is left each October with this commemoration of their horror; with an inevitable reverence for such conviction even unto death; with an uncomfortable humility in the face of such sacrifice; with an almost clutching gratitude for the liturgy and the dogma that have mothered and sustained so many lifetimes of Christian practice; and with the godly imperative to see that all of these emotions are forged into a grace of mutual guilt and mutual love that is worthy of their fire.

OCTOBER 17   THE MINISTRY OF COOKIES

Mid-October is gingerbread time at our house. By virtue of years of tradition, Sam makes it—generally all over the whole kitchen and half of the farm, but then that's just the way the man cooks. He can't help it.

He grows the ginger in a pot in front of our dining room window and mixes it in great quantities into his bowls of dough. In the days of our youth, he used cookie cutters to push out the gingerbread boys and girls. Now, older and wiser, he free-hands it. Paring knife in hand, he slices and swishes and slides the flattened dough away to expose a veritable world of dancers in pirouette, sunbonnet Sues, little Dutch boys, toasty-colored snowmen, and incongruous scarecrows. He makes them as gleefully as I used to make babies and, for all I know, as God made Adam, though I am deeply suspicious of that kind of easy analogy.

When Sam is finished, the "people" will go a dozen different directions, leaving us by hand, by car, by mail, by UPS, and by belly, according to the circumstances. This year a box will even go as far away as New York to a room in the Helmsley Plaza where Nora has been for weeks and will be for weeks more while her firm represents the *Tribune* in the *Daily News* strike.

What arrests my attention about all of these matters this morning as I seal the New York box for the UPS man is the ministry of cookies. In and of itself it is an act of faith for a grown man with grown children to continue to make gingerbread people. In and of itself it is an act of fathering in metaphor as well as content. In and of itself it is the kind of godly analogy I am not suspicious of.

OCTOBER 18   .BECAUSE I KNOW

Today is the Feast Day of St. Luke, the Evangelist. All over Christendom today, Christians, especially those of us who are liturgical ones, will stop and pay homage. Many of us will attend special services in honor of St. Luke or share the Eucharist offered in thanks for his life among us. In our various ways, whatever they are, we will remember.

Luke, the only shaper of the early communion who was not a Jew, has fascinated history and doctrine for two thousand years. He was a physician by training, which makes him a kind of patron saint for our own household. By popular tradition he was also an artist, which reinforces our private sense of his domestic appropriateness. And to compound the personal, five of our seven children were born either in or received their early instruction in a parish named for him.

On St. Luke's day, however, none of this seems as significant as it does mildly charming. What I am engaged by each year on

St. Luke's Day are those very direct and elegant sentences with which the saint began his Gospel:

> Forasmuch as many have taken in hand to set forth in order a declaration of those things which are most surely believed among us, Even as they delivered them unto us, which from the beginning were eyewitnesses, and ministers of the word; It seemed good to me also, having had perfect understanding of all things from the very first, to write unto thee in order, most excellent Theophilus, That thou mightest know the certainty of those things, wherein thou hast been instructed. (Luke 1:1-4 KJV)

And always I feel the hand reaching, warm and human and real, across history and down upon my shoulder. "It is all right," Luke says. "You may believe because I know."

OCTOBER 19   WATER

The rains have begun for us, the deep long rains of October that still the fallen leaves with water and hold back for days any breaking of the light. It is my favorite time of year: a time for reading, a time for soups and warm bread, time for slipping over into the other world of thought and prayer, a time to go to the dark side of the moon and be afraid there.

The boundaries and anchor rope of chores and planting and doing cannot hold against these silent, seductive rains. The air is so thick with them it cannot nourish us; and the body, like the eye, falls victim to its own lethargy. Outside the world grays as fenceposts and tree trunks blacken before the steady progress of the rain, and colors become only shades in the pervading wet.

We are told that a man of the Pharisees, Nicodemus, came to the Christ by night, believing in his divinity because he was persuaded by his miracles. Ah no, says the Christ of St. John, the kingdom of God can be seen only by those who have been born again. Nicodemus, a wiser man than we and taking the miracle-worker literally, asks how second birth may be, since no man can twice be birthed by his mother. And when the Pharisee

277

receives his answer, it is the most haunting one possible: "Verily, verily, I say unto thee, Except a man be born of water and *of* the Spirit, he cannot enter into the kingdom of God" (John 3:5 KJV).

It is well, Christian, that we spend these days of October considering the properties of water.

OCTOBER 20   JOY AMONG THE ANGELS

Both Jewish and Christian Scripture talk a great deal about friends, as well they should. We all are central to the well-being of one another, a necessary part of one another; and friendship is the rubric which bonds us to one another.

Friends, for most of us, are of both sexes, and that too is as it should be. Yet as I have grown older (and perhaps lazier), I have discovered myself yearning more and more toward the affection and support and wisdom of other women; toward those whose emotional terrain is more similar to my own, whose summations and prizes I share, whose rhythms and metaphors require no prior explanation. The company of other believing women has, in fact, become for me one of the great proofs of the kingdom of God on earth, as well as one of its strongest gifts. Jesus knew this phenomenon, recognized it, honored it.

Only one time in all of Scripture does the koine word *philos* ("friend") appear in its feminine form *phile* (meaning "woman friend"). That time is when Jesus uses it to tell the story of the woman who, having lost her silver coin, lights a candle, sweeps her house, and finds her missing treasure. Immediately upon finding that coin, the Master says, she calls her *philes,* her women friends, to her and commands them to rejoice with her. This parable Jesus told to explain and define the joy among the angels when one sinner repents.

Increasingly when I sit at this table, or any other, and am joined by my *philes,* I am compelled to think of what we do and say and share in terms of the power of Christ's words about us: that our joy is such that it can be likened unto that of the angels in heaven and is as redemptive as that occasioned by the repentance of a sinner.

Rebecca and I have been bitten by the flea market bug. Her father is horrified, so we try to keep our excursions as oblique as possible and their results as unobtrusive. (Both are a little hard to do, may I say, if one has truly become an addict.)

Actually, I'm not much of an acquirer. Sam has always done that in our family. But I am cheap, which makes shopping for things I'm going to have to buy anyway ten times more exhilarating at the markets. Also, I'm a sucker for my daughters, and to see the excitement on the face of this one when she discovers the perfect "gee-gaw" or "most completely camp" purse is reward beyond description—as is the loud conversation about everything from prices to the condition of the world, which the vendors constantly shout back and forth to one another as well as to those of us buying.

The market's bantering is as revelatory and sincere as any you'll ever hear around a dinner table, and very similar in its exercise of impunity and directness. In fact, as an experience, going to the market totally reaffirms my notion that the human animal simply likes to congress with his fellows just as much as he likes to eat, and more than he likes to sleep.

. . . Which is, no doubt, why Jesus himself spent so much time in marketplaces and at dinner parties. His accusers, of course, said it was because he was a glutton and a wine drinker. I myself know at least two dozen well-intentioned preachers who would say it was really because he was smart enough to know where the people were and to go there. But as for me, as I head out the door with Rebecca this sunny Saturday afternoon, I prefer to think it was simply because he was human.

OCTOBER 22   THE GREATEST ACT OF PRAISE

I am obsessed by papers and pens and writing supplies. It is all well and good to observe that those things are the tools of my trade. Undeniably they are the accouterments of it, as well as almost the sum total of its physical environment. But I am speaking here of something far more subtle than that.

Over the years, as I have read more deeply into Eastern wisdom literature and especially more openly in Japanese tea literature, I have begun to identify in my obsession something close to the tea masters' reverent respect for utensils and their exquisite care for the proper selection of scroll and ladle, whisk and bowl. In giving themselves to every detail, the masters invest themselves in the actuality of the moment. Only when all parts of the ceremony are so realized can the tea begin, progress, and conclude in harmony and with benefit to all.

It is a carefulness that Alex Haley knows and that my obsession with paper first led me to appreciate in him. Haley's is a simple stationery, thick to the touch and faintly shaded with beige, but unpretentious almost to austerity. Each sheet's only decoration is a line across the bottom in small but dignified type. It reads: Find the good and praise it.

Alex Haley's life has been a generous one, well-lived and as broad in its sympathies as in its accomplishments. But every time I receive a letter written on that paper, as I did this morning, I am taken all over again by how powerfully the man has lived toward the tool and how perfectly the tool has been selected to reflect the man.

Such care in the *things* of our time here is an important discipline for the human spirit, wherever it may be incarnated and in whatever role. In and of itself, in fact, it can become the greatest act of praise.

OCTOBER 23   THE PROOF AND THE SYMBOL

If one is Anglican, today is marked on the liturgical calendar as a Holy Day. It is, to quote that calendar, the "Feast of St. James of Jerusalem, Brother of Our Lord Jesus Christ, and Martyr, c. 62." If one is Roman, one would have to wait until May 3 to observe the Feast of James the Less. The days are different; the titles are certainly different; the man is the same, and the martyrdom in approximately A.D. 62 is fact.

Having been physical and genetic brother to incarnate God is an existence so far beyond the reaches of my spiritual imagination that for years in my youth I refused to engage it. Yet

October is, as I have said from the very beginning, a time of life and a point of view as well as a month. And with each passing October, I approach, pass through, and recall the Feast of St. James, Brother of Our Lord Jesus Christ and Martyr, with fewer words and greater awe. The role he played, I am convinced, is our role; and having been the first to play it out to its completion, he became the proof as well as the symbol of our vocation.

OCTOBER 24   JONAH'S STORY

Over the years of their growing up, our children, like all children, gave me dozens of things. Like all mothers, I kept those things in prominent use for a sufficient time before discarding, storing or enshrining them according to the item, the child, and my commitment to the particular object. As the children grew, their gifts changed from what they were capable of or were delighted by to what they perceived would please. Gifting, like any human skill, has to mature; and in their maturing, our children have developed an almost exquisite sense of accuracy in matching the gift to the receiver. Only once, as far as I can remember, has that subtle perceptivity ever seared me.

When Mary was an undergraduate at the University of Maine, one vacation she brought home to me a small glass whale, inside of whose clear belly sat a hunched over and desolate Jonah. She regarded the thing as "perfect" for me, remarking on her own delight in having "found the old boy" in some seaport shop "because you used to tell us that story so much I knew you loved it."

She set the Jonah and his whale in the living room and I endured it there for over a year before the whale's tail fell victim to Rebecca's dust rag. But even broken—too broken for public display, anyway—I could not discard the Jonah. Instead, I put it away where, upon occasions like this one, I can take it out and look at it. You see, Mary had been right about my involvement with Jonah, but wrong about its definitions.

Jonah's is the story in the Old Testament that is most reflective of the sins I fear in myself. Given the commission to speak, Jonah resisted lest those of another town should enjoy salvation and prosper as he himself was prospering. Having been rescued, as Jonah himself said, from "out of the belly of hell" (Jonah 2:2), he sulked before God for Nineveh's good fortune. Having been consoled by the favor of a shade tree, he accused God of inconsiderateness in wilting the innocent and harmless tree a day later. And most gripping of all, having chastised God and been mildly answered, Jonah and his story simply end. There is no resolution, no clue as to whether or not Jonah himself ever gained grace or simply remained a petulant, envious, and unpruned tool of choice.

It is a scary story and the reason I have kept Mary's broken gift.

OCTOBER 25   A MYSTERY

The time changes today; or rather, it *has* changed.

While Sam and the children slept last night, I sat, wrapped in my shawl, in the kitchen. At that unnameable time that was 2:59 A.M. until the exact moment when it became the unnameable and slid back somewhere into being two o'clock again, our moorings changed. Where the minutes and their seconds came from, how the clock's face opened a slender slice of itself and admitted their dark time—these are a deep magic. But they are real.

The old three o'clock and the former two o'clock parted to permit a purity of time-without-name, a unit of loving that was measured with a measure we use and agree upon but cannot call even by itself, for it lies beyond us in unknowing. A mystery.

OCTOBER 26   ALFRED THE GREAT

October 26 is the commemoration of Alfred the Great, king of the West Saxons, who died on this date in 899.

At first blush it may seem strange that an American denomination should mark a day in its year to recall and be instructed by the life of a king. But there's a good reason for remembering Alfred, a reason that extends far beyond the bounds of Anglicanism.

Alfred the Great, while he knew no forms of Christianity

other than Roman Catholicism, was in many ways the man who prepared the way for the coming of Protestantism among English-speaking peoples. Alfred, a devout Christian, had a strong and passionate commitment to the worthiness of his own people and his own culture.

Combining his two belief systems into one, the young king set about translating all monastic and holy writings from Latin into Anglo-Saxon (a massive undertaking which he so effectively instituted as to have his effort continue uninterrupted for three hundred years after his death). He demanded that the clergy, if they were within his domain, be literate—and educated, as well. He established schools within castle walls and required that both his nobles and the youth of the countryside accept instruction there. Later he even recodified the laws to incorporate Christian doctrine into a centralized monarchy.

These are strong statements of faith and strong practices of belief from a strong man, but they also are values and connections that are possible for even the least influential of us. Whatever it was that Alfred the Great accomplished or strove for, it could be subsumed under his abiding belief that every believer must read and know for himself the Scriptures. Alfred's life is a historical imperative to us as churched people to pick up the cause of literacy within our walls and as part of our own vocations. Alfred the Great—until his job is done, may we never forget.

OCTOBER 27   MOONS OF OCTOBER

October is the moon's month; for though it comes and goes, waxes and wanes, along its natural course through every month, it is only in October that the moon rests so full and lush and reddened just at our horizon. Equal in diameter to our sun, it is the other statement of our light—cool, human-faced, apprehensible to the eye, sterile user of the dark . . . sterile user of the dark and present only by its contrast.

I hail you hanging there above the fence line of our October. My woman's body pulls toward this autumnal braking of your cycles, feels against itself the fullness of your rim, welcomes the shadows cut into being by your light. Before memory was Christian, it was human; and memory stirs tonight—aches into my ribs and burns me with the call of you. Celebrate me now, Moon, and let me dance until frenzied I can forget that other, less lovely light that brings me life . . . Lucifer, bearer of the light, fallen beauty from before the throne of God, walks abroad in time and, Christian, we would do well if we learned from the moons of October the subtlety of his light.

OCTOBER 28   THE BLESSING OF ST. JUDE

October 28 is the Feast of St. Simon and St. Jude, apostles. As far as I know, almost nobody stops these days to say much about St. Simon. He is vaguely interesting to me because he was, according to Luke's Gospel, a Zealot, which means yet another politician among the chosen twelve. The Zealots were Jewish patriots sworn to the overthrow of Roman rule. What intrigues me occasionally, therefore, is that he and Iscariot, a known plotter, and Matthew, a public official, were all three in the same holy group—constituted, in fact, a quarter of its manpower. But that is only a tidbit to chew upon, like poor Simon. It is Jude who holds me.

Jude himself, again like Simon, is historically vague and rather unremarkable personally, or at least tradition seems to have thought so. He is also, peculiarly enough, the only writer of Scripture whose words are not included in the propers assigned for reading on his feast day. The irony of that fact is overwhelming to me every year. Talk about anonymity!

There is—isn't there always—a reason for not reading Jude on Jude's day. The reason is that no one is really certain that he wrote the epistle assigned to him. There does, however, seem to be a general acceptance that his were the words which somebody paraphrased in the concluding verses of the Epistle of St. Jude; and they still stand in Christian tradition as "The Blessing of St. Jude." For me, those words compose some of the most powerful sentences in the New Testament. I give them to you now with my own Christian affection:

Now to him who is able to keep you from falling and to present you without blemish before the presence of his glory with rejoicing, to the only God, our Saviour through Jesus Christ our Lord, be glory, majesty, dominion and authority, before all time and now and for ever. Amen.*

Amen.

OCTOBER 29   THE FAMILIAR

The dusk comes early now, closing off the fields from view long before I have finished with our supper. I flip on the fluorescent light over the sink, give the soup another stir, set the oven dials, and go to lower the bedroom shades against the cold. Soup and biscuits with salad and custard. They know that already, even before they get here, just like they know the lowered shades and the two lamps already lit in the dining room. I turn on the coffee pot to brew, and I fill the glasses for their tea. They know this too.

The first car pulls in the driveway. From the sound it will be Sam and Becca. I hear the door and then the sacks. He has stopped at the store. I knew that too. He always does in winter. When there's no garden to harvest, he feels bare and shops for other men's wares to fill the void.

The biscuits rise and another car—John's this time—turns and parks, facing out for in the morning. I ladle soup, and Sam, Jr. comes. I see his lights piercing the dark through the kitchen window. The biscuits brown and I turn off the coffee. Without more invitation than that they come, gathering at the table, each in his or her accustomed place. They all know that.

The talk is desultory, routine, the same as last night, except for the snippet here or the tidbit there that made today's variation. They eat, but before the soup is done, they smile. The biscuits warm them and the first taunt passes from young Sam to Rebecca, the first hospital story from old Sam to me. The coffee

---

*As translated by James Bentley, *A Calendar of Saints: The Lives of the Principal Saints of the Christian Year,* Facts On File Publications, New York and Oxford, 1986, p. 211.

steams in their cups while I dish up custard, and John asks his father a question about one of his chemistry seminars.

I will not be here next week. I will be gone, as I am so many weeks, to a series of meetings and seminars, speaking, talking, writing. They know that too. Somebody else will make the soup. Sam will make the biscuits. They will forego the custard. But always just at dusk I will see us this way and so will they, knowing as each of us does, that what is real is not nearly so true as the familiar when it is remembered.

OCTOBER 30   THE HOUR OF COMPLINE

Outside the window beyond my favorite chair, October is aging. The month that began still bearing squash and peppers and green tomatoes has no color now except the studied browns of fields about to sleep. The ordering of the seasons calls them to that act of final preparation.

We who keep the faith of Christendom by the practices of the Anglican communion follow such an ordering too. In our common life, our liturgy and our private devotion, we, clergy and laity alike, still accept the basic disciplines of the Benedictine Rule, albeit in modified form. Where once the canonical hours of matins, lauds, prime, terce, sext, nones, vespers and compline circumscribed the movement of our ancestors' days, we now follow simpler devotions: Morning Prayer, Noonday and Evensong. But before each day's resting, still we keep the ancient rite of Compline. "The Lord Almighty grant us a peaceful night and a perfect end," the words begin. "Our help is in the Name of the Lord." To which comes the response, "The maker of heaven and earth."

After a psalm and meditation, the office continues with the words of St. Peter: "Be sober, be watchful. Your adversary the devil prowls around like a roaring lion, seeking someone to devour. Resist him, firm in your faith."

After our Lord's Prayer, we offer the words of the evening collects: "Keep watch, dear Lord, with those who work, or watch, or weep this night, and give your angels charge over those who sleep. Tend the sick, Lord Christ; give rest to the weary, bless the dying, soothe the suffering, pity the afflicted, shield the joyous; and all for your love's sake. Amen."

And then, as we pray silently, whoever leads us, or we ourselves if we worship alone, begins the reverenced words of the *nunc dimittis,* the words of Simeon as he turned from seeing the Holy Infant:

> Lord, you now have set your servant free
>   to go in peace as you have promised;

> For these eyes of mine have seen the Saviour,
>   whom you have prepared for all the world
>   to see.

> A Light to enlighten the nations,
>   and the glory of your people Israel.

> Glory to the Father, and to the Son, and
>   to the Holy Spirit: as it was in the
>   beginning, is now, and will be forever. Amen.

Together we speak the final words: "Guide us waking, O Lord, and guard us sleeping; that awake we may watch with Christ, and asleep we may rest in peace."*

October is the hour of Compline in the year's day. I know of no better way for us to remember that throughout the pages after we have parted than to share the office now while we are still together—which is why I have recorded it here and why I invite you to speak with me again the words you have just read.

Go in peace to know and serve the Lord.

OCTOBER 31   OCTOBER'S LAST CITIZENS

October draws to its end, and only a sixth of measured time remains to us before the year, that miniature of life, does likewise. We go tomorrow into the dark days of winter.

And if we should chance then to dream, as surely we must in

---

*All quoted materials are taken from *The Book of Common Prayer,* 1979, pp. 127-35.

the long, quiet night, our winter dreams will come to us as summaries of October. Broken, if we are blessed, by her retreating colors and natural process, humbled by her fools and saints, fear-filled and cowered to the end by her pagan gods and devils, redeemed only by hope and the symbolism of half-remembered springs, we pause one last time before our sleep. We pause because we have yet to meet the shadowed dead, the final citizens of October.

Our children, costumed by ignorance, will protect themselves tonight with mimicry and sound, but we are not so innocent, we who have lived into and through October. October's last citizens are those whose company we now prepare for, whose communion our dreams teach us how to join. They are the meaningless dead, the unsung and uncelebrated, held in time only by our love and by an acquired respect. They are the ones who without great purposes to hold to or great causes to serve lived anyway, sustained by faith. And to move finally from October to our winter we must now pass through that great cloud of witnesses.

NOVEMBER

Thoughts on Simple Things

ANNE KILLINGER

NOVEMBER 1　　　A THANKSGIVING HOUSE

When it is time to buy a new house, what do you look for? Several women recently were discussing house-hunting. One wanted a large house to accommodate two offices. She and her husband are college professors and need their own spaces for research and writing. Another woman is a gourmet cook and dreams of having a house with an enormous kitchen. "A music room is a must for me and the children," said a third. Another quickly chimed in to say she wanted a two-story house with lots of insulation between the floors to dampen the noise of the loud rock music her children constantly play upstairs.

Some wanted other things—large trees, a nice yard with space for a vegetable or flower garden, compactness and easiness to care for. Price and location were mentioned more than once.

When my turn came, I said, "I like all the things you've mentioned, but my house has to be a Thanksgiving house."

All of them wondered what I meant. What does a Thanksgiving house look like?

My husband and I have always liked driving through the country. Whenever we do, and I see a two-story farmhouse nestled in a clump of trees surrounded by beautiful meadows, I always say, "That's a Thanksgiving house!" Or sometimes we see a log cabin with smoke curling from the chimney, a stack of wood in the yard, and a dog or two on the porch, and I say, "That's a Thanksgiving house!"

Through the years of sighting such houses, I've learned that a true Thanksgiving house can be of almost any style. It can be large or small, Colonial or modern, brick or board.

Perhaps I can explain it better. A Thanksgiving house is the kind that puts a glow over the people we love. It's a place where sorrows are quickly turned into joys; one that lets us be childlike and allows laughter to permeate its structure; one where holidays and holy days are shared, where memories are made and traditions grow. It's a haven of love, warmth, and security.

A Thanksgiving house can be any type of house, but there is one rule that is set in concrete: It has to be a house built on a solid relationship with God; a place where God's promises and presence are duly noted; a house where celebration seems natural because God is there.

Bless this house, O Lord, we pray;
Make it a Thanksgiving house by night and day.

NOVEMBER 2   DOORS

Have you ever thought about how many doors we pass through in a day, in a year, in a decade?

It staggered my mind when I counted how many doors we have in our house and how necessary each one is. Wherever we go, there are doors to pass through. They are an essential part of our lives. Did you know there is a secret to doors? We must learn when to use them to shut out and when to use them to let in.

Closing doors can be very difficult and painful. This was brought home to me after a visit to a former parish my husband and I served. The members of the congregation greeted us with love and warmth. The Sunday service was pretty much the way it had been when we left. There were parties and dinners shared with special friends, but something wasn't quite right. Nothing seemed to be exactly the way I remembered it. After a few days' visit, I sadly realized that we and the people there had moved in two different directions in our lives. It was time to close a door.

When my mother and my husband's parents died, it was a traumatic door to close. When our children left home for college and eventually to marry, it was a lonely door to close. When our friend lost his job, his family, and his health, it was a diminishing door to close.

Closing doors can be life-changing, but it isn't always a bad thing to do. Sometimes we need to do it in order to stop living in the past and get on with our lives. And, at the same time, some closed doors are waiting to be opened, often with exciting adventures on the other side.

A friend who has been struggling with cancer gets a clean bill of health. A door is flung open to a new and happy life. A neighbor brings a freshly baked cake to welcome you to the neighborhood. A door of friendship is opened. You volunteer to tutor a child with a reading disability. A door of learning and encouragement is opened.

The world is full of wonderful doors just waiting to be opened. Praise the Lord for doors!

When I try to open a door before it is time, Lord, please keep it locked. When I close a door on life too soon, please keep your foot in it.

NOVEMBER 3   THE MAILBOX

So many times a day people ask, "Has the mail been delivered?" Most of us rush expectantly to our mailboxes when we hear the letter carrier leave the porch or the mail truck drive away. Getting the mail is an important daily event.

If your box is like ours, it is usually stuffed with throw-away mail such as circulars, advertisements, and catalogs. But occasionally there are letters from family and friends or special-occasion cards that bring warmth and cheer into the house—mail you want to settle down with and read in a leisurely fashion; messages that make you feel as if you've had a good personal visit with the sender.

The mailbox can contain things that bring joy. They make the day brighter. Your heart smiles. Life couldn't be better.

Or the mailbox holds things that send your spirits down.

There can be an envelope from the IRS saying that you owe more taxes than you anticipated on your tax forms. Maybe somebody has become angry with you and cowardly puts negative feelings in an anonymous letter. Perhaps a friend sends a note about her troubled thoughts or, worse, information about the death of a mutual acquaintance. The note brings discord into the music of your world.

The mailbox can produce sorrow. The day is mournful. Your heart feels blighted. Life seems withered.

That's when the mailbox reminds me of a beautiful field of autumn wheat waving in the warm sunshine. It's almost harvest time, and there promises to be an abundant crop. Then the clouds bring rain, and the rain turns into icy sleet. The wheat freezes and becomes a ruined, sodden mass when it thaws.

Isn't that the way life is? The joys of yesterday get mixed with the sorrows of today. The wise person who wrote "for everything there is a season" was correct. Sometimes sorrows come when we expect sunshine. Then things change abruptly, and sweet music breaks into our weeping.

The point is that we mustn't allow the mailbox, with its messages of joy and sorrow, to dominate our emotions. Life is much bigger than the mailbox. We have been given a hope that doesn't depend on the post of the day. Whenever I am tempted to feel despondent over what our mailbox holds, I remember a message sent by the heavenly Postmaster General's Son. It reads, "You will weep and lament; you will be sorrowful, but your sorrow will turn to joy."

And that happy message was delivered without a postage stamp!

NOVEMBER 4   APPLES

Autumn is a time for harvesting apples. I hadn't thought much about this until the year I was teaching in a church's day school. That fall, the teachers spent several days planning a field trip to an apple orchard nestled in a beautiful valley of the Blue Ridge Mountains. We drew pictures of apples, sang the "Johnny Appleseed" song, and shared dreams with the children about

292

what the orchard would be like. The children themselves came up with imaginative stories about things that happened in the great "apple forest."

The day of the big adventure arrived. The cars were lined up to go. Children piled into the vans and station wagons, with adults calling inside to say, "Buckle your seat belts!" Being buckled in didn't put a damper on the little hearts brimming with laughter and eyes sparkling with delight.

The vehicle I drove was filled with merry, chattering children. Apple talk was the big thing all the way to the orchard.

The orchard met everyone's expectations. It was a beautiful place. Both children and adults eagerly gathered big, Red Delicious apples, placing them in bushel baskets provided by the owners of the orchard. Someone said that almost as many apples went into our stomachs as went into the baskets. We all agreed that we knew why they are called delicious apples.

When the outing was over, our troops of tired, happy children and grownups buckled up for the journey home. The trip had been a tremendous success.

In the dining room of our home, we have a silver bowl filled with wooden red apples. I used to keep fresh apples in the bowl, but someone was always destroying the arrangement by taking an apple out and eating it. Or sometimes the apples were not eaten, and they became soft and overripe and had to be removed. The wooden ones remain the same day after day, month after month, year after year.

Now, years after the apple outing, these wooden apples remind me of that special visit to the Speed-the-Plow apple orchard in the beautiful Virginia mountains. I remember how the heavily laden boughs of the apple trees spoke of the blessings of God, and how the fruit was a symbol of hope and bounty for the future.

My memories make me want to sing again the little song we taught the children. "The Lord is good to me, and so I thank the Lord. . . ."

The Lord has been very good to me, and so I thank the Lord for giving me the autumn gift of apples.

When Jesus said "When you pray, enter into your closest," he must have been talking about my friend's closet. It is a huge walk-in closet where her clothes are on one side and her husband's on the other, and she fastidiously keeps everything in order.

All of her husband's clothes are color-coordinated. She places a shirt by the correct suit, and a matching tie hangs over one side of the jacket. Shoes are on the floor beneath the suit. Business clothes and sport clothes have their separate sections.

It is the same for her clothes. They are lined up neatly according to both colors and accessories. There is a place for everything, and everything is in its place. My friend's closet is the topic of conversation—and the envy—of all who have seen it.

I like a neat closet. Periodically, I discover that the walk-in closet my husband and I share can't hold another thing. It is time to weed out and reorganize things. After a good morning's work of filling garbage bags to give away and to throw away, I manage to restore the closest to a state of peace and order where one could probably retreat for prayer.

But somehow I don't necessarily feel that the closet's tidiness is what matters when I pray. Instead, I think it's the clutter in my own life that needs to be rearranged or thrown out to make room for God.

I need to begin by weeding out worries to make room so I can see the glories of God's handiwork on this glorious autumn day.

I need to pack away sadness so I can hear God's beautiful symphony of laughter.

I need to toss out fears to make room for God's visions and dreams for my life.

I need to get rid of time-consuming busy work and replace it with precious moments spent letting God know how grateful I am for his love and support.

I need to crate up doubt and fill my heart with the knowledge that God accepts me.

Dear God, help me to keep my personal closet in order. But, when I fail, please don't stay away.

One bright, cool autumn morning, I discovered I had some spare time and decided to clean out my long-neglected kitchen cabinets. I began with a cabinet that held an assortment of cake pans. There were all kinds of pans.

There was one in the shape of a lamb for Easter.

There were heart pans for Valentine's Day.

There was a pan in the shape of a Christmas wreath and one made like a turkey for Thanksgiving.

There were wedding cake pans, cheesecake pans, and just plain round and square pans in all sizes and depths.

In fact, there were so many pans that I could have opened a pan shop. As I sorted out the pans and refitted them into the cabinet, I was reminded of the many fancy cakes I had baked and decorated through the years.

I had to smile when I recalled my first attempt at cake decorating. I tried to master the art alone. Finally, I admitted that my roses looked like splayed-out versions of tired cabbages, so I enrolled in a cake decorating class.

It was a wonderful class. After several weeks of listening carefully to instructions and practicing what I had learned, I found that it was amazingly simple to turn out acceptable flower and leaf designs. I was ready to tackle the most elaborately decorated cake one could imagine. It would turn out to be a lavish masterpiece!

But it didn't take this novice long to discover that more advanced lessons and a lot more practice were needed before I would be capable of doing all that I had dreamed of doing. The cake I wanted to make and decorate still lay far beyond this beginner's skills and abilities.

Many times I forget that I am only an amateur when I deal with some of life's situations. In committee meetings, I am prone to plunge in and volunteer for things that are far over my head. *Give me lessons in humility, Lord.*

Sometimes, in a sharing group, I leap in and start expounding on some deep or troubling subject without finding out first if I really know how to handle it. *Give me lessons in discernment, Lord.*

When people I love are struggling with problems, I want to rush forward and solve the problems and protect the persons without giving them a chance to grow by forging their own ways. *Give me lessons in releasing things, Lord.*

There are so many lessons I need to learn about your kingdom, Lord. Sometimes I make as big a mess of doing things for you as I did in my early attempts at cake decorating. Lord, help me to listen to your Spirit until I really know what I'm doing.

NOVEMBER 7   LOCKS

A few years ago, our family moved to another city and had the good fortune of looking at houses with a wonderful real estate agent. In a week's time, we must have gone through at least seventy-five houses.

At every house, the agent rang the doorbell. If the occupants were not at home, she worked the combination on the lockbox attached to the house, removed a key, and proceeded to open a lock on the front or side door.

After we entered the house, we encountered more locks. There were sliding locks on windows, safety locks on patio doors, deadbolt locks on basement doors. Sometimes there were locks on garages or outbuildings.

In some homes, we were shown sophisticated security systems that ensured the house's safety against intruders who might attempt to break through one of the many locks.

Locks are, unfortunately, a necessity in our homes, cars, stores, and churches. I know of one church that not only has locks and bolts on all its doors, but also has five security guards who patrol the parking lots and building at all hours of the day and night.

Anywhere there is a threat to safety, we need the protection and security of a system of locks and safeguards.

But there are some locks in life that are a disadvantage. These are the locks on our personal lives that are so tightly fastened that growth, caring, and sharing are inhibited and stifled, if not totally eliminated.

Think how people become when icy locks around their hearts keep out love. Or maybe you know some folks who maintain a grudge lock that keeps out forgiveness. There are some people who hold tightly to a stingy lock that forbids the entrance of compassion and generosity. And many people lock up the rooms of their lives with a restrictive lock to keep out the presence of God. Sometimes locks cause us to lose our real sense of perspective on life.

Father, you have the key to open the locks of my heart, mind, and being. Give me the wisdom, humility, and courage to place my complete trust in the Master Locksmith and to leave my house wide open to you at all times.

NOVEMBER 8   BOTTLES

There is an assortment of antique bottles, vases, and pottery objects sitting in my kitchen windows. This morning the autumn sun is shining brightly on them, and they give the room a glowing, added dimension.

A rainbow of colors streams across the floor from the sunlight pouring through a crystal prism. The Depression glass looks as if it is decorated with glistening, ruby-red teardrops. A cobalt blue vase appears to be wearing a golden crown as the light reflects from the halo of goldleaf around its rim. Pottery rabbits and chipmunks look happy and contented as they bask lazily in the warm sun.

From across the room, the entire area of the window appears to me as a colorful scene of peace and beauty. If I look closely at these old pieces of glassware, however, I see certain irregular-ities—a bubble here, an odd indentation there, varying shades of color, no two painted flowers exactly alike. It is these little imperfections that make antique glassware valuable and authentic treasures.

I am grateful that the Bible tells us about people with imperfections.

Jesus seems to have had a knack for searching out persons with flaws in their makeup. We read about his ministering to the handicapped, the diseased, the brokenhearted, and the emotionally disturbed. He always had a way of reminding them that, no matter what imperfections they had, God loved and cared for them.

It's the same today, isn't it? When the sun shines on us, revealing our flaws, Jesus still assures us that we are acceptable to God. Not just acceptable, really, but valuable.

Lord, can you really make a valued and treasured servant out of this chipped earthenware vessel? If you can, I'm yours.

NOVEMBER 9   SPINNING WHEEL

I have spent months trying to locate an affordable spinning wheel. Last fall some friends and I were going through an antique store in California where there was a little room filled with assorted spinning wheels. Some were very old, and others were new. Some were large, and others were small.

The owner was carding some wool in preparation for spinning it into yarn. When she finished the combing process, she spun the strands on an old-fashioned wheel that would take only one thread at a time. Fortunately, this wasn't her only method of getting material, as it was for women in colonial days.

When I showed an interest in the wheels, she asked if I knew how to spin. I admitted that my sole interest in owning a spinning wheel was to have it as a decoration in my den. But my inability at spinning wool didn't lessen the fascination I felt at watching her expertly turning raw wool into usable yarn.

As I watched, I let my imagination take over. I imagined that God was sitting at a giant spinning wheel and that we were the raw material out of which he was to make something. I imagined God carefully combing out our matted, unusable traits of selfishness, jealousy, and malice; and doing it with gentleness and patience.

I could see God bringing order as, one at a time, he spun out and untangled our knotted threads of pride and self-importance. I visualized God delicately coloring each thread so that we would coordinate with the overall design he had planned for us and our world.

I thought what a big difference it would make if only we allowed God to be the Master Spinner in every aspect of our lives. He has done so beautifully with so many things.

"Consider the lilies of the field," said Jesus, "how they toil not, neither do they spin; yet Solomon in all his glory was not arrayed like one of them."

If we let the heavenly Spinner take over for us, we will become material for his beautifully hand-crafted products. Who knows? Our lives may even be more beautiful than the lilies!

NOVEMBER 10   BOOKS

I can't remember a time in my entire life when I wasn't surrounded by books. My mother was an avid reader and generously passed on the love of books to her children.

When I was a child, I loved the afternoons when she and I walked to the library to return a stack of books and pick up some more. I savored the smell of the old books, especially those with leather bindings. I enjoyed looking through new editions and finding pages that had not been cut apart. To think that I would be the first person to read a particular book! I reveled in the rows and rows of children's books, imagining they had all been written just for me. Mother and I would gather up our newly selected treasures, carry them home, and quickly head for the shaded side yard where we sat and read when the weather was nice.

Today books line the walls of our home. My husband and I have a great love of books. I often describe us, in fact, as being "book poor."

Yet, with all my involvement with books, I never fully understood their importance until the year our church began a literacy program. I volunteered as a teacher and took the Laubach course in preparation for my new work. When I completed the course, I was assigned to two students, both of whom were from Latin America.

One student could not read or write any English at all. She couldn't even read or write in her native language because she had gone to work as a small child and had never been able to attend a school. Teaching this young woman was a challenge. It was also very sobering, for it made me think what it would be like not to be able to read books.

I discovered that people who can't read miss so much of life. Every day for them is filled with dozens of "I don't know" and "I can't" responses to other persons. They may not know simple things like the names of colors or the names of pieces of furniture in their homes. They can't read directions on food cartons and medicine containers. They can't interpret street signs and road signs. They live with enormous fear and hesitation. They don't have much self-esteem. They are always uncomfortable in their jobs, for they are afraid of having their illiteracy discovered and used against them.

What happy transformations occur in the lives of those who learn to read after years of deprivation and ignorance. They become like butterflies shedding their heavy cocoons. God's entire beautiful world begins to open up to them. They are like children in paradise.

Almost invariably, when a new reader is asked which book he or she enjoys reading the most, the response is "The Bible." That book, above all others, is the one they have desired to read.

One Sunday, we had a literacy celebration in our church. One of the participants was an important, middle-aged businessman who had been illiterate until he was almost fifty years old. As he stood at the lectern and started to read the Scripture, he had to stop and fight back tears. When he could speak, he said he wasn't crying because he was afraid or embarrassed; he was crying because he felt so emotional, after all those years, about being able to read the Bible.

Imagine reading about God's love, forgiveness, and compassion for the first time when you are nearly fifty years old!

I am grateful for all the many books that have influenced my life. But now I have a better understanding when I read in the Scriptures: "Blessed are they who read." Being able to read enables us to enter more fully into the mystery of Christ. In fact, it really does help to turn the world into a paradise.

I was clearing cups out of the dishwasher one day, and because we are blessed with a variety of them, an interesting thought struck me: Cups have their unique and individual personalities.

One of our sons, for instance, has a collection of humorous cups. One of them has a gloved hand for a handle. Another has a little head in the bottom of the cup that looks up at you when the cup has been drained. Several have funny slogans or comical pictures on them. They are all delightfully different, and each has the capacity to make you smile on a down day.

Cups can bring a lot of warmth.

On winter days when my husband is working at home in his study, four o'clock signals tea time. He lights a fire in the living room, and we relax for a few minutes while sharing our thoughts over a cup of tea. I don't think he ever fails to comment on the beauty of the porcelain cup from which he drinks. He likes to recall when we bought it in a tiny shop in England. He remembers the many times he drank from it in our summer apartment in Oxford before bringing it back to the States. For him, it is a cup brimming with memories.

Cups can make you feel secure.

After dinner, we like to have a cup of coffee in the den while watching a favorite BBC program on television. We especially enjoy hazelnut coffee. While holding a half-empty cup, my husband almost invariably says, "There is something about this cup of coffee that makes me feel so happy. Life is good."

Cups can promote feelings of endearment.

There is one special cup I love above the others. It is a chalice our son gave us. I look at it and think about the many chalices artists have designed through the ages. They must have loved their work. Some of their cups are so beautifully and intricately fashioned with gold and jewels that they are placed in museums.

But a chalice signifies much more than beauty. Its meaning has for centuries been related to the Lord's Supper. This special cup embodies a lasting devotion to the blood of Christ, which was poured out for the sins of the world.

Whenever we participate in a communion service, there is something about taking the cup that lifts us up for the moment and gives us everlasting life for the future. "All of you drink of it," said Jesus. It is a wonderful command, even breathtaking when you think about it.

Thank you, God, for a cup that warms my soul as often as I drink from it.

NOVEMBER 12   SEWING ROOM

In my mother's day, one room of the house was set aside for sewing. That's where the majority of the entire family's clothes were made. If a sewing room was large enough, the women also gathered there to knit socks and sweaters, crochet afghans and bedspreads, and piece together quilts.

Not many houses have a sewing room anymore. Most working women can't find the time to devote to the nearly lost art of sewing. Even if they could find the time, most families can't afford the extra expense of a special room for making clothes and crafts.

I thought the sewing room was passé until we visited some friends in North Carolina. They designed and built their home with a huge room solely for sewing and making things. There are cabinets for yarns and cloth, bins for buttons and thread. Two sides of the room are solid windows so that there is sufficient light even on rainy days.

My friend who uses that room has the dream room every seamstress and crafter desires, and she uses it daily for her lovely creations. She is a remarkable seamstress who deserves her special room in the house.

God, too, is a remarkable crafter, but God doesn't need a sewing room. God makes a cloak out of love and protection; God knits a comforter of promises. God mends broken dreams. God sews a fine seam of blessings. God takes torn and tattered lives and weaves them into whole new creations.

Everything God makes carries the label MADE IN HEAVEN.

302

NOVEMBER 13   CLOCKS

What time is it? Are we going to be on time? "I'm late, I'm late, I'm late," says the rabbit in *Alice in Wonderland.*

Most of us are driven by anxieties about time. It sometimes seems to me that our entire household, maybe even the world, is built around one gigantic clock, and our lives are mechanically impelled by the gonging of the hours.

Clocks may be a nuisance, and we may despair of the hold deadlines and schedules have on our lives, but we can't deny the importance of time. It is of the essence to the person who has had a heart attack and must be rushed to the hospital. It spells the difference between life and death for an infant who is choking and needs immediate attention from a parent or babysitter. It is necessary to the relationships between husbands and wives, parents and children, and friends.

And the regulation of time is important, too. School classes begin and end by the clock. Factory workers, hospital employees, secretaries, and bank clerks begin and end their work by the clock. Doctors keep appointments by the clock. Most of us get up and go to bed at certain hours.

Our whole lives are dominated by a concern for time, for being punctual, for getting things done, for meeting our deadlines.

But one thing troubles me in all of this. Do I manage to make time for everything but God? Do I keep all my appointments except with him? Did I call on him today, or am I waiting until I'm all caught up on my work and have the leisure to think about him? Have I taken time, in the midst of my other activities, to reflect on his presence and thank him for his inexpressible gift to me?

O dear God, please don't let the clock run out before you are restored to top-quality time in my life.

NOVEMBER 14   NURSERY

In the fall of the year, when I was expecting our first child, we turned the spare bedroom of our small house into a nursery. It

303

was so much fun planning it and, bit by bit, getting it ready for our new baby.

We bought a Boston rocker. My father-in-law found an antique cherry cradle and refinished it for us. I made a baby-sized, pastel patchwork quilt. My mother-in-law brought us a bathinette with built-in storage space under it. My mother and I sewed an extensive layette. We hung pictures and mobiles suitable for a baby's environment.

The finished room looked like a little bit of heaven, and the arrival of the baby only reinforced that impression. What a joy it was for us to rock, clothe, feed, and comfort our wonderful son in a room that was lovingly prepared and decorated just for him.

Sometimes I need God to have a nursery room specially outfitted and decorated just for me. I know I'm an adult, but when I cry over hurt feelings I want to crawl up into God's lap and be rocked. When my soul is dry and hungry, I long for God to feed me soothing words. When daily cares have exhausted me and made me anxious, I need God to sing me to sleep. When I feel unsure of myself, I yearn for God's strong arms to steady me and hold me up.

When I am feeling alone and unlovely, I desperately need to hear God say, "I will never fail you nor forsake you." When I feel afraid, I want to cry out, "Come into my life where I am hurting, Lord. Please hold my hand. You know the joy your comfort can bring. You understand."

It is amazing how all the burdens and cares of life can disappear when I become God's little child.

NOVEMBER 15   BASKETS

I love baskets. Because of this, we have quite a collection of them in our home. There are baskets filled with flowers, baskets holding magazines, baskets merely sitting around. One of my favorites is a lovely fluted basket handwoven by my niece in colors that match my kitchen.

Almost any basket makes me think of a trip a friend and I made a few years ago to serve lunch at a school for the blind. We were both nervous about going to the school. The teacher who met us when we arrived understood our nervousness and suggested a tour of the classrooms before lunch. I'm not exactly sure what we expected, but, whatever it was, we weren't prepared for what we discovered. We soon were standing speechless with awe as we saw class after class in which blind persons were producing beautiful, intricately fashioned crafts.

There were woven baskets of delicate designs, dolls with hand-embroidered faces, table linens with perfectly executed handpainted patterns, wooden ornaments with whimsically painted designs on them, and many other beautiful things.

The students were of all ages, but they shared laughter, joy, and song. They all worked industriously, happily, and lovingly.

When the bell rang for their lunch break, my friend and I quickly put the food on the table and prepared to serve it. An elderly gentleman was called on to offer a blessing over the food. He prayed a beautiful, lengthy prayer of thanksgiving, including an invocation of God's care on "those less fortunate than we." My friend and I were touched by this reference. And it didn't really matter that we served lunch that day with tears running down our faces, because the students couldn't see them. They knew only that we were there and that we cared about them.

After that prayer, I kept thinking that I needed their kind of vision when my world goes dark—when I don't take time to see and my sense of wonder is gone.

The students finished their meals and thanked us for bringing them. Then they went back to their projects.

Before leaving the school, my friend and I purchased several of their wares, including some baskets. I still treasure those baskets. They are among the most special ones I own. They remind me that, even in a world where a person doesn't have eyesight for seeing everything, the heart can still have 20/20 vision.

Thank you, Lord, for the lesson of the baskets.

NOVEMBER 16   PICTURES

My husband and I are art collectors. There are very few originals on our walls, but a variety of prints have taken over almost every room. They range from European masters to early American unknowns to contemporary paintings and drawings. Each picture was lovingly purchased with an eye to its particular beauty, color, and subject matter.

Pictures are supposed to be inanimate objects, but ours speak to me in many ways and share with me some of life's greatest gifts.

My favorite picture hangs in our dining room. It is an oil painting made by our younger son of his great-grandfather, whom we all called Papa. Papa is dressed in a straw hat and overalls and is standing before a background of farmlands and outbuildings. The picture speaks to me of Papa's great strength of character and dignity. I can see these characteristics in his face and the way he stands.

In the sun room is a painting of Bellingrath Gardens in Mobile, Alabama. The flowers in this picture are breathtakingly beautiful, and they speak to me of warmth and wonder—wonder at the skill of an artist who could paint such a feast of colors, and wonder at a God who could create such an array of flowers in the beginning.

In another room hangs a picture of an old woman making a flower-garden quilt. Her gnarled hands almost make me cringe for the pain I know she must be enduring to sew such an enormous quilt. But the pang of sympathy is soon dispelled by the beauty of her kind, peaceful, heavily lined face. It says: "Forget about my infirmities. Celebrate with me the wisdom of wrinkles."

In yet another room hangs a marvelous print of an early American village at holiday time. Horse-drawn carriages are filled with people on their way to visit family and friends. Autumn colors dominate the landscape. People are waving from windows and doorways of two-dimensional houses and shops. In its primitive way, this painting says, "Come with us to celebrate the thanksgiving of life!"

In our living room there is a sensitive print of the Madonna and Child painted in the seventeenth century. The scene appears to be illuminated by candlelight and creates a very warm, personal aura that says, "Join my spirit of faith, hope, and dreams."

As I listen and meditate on our pictures, they have a way of becoming my prayer gallery. I see a touch of God's artistry in every painting. I experience his presence in the purity of color. I appreciate his sense of humor in the whimsical designs. I value the importance of his truth in the beauty of line and form. I feel refreshed, and say, "O give thanks to the Lord, for he is the rarest of artists!"

NOVEMBER 17 WINDOWS

Have you ever tried to imagine a house without windows? It's almost impossible, isn't it? Windows, after all, are the eyes of a house. And what wonders they allow us to see!

There is autumn, for instance, which is one of my favorite seasons. During the months of October and November, the windows bring bright, colorful pictures into every room of our house. Some mornings, when the sun is bright and the colors are especially vivid, it is almost more than I can bear.

But windows don't play favorites. They are there for all the seasons. How beautiful it is to look out in winter and see the first snowfall. The fir trees are wrapped in ermine, and one has a bright red cardinal perched on its branch. What a glorious scene it is!

In the spring, windows frame the first lovely blossoms on the apple trees and pear trees, and the world seems to be bursting forth with life after its long dormancy in the winter months. Everything is undergoing a thrilling rebirth!

In summer, windows reveal the bright bolts of lightning that cascade through the dark storm clouds, as heavy rains come to quench the thirst of the hot, dry earth. It is a totally natural sight that surpasses even the fireworks at Disneyland!

Windows are a blessing from God. At least they are to eighty-year-old Mrs. Ormsby. Mrs. Ormsby lives with her son and his wife in a big old house on the edge of a village in New England. For years now she has been severely crippled by arthritis.

Every morning before he leaves for work, her son carries her from her bed to a chair by the window, where she can take part in what is happening in the world outside.

She loves to watch the changing seasons, and she can tell you the names of every tree, flower, and bird within her line of vision. She "reads" the signs of nature and knows when things will blossom and when the migrating birds will begin passing overhead.

The window permits many friends to come into Mrs. Ormsby's life. The letter carrier greets her each day with a big wave as he walks from house to house. The children playing in the yard after school stop to watch her throw them a kiss, and they respond with big smiles. Couples out for an afternoon stroll pause to greet her. If the window is open, they call to her. Sometimes they even stop for a chat.

Mrs. Ormsby's favorite pastime is to pray for everyone and everything she sees through her window. She prays for the Downs child next door. She prays for anyone she doesn't see for a day. She prays for the health of the letter carrier. She prays for the joy the new baby will bring to her friends across the street. She prays that the early November snowstorm won't harm anyone.

Praying for the world outside her window, she says, eases her pain and helps her to feel that she is a part of everything. It is her way of having communion with God's universe.

Her window is a kind of miracle.

Lord, help me to see the world through my window the way Mrs. Ormsby does.

NOVEMBER 18   ATTICS

I grew up in a neighborhood of older people. Even my own parents were older when I was born, as I was the youngest of seven children. All the other children in the neighborhood were the ages of my brothers and sister and had left for school or military service or to get married when I came along. Therefore, I was a sort of mascot to almost everybody around my home. Mrs. Gooch played cards with me; Mrs. Kennedy read books to me; Mrs. Fry baked cookies and set them before me as if I were the taster at the county fair.

I suppose they really spoiled me, and I enjoyed every minute of it. The treat I loved most was getting to rummage through neighbors' attics. Most of them were fraught with cobwebs and some with coal soot, but that only added to the magic.

One neighbor was more prosperous than the others, and her attic was filled with untold treasures. There was an old-fashioned wicker doll buggy with rubber wheels that didn't make a sound when you pushed it. In a big cardboard box there was a beautiful Shirley Temple doll. There were wooden soldiers, silver dresser sets, and a doll house furnished with everything, even a miniature silver tea service.

I could spend hours upon hours in this haven of delight.

Another neighbor's attic was filled with trunks of old clothes and costume jewelry. I would while away whole afternoons dressing up in fancy dresses, high heels, hats, and jewelry, and pretending I was a movie star or a famous lady.

Even today, attics fascinate me. I love to go through the boxes in our attic. It is always like a walk down memory lane.

There are pictures of our families that go back three or four generations. Some of the people in them I have never seen, yet I feel inexpressibly close to them.

There are boxes filled with our children's clothes. In one, I find a ceramic baby bootie that was filled with flowers and sent to the hospital when our first son was born.

One large box is filled with drawings and paintings made by our children. And there are toy chests bulging with G.I. Joe dolls, Hot Wheels cars and tracks, chemistry sets, stuffed animals, and all the other leftovers from those wonderful days.

I think I love the attic most on a rainy day. I sit there and listen to the steady beat on the roof and give thanks to God for all the wonderful memories and joys the attic holds for me.

It's more than that.

Thank you, God, for the comfort of this attic, and for the way I feel your loving arms wrapped tightly about me here.

NOVEMBER 19   FLOWERS

I've spent most of my life admiring flower arrangements. What a gift it is to be able to take a bunch of flowers in all shapes and colors and sculpt them into a work of art.

My flower-arranging ability had always been to plunk a lot of flowers in a vase, with the result that they usually looked as if they have been plunked in a vase. Once, I joined a garden club in hopes of gaining skills in flower arranging, but, alas, no hidden talent emerged after all my lessons. I had to be content as an admirer of others' floral endeavors.

But all of that changed when we moved to California and I met Win and Kay. Win has the greenest thumb I have ever seen, and he grows the most beautiful flowers imaginable. His roses are simply breathtaking. They put the efforts of greenhouses to shame. And Kay is a genius at arranging flowers. She knows just what to put where and how to make everything complement everything else.

Week after week, Win and Kay brought gorgeous bowls and vases of flowers to our church to decorate the hallways, parlors, and chancels. My husband and I always loved seeing them come in from the parking lot on Sunday morning, their arms laden with magnificent creations. It didn't seem possible, but every week they appeared to surpass their efforts of the week before.

From time to time, the church had special holidays when volunteers were needed to help decorate with greens and flowers. I appeared on these occasions, and I began to learn some tricks from Kay. With her instruction, I could at last arrange flowers in an acceptable manner. Her expertise with flowers and her love of beautiful arrangements gave me the confidence I needed to make passable bouquets.

Today, whenever I falter on a difficult arrangement, I ask myself, "How would Kay arrange this?" Then it always falls quickly into place.

Life is so much like a flower arrangement. When you know how to manage, it can be simple and natural, colorful and graceful. It can have balance and harmony. It can even be full of wonderful little surprises. But if you don't know how to approach it, life can be like a bunch of flowers plunked in a vase. It falls into a helter-skelter pattern. It lacks unity. It doesn't satisfy. It isn't inspiring. It droops and sags like the bent stems of heavy-headed chrysanthemums.

Whenever things are not going well, we need to stop and ask,

"What would God do in this situation?" It's amazing, if we do this, how beautifully everything begins to fall into place. It needs only the touch of the Master Arranger.

Help me to remember to call upon you, Lord, whenever my life is in disarray. You know how to make everything beautiful again.

NOVEMBER 20   THE SINK

I can't count the number of times when I have been in the middle of reading a good book and my mental clock would ring, signaling me that it was time to prepare dinner. Reluctantly I would put the book down and drag myself off to the kitchen, where my duties at the sink would begin.

The same thing usually happens when I am playing the piano or having an interesting phone conversation with someone. It's back to the sink. And often, when I'm having a good time shopping, the big clock says, "Go home, it's sink time again."

And always, after a nice family dinner, the family members seem to scatter, and I find myself once more at the sink. Talk about something as inevitable as death and taxes!

Then one day I said, "What is this thing with the sink? It isn't picking this fight. The sink isn't my enemy." My bad attitude about the sink began to change. I started thinking about all the alone time the sink had afforded me through the years. It was a little corner of the world that was really mine.

In that light, everything looked different. I began to relish the time I spent at the sink. It was really quite a pleasant time. I could think and ruminate about things. I could even sing to myself if I wanted to. It was a good place to be. It was comforting. It made me feel secure and necessary. In a sense, I felt as if I was serving my family by being there. I prepared gifts of food there for the ones I loved. I cleaned up after them, further showing my love.

I also discovered that the sink is a pleasant place for daily meditations, for pondering the miracles of God. I looked out the window and saw the sunset or beheld the tinges of color on the trees, signaling the onset of autumn. Sometimes I saw small animals scurrying through the woods or birds flitting from tree to tree.

I have a friend who has arthritis in her hands. She says she can hardly wait to wash dishes at the sink because the warm water has a soothing, healing effect on her knuckles and wrists. For a few moments, she enjoys pain-free mobility again.

My sink, I realize, has been a place of healing for me. It has often served as my psychiatrist. Standing there, I have repeatedly thrashed out problems that seemed insurmountable when I started but that have dissolved like soap bubbles as I worked in the steaming water.

The battle is over.

Forgive me, God, for thinking the sink is one of life's interruptions or irritations. How can it be, when it always gives me time to center my thoughts on you?

NOVEMBER 21   JEWELRY BOX

Some people collect jewelry boxes. They don't necessarily put anything in them; they simply enjoy the unique characteristics of the various boxes they have.

Jewelry boxes are fascinating. Some have small sealed divisions that hide secret compartments. Boxes with musical mechanisms give a special kind of pleasure each time they are opened. And some boxes are beautifully handcrafted, with wooden inlays, dovetailed joints, or carved figures.

My jewelry box isn't anything particularly unusual, but it holds many fond memories. It is filled with trinkets I have acquired through the years. A few are valuable, I suppose, but most are simply enjoyable ornaments given to me by family members and friends.

When our youngest son was a small child, it delighted him to have the task of straightening mommy's jumbled-up jewelry box. He would get into the center of the bed with the box and begin his work. After carefully untangling the chains and beads, he would lay each item out with special care. Then he would bestow on the assembled lot the kind of admiration usually reserved for the crown jewels themselves.

Then the questions would begin: "Mommy, where did you

get this necklace? Who gave you this bracelet? When did you get these earrings?"

Every time, he asked the same questions, persisting in the litany until the very last trinket was replaced in the box. But when he had completed his task, order was restored to my jewelry box for a while, and we had a wonderful time of sharing.

Sometimes, I confess, I feel as if my life is like a jumbled-up jewelry box. I keep anger stored up in little secret compartments. I grope through a maze of partitions in search of parts of myself I can't find. I get tangled up in frustrations. I feel trapped because the key to my existence seems to be lost.

That's when I need God to step in and straighten out everything. I need to hear: "Child, vent your pent-up anger by praying for the people in situations that have hurt you. You'll be amazed at how quickly your anger will vanish.

"Little ones, when you feel that you are at a dead end, follow my road. Its sign clearly reads, 'I am the way, the truth, and the life. Follow me.'

"Try to replace your frustrations with a little more self-esteem. Remember, you are worth more to me than precious stones.

"You may have thought you lost the key to your life, but the Creator always holds the master key. Keep your faith in me."

It is amazing what God can do for our complicated situations if only we let him.

Thank you, Lord, for the order you restore to my life.

NOVEMBER 22   TELEPHONES

Mark Twain wrote, "It is my heartwarm hope and aspiration that all of us throughout the whole earth may eventually be gathered together in a heaven of everlasting rest and peace and bliss, except the inventor of the telephone."

For Twain, who needed peace and quiet for constant concentration, the interruption of a ringing telephone must have been a curse and an abomination.

At times, it can still be an annoyance. Think about the woman who works in an office all day, rushes to the grocery store after work, collects her children from a day-care center, and goes home to prepare dinner for her family. She certainly doesn't need calls in the evening from magazine salespersons and donation solicitors. Her stress level is elevated enough without having to cope with unwanted interruptions during what she hopes will be quality time with her family.

To me, there is nothing more bothersome than having the spell of a lovely candlelit meal suddenly broken by a telephone call about getting my carpets cleaned or having my fireplace inspected by an enterprising chimney sweep. I know that whenever I answer a call of this kind, I always return to the dinner table with a grumpy attitude and the feeling that someone has encroached on my privacy. At this point, I am quite willing to agree with Mark Twain.

But there is a sense, on the other hand, in which the telephone is a real blessing. I have a friend whose husband is often out of town on business. They have a two-year-old son who is prone to earaches. Several times he has awakened in the middle of the night with a throbbing pain. When something like this happens, it is an immeasurable comfort to my friend to know that the pediatrician is only a phone call away.

An elderly relative of ours is a shut-in. She sits alone all day in her living room, unable to get out of the house. The telephone is a great comfort to her. The monotony of a blustery, fall day is often broken by the calls she receives from her friends across town or her daughter at work, asking if there is anything she can bring her in the evening. The telephone is her contact with the outside world.

When I answer the phone at the end of a long, trying day, there is nothing that makes my heart smile more than the cheery voice at the other end of the line that says, "Hi, Mom! What are you up to?" At this point, I don't agree with Twain. All the obvious disadvantages of having a phone give way in an instant when I think of the times I have picked up the receiver to hear the voices of friends or important information about things that are happening or simply spend a little time with loved ones.

All of this business of earthly telephones aside, I think of my

314

eternal Best Friend who waits for my calls to him. Sometimes I listen for his to me as well. These calls are made a little differently from the ones to my friends across town or out-of-state. They are made through the communication process known as prayer.

God is always there to take my calls. I've never known him to be away from the phone. But I have to confess that I am often doing something in the next room when he calls for me, and sometimes I pretend I don't hear the ringing of the phone. Even when he does get me, I sometimes fail to take the advice he has for me. And frequently, when he has done something especially nice for me, I forget to ring him up and thank him. I guess I'm really pretty rude about the relationship.

Come to think of it, I haven't heard from God in a while. I wonder if I've left the receiver off the hook again, and missed his call.

NOVEMBER 23   QUILTS

"Quilting," said an emcee on a morning TV show, "is taking over the country." He was promoting a recently published book about quilts, and he couldn't hide his amazement at the many uses to which they are currently being put. He had thought that quilts are used only on beds for warmth. But the book he was holding showed them being used as wall hangings and tablecloths, and it suggested that their colorful patterns are easily adaptable for placemats, pillow covers, and many other decorative and utilitarian purposes.

Certainly quilting is not a new art. Museums exhibit quilts from the earliest days of our country.

In our home, we have some very old handmade quilts that were passed down from my husband's grandmother, who lived on a farm in Iowa. She was an accomplished quilter. As I look at her handiwork, I marvel that her eyes could see and her hands could sew such tiny, intricate stitches, and that, years ago, in a place where there were so few fabrics to choose from, she could form such spectacular creations.

One of my favorite quilts is one that now adorns the back of a Boston rocker in our kitchen. When our children were babies, we used the rocker to rock them to sleep. The quilt isn't an antique. It was made by my mother and a group of her friends from bits and pieces of fabric left over from my maternity clothes and the layettes sewn for the new babies.

These energetic quilters worked together each week on this special quilt. For them, it was a time of fun and laughter, gossip and sharing. They sewed and talked, talked and sewed, until it was finished, and then they went on to something else. I have to admit that there are a lot of little bobbles in the quilt. Some of the ladies were not very talented. And sometimes they got so interested in the gossip they were telling or a joke they were sharing that I am sure they missed a stitch or two. There are even a couple of spots where their stitches take a crooked path and form a design totally unrelated to the rest of the pattern.

But these little inconsistencies don't bother me. In fact, they are now part of the charm of this particular quilt. I smile when I see them and remember the happy, laughing faces of the women as they chattered and worked on a labor of love.

The real secret of quilting, of course, is the way the quilter takes the variety of fabrics and colors and works the pieces into a mosaic of beauty and interest. It is a godlike thing to do, because, after all, this is what God does with the brokenness of our human experiences.

God sees the fragmented lives of those who are hurting from loneliness, hunger, disease, stress, broken homes, lack of work, and a hundred other things. Like an expert quilter, he lines up all the little segments of suffering existence and then gently pieces them together into a pattern of order, symmetry, and comfort.

God is the best quilter I know. His handwork will flourish forever. We can trust him with our lives, and with our country's life, and with the world. His designs will eventually win all the prizes and adorn heaven itself.

NOVEMBER 24   FIREPLACE

"It takes a heap o' livin' in a house," says the poet, "t' make it home." In our house, a lot of the livin' is done around the fireplace. If we had to name one place that is the heart of the house, I think it would be the fireplace.

There is nothing like a roaring fire to spread warmth to the far corners of a room. In a lot of old houses, unfortunately, that was as far as the warmth went. I have heard my father, who is ninety-six, talk about the freezing winter mornings when he was growing up in a simple farm home. He would make one leap from his featherbed, dive down the stairs, and stand in front of the fireplace to get dressed. Now he chuckles about those cold mornings as he sits in front of a blazing fire in a house that is centrally heated by natural gas.

My husband and I have often enjoyed cooking hot dogs and roasting marshmallows in the fireplace on winter days when there was a power outage. But my father doesn't see anything unusual in that. He says his mother often placed a pot of meat, vegetables, and herbs over the open fire to cook. It simmered there until dinner time, filling the house with delectable aromas At just the right time, she would put an iron skillet of corn bread into the ashes to bake. My father recalls that as "real good eatin'."

In the evening, my family likes to turn out the lights and watch the light from the fireplace dancing around the room, playing games on the ceiling and walls with the shadows cast by the chairs and tables. When my father was a boy, the fireplace was the primary source of light after the sun went down. The children sat in front of it, their backs to the hearth, to read their school books and do their lessons.

We have come a long way from country livin', but some things remain the same. The fireplace is still the heart of the house. Food still tastes better with the crackling flames of the fireplace in the background. Conversation still seems magical when a log drops and new flames spurt up around it. We still get a comforting feeling from seeing the glowing embers of a dying fire and smelling the pungent odor of wood smoke lingering in the room.

And there is still no better place to read the Bible and meditate. Jesus said, "In my Father's house are many rooms." Do I dare to hope there is a fireplace in every one? That would be my idea of Paradise, seated at the feet of the Master by a fireplace.

Oh, what glory that livin' would be!

Buying a new chair for our home is a task that can take from one or two days out of a week to the entire week itself. Just thinking of my husband as he goes from store to store, sitting in every chair to see if it's comfortable, makes me think of Goldilocks and the three bears.

The chair can't be too soft or too hard. It must be exactly the right height and width. The color mustn't be too bold or too subdued. In other words, it has to be just right. But I have to hand it to my husband: he is a genius at selecting comfortable chairs.

Every morning I sit in one of his chairs to have a quiet time of meditation. It is located in front of a big bay window that gives me a panoramic view of the woods behind our house. I watch the squirrels scamper from one tall tree to another. At this time of the year, they are busily gathering nuts and scavenging for suitable materials to winterize their nests. And I see the leaves on the dogwood trees turning bright red. Sometimes in the early morning there is a touch of frost on everything, promising to make the woods even more colorful than they already are.

Today, while I was sitting in the easy chair and basking in the wonders of God's world, I remembered the comfort of another chair in my life. I was eleven years old. Our church was sponsoring a youth revival. The service had ended and I was sitting in a chair waiting for the organist. She lived a block from my parents, and we always walked home together after the evening service.

The guest minister, a young man, was leaving the church and stopped to speak to me. During the conversation, he asked if I was a member of the church. I told him I attended all the services, but no, I wasn't actually a member. He asked me some questions about God, faith, and spiritual commitment.

I must not have given him very clear answers, because he asked if I believed the chair I was sitting in would hold me up and not let me fall down. It was a massive chair that would require at least two persons to move it; so I answered yes to what I thought was a pretty silly question.

Then he asked, "Do you believe that chair over there will hold you up and not let you fall down?"

The other chair was the mate to the one I was sitting in. Again I said, "Yes."

"God," the minister said, "is like these chairs. He will hold you securely forever. You only have to have enough faith to believe and trust him."

That may have been a rather simplistic view of what faith is all about, but it made a deep impression on me. I soon accepted that faith, and all because of a chair.

Sometimes when I feel my faith slipping a little, I remember what the young minister said and I pray, "No matter what chair I am sitting in, God, help me to believe you will never let me fall. Give me the comfort of knowing that your chair is always *just right* for me."

NOVEMBER 26   TABLE

Over the river and through the woods,
Now Grandmother's cap I spy.
Hurrah for the fun, the pudding's done,
Hurrah for the pumpkin pie!

I never went to my grandmother's house for Thanksgiving, so all my mental images of the festivities at her table would be fictitious. My parents didn't make much of Thanksgiving either—at least, not while I was growing up. My childhood fell during the days of World War II, and, between wartime rationing and my parents' awareness that they had four sons away in military service, they weren't in the mood to celebrate.

It was after I married that I began to learn what Thanksgiving joy is all about. That's when I fully understood the meaning of "Hurrah for the fun" and "Hurrah for the pumpkin pie."

Thanksgiving week at our house is a major production.

Monday, I make out a gargantuan list of groceries to buy and things to do to make the big day a notable success. I even work out timetables to remind myself when things have to be done in order for everything to come out together in the end.

Tuesday, I make the rounds of the markets, filling shopping carts to overflowing with good things, as if the next Great Depression were round the corner and I were preparing to hoard everything I would need for months.

Wednesday is baking day, when the ovens go full blast and I am mixing and stirring and filling and putting pans in and taking them out all day. Whenever possible, I arrange to bake the breads and pies and cakes at times when the family will be around to smell the delicious yeasty and spicy aromas wafting out of the kitchen into the entire house.

Thursday morning, after the turkey is stuffed and placed in the oven, we go to church to thank God for his bountiful gifts to us during the entire year. Following the service, we rush home. Snacks are passed around to pacify eager appetites. Then I settle down to the final preparation of the feast, coordinating the corn, beans, potatoes, gravy, oyster casserole, dinner rolls, and everything to be done just as it is time to take the turkey from the oven and set it in the middle of the table.

At long last, the waiting is over. Everyone is called to the dining room. There it is, the table filled with good things that seem to stretch from wall to wall! The golden, basted turkey presides over everything like a proud monarch. The bright red cranberries, plump and juicy, glisten like jewels in the bowl. Vegetables send up steam from half a dozen dishes. Homemade breads and rolls drip with melted butter. It's time for the happy feast to begin.

Several years ago, a strange thing would always happen at this point. Our youngest son would suddenly burst into tears. The first time it happened, we were alarmed. Then we realized what was happening. The little fellow would become so expectant and excited about the celebration that his emotions couldn't stand it. He would have to cry in order to release them. After hugs and reassurances, he would be all right again, and then we would all sit down at the table and hold hands as we offered our thanksgiving to God. We still think about it as we gather around the table. It is part of our family's Thanksgiving lore, part of what binds us together. And we still hold hands when we voice our thanksgiving.

Thank you, God, for the Pilgrims, our country, freedom, and peace.

Thank you for our home, our health, and our loved ones.

Thank you, Lord, for soft voices, whistling trains, and the smell of burning leaves.

Thank you for the abundance of food on our table, and for the five kernels of candy corn at each plate to remind us of how little the Pilgrims had that first winter in New England.

And last of all, we thank you for a little boy who was always filled to overflowing with love, joy, and tears of excitement.

You have prepared a table before us—a wonderful table—and it isn't even in the presence of our enemies!

NOVEMBER 27   DECORATIONS

It's beginning to look and sound a lot like Christmas!

We observe a yearly ritual at our house. The day after Thanksgiving, we play Christmas records on the stereo and haul box after box marked "Christmas" down from the attic to the various rooms where they're supposed to go. There we unwrap all the gingerly packaged decorations and set them in their proper places to preside over the Christmas holidays. Thanksgiving Day is past, and the gladsome weeks of Christmas are ahead.

I must have grown up hearing the Christmas carol "O come, let us *adorn* him," because I have an absolute passion for decorating everything. My husband says he can't sit still very long in one place or I will put a string of lights on him!

Decking the house in holiday tinsel, twinkling lights, lovely crèche sets, wreaths, bows, and candles isn't a commercial thing to do. For me, it merely signals the beginning of happy days to come. The decorations are all reminders of many precious memories from the past and express the hope that we will create many new ones in the future.

As parents, my husband and I can't resist cheerful smiles when we look at the nondescript ornaments our children made when they were in their preschool years. Some of them are very odd looking today. But, even though our children are now grown, the ornaments still hold a place of prominence on our hearth and in our hearts.

A feeling of nostalgia always floods over us when we unpack our Dresden porcelain crèche set. We purchased it in Germany many years ago when our money was very scarce, and we debated at the time about whether we were being too extravagant in buying it. But what joy it has brought us through the years!

When we set candles in our windows, place wreaths on the doors and greenery and fruit on the mantle, we feel a closeness to our colonial past. These warm old traditions are like loving arms stretching across the intervening years. Their simple, uncomplicated nature allows us to celebrate the birth of our Lord with a sense of uncluttered wonder and reverence.

That's what it's all about, isn't it? Wonder and reverence. So, let's deck the halls with boughs of holly and anything else we can find. We're celebrating the birthday of the Christ Child, who came to give so much to so many. I can't help thinking God would approve of our decorations.

NOVEMBER 28   CARDS

I am sitting at my desk with boxes of Christmas cards piled up before me, looking over our list of friends and relatives to whom we always send cards and letters. My heart fills with tenderness as I begin reviewing the list. Here are the names of former parishioners, with whom we lived and loved for years in the past. Here is the name of an old girl friend. We had so much fun together in high school, but now I see her only once every five or ten years. Here are the names of some of my husband's friends. He brought them home to dinner once when we were living in Nashville, and we have been exchanging Christmas greetings ever since.

My husband always writes an omnibus Christmas letter to send to everyone on our list. We make a list of the outstanding events and occurrences of the year, and then he weaves a letter around the list. It has gotten shorter as we have grown older, partly because we don't want to bore our friends and partly because the children are no longer at home and we don't feel the need to expound on their beauties and virtues the way we once did.

Despite the letter, though, I can hardly restrain myself from adding notes and even whole paragraphs on some of the cards. Our friends are that dear.

I have to chuckle when I think about the letters our youngest son used to write to people, usually in response to a birthday or Christmas gift he had received. Invariably, he would write: "Dear So-and-so, How are you? I am fine. I hope you are too. Well. . . ." Sometimes he would remember to add a line of thanks he had meant to add when he started, and sometimes he merely wrote, "Well, I had better get back to my homework" before signing off.

I wish it were that simple for me. I only have to think about some of our friends and I get all wound up and want to write volumes to them. There is something about Christmas that makes all my memories of them come alive, and I want to reach out and hug them and tell them everything. And since they are not here to hug, I want to tell them everything on the Christmas card.

Maybe this is what Christmas is all about anyway—the sweet, wonderful fellowship we have with friends everywhere because God has shown us in Christ how to love. I do know that what I am about to do is a sacrament for me. I will feel God's presence very real to me as I inscribe each card, and even as I lick the stamps and seal the envelopes.

Thank you, God, for the host of friends we have. Bind us a little closer with these cards and letters I am preparing to send. And bless that little boy who once wrote "How are you? I am fine" with a merry Christmas. He is a man now, but my heart still goes out to him.

NOVEMBER 29   ADVENT WREATH

The first Sunday of Advent almost always catches me unaware when it falls in the end of November. My mind automatically thinks of December as Advent month, so, belatedly, my husband and I have been known to light the first candle of the Advent wreath on December 1, whether it's a Sunday or not.

We don't follow very strict rules about our Advent wreath.

We generally use four red candles with a white one in the middle, instead of the usual purple and pink candles surrounding the white one. The wreath is set in the middle of our round kitchen table. On occasion, we have even burned all four candles the first Sunday and every day after that, replacing them when they burn down. My husband likes the extra light when eating his evening meal.

This may sound as if we don't take the Advent traditions very seriously. I suppose we are rather free with them. But we always wait to light the central white candle, the one that honors the birth of the Christ Child, on Christmas Day. That is really the special candle.

That white candle refreshes our memories of the One who is the light shining in the darkness, the light the darkness could not overcome. Its beautiful radiance reminds us of the love that led God to send his one and only Son into the world. As it touches on the shadows of our minds, it lifts us out of our lethargy and makes us want to break forth in joyous singing, which is the only proper response to the wondrous comfort God has brought us through this special Baby.

Lord, thank you for the candle of gift and sacrifice that burns brightly for the everlasting renewal of the world.

NOVEMBER 30   PATIO

The patio had a somber look yesterday. The furniture was covered in plastic for the winter. The barbecue grill was packed away in the basement. A few late-blooming chrysanthemums drooped on their tired, drying stalks. It was a lonesome sight.

The sky had a dismal look, too. The normally blue background with fluffy white clouds gave way to a dull pewter color with dark, heavy clouds hovering so close to the ground that you felt as if you would freeze if you touched them.

My spirit had a dejected feeling. There was a sense of constriction around my head, as if I were wearing a cap of depression. My energy level dropped to what must have been an all-time low. The sounds of music in my heart fell silent. I was grateful for the arrival of evening and the chance to go to sleep and shut out the melancholy day.

Today the patio looks different. The snow that fell stealthily during the night left a coat of white icing on the plastic furniture covers. The old chrysanthemums now appear to glow as beautiful bronze blossoms under a generous sprinkling of powdered sugar. The entire patio looks radiant.

The sky looks different today too. The sun, shining golden white against a field of azure blue, bestows its gentle warmth over the whole enchanted world.

Best of all, my spirit has a different feeling today. Winter arrived so softly and quietly on our late autumn patio last night. How beautiful it is this morning! God has sent a miracle from heaven that makes my heart lift with love and cheer. My spirit is sparkling!

> *Blessed be the name of God forever,*
> *for he changes the seasons.*
> *He reveals deep and mysterious things;*
> *and the light dwells within him.*

DECEMBER

The End and the Beginning

MINERVA GARZA CARCAÑO

DECEMBER 1   **MY FATHER'S GIFT**

*For God so loved the world that he gave his
only Son, so that everyone who believes in him
may not perish but may have eternal life.*
                              —John 3:16 (NRSV)

(Read John 3:16-17.)

As I consider the seasons of Advent and Christmastide, I remember the first of such seasons that my memory recalls. I was five years old. That year my father had assumed the responsibility of setting up the Christmas tree at our local church. He took my younger sister and me to help him.

The sanctuary in that place is large, and the Christmas tree seemed to us huge. Father gave us a few decorations to place at the bottom of the tree while he placed other decorations and strings of lights higher up on it. My sister and I were fascinated by the intricate shapes of the decorations and their beautiful bright colors—stars and globes, tiny mangers, and long strings of shiny tinsel. As we worked and played, Father told us the Christmas story of Mary and Joseph and the birth of baby Jesus. Jesus, he said, had come to let us know how much God loved us.

When all was done Father turned off all the sanctuary lights and then helped us turn on the strings of Christmas lights on the tree. At that moment, the tree was the most wonderful vision we had ever seen, and with the Christmas story alive in our minds and tender hearts, it was truly an experience of God's love.

Of all the Christmas gifts that I have received over the years, my father's gift of that day is still the greatest.

DECEMBER 2   THE INVITATION

O house of Jacob, come, let us walk in the
light of the LORD!
—Isaiah 2:5 (NRSV)

(Read Isaiah 2:1-5.)

Isaiah speaks of the time of the Messiah. Zion will be raised up, and all people will come to know the Lord through her. Judgment will also come as the Lord helps the nations learn to live in harmony. It will be a time of peace when the light of the Lord will shine.

During these days of Advent, we prepare for the Messiah of peace and light. Our homes are lit with candles and special lights that remind us of the coming of the Messiah. Our actions during this period of the year are often more benevolent as we attempt to live the peace of the time of the Messiah. But living in the time of the Messiah is not something that we accomplish for ourselves. It is rather a divine gift given to all who desire it.

This Advent, we are all invited to the house of the God of Jacob to share in the gifts of peace and light. It is there that the Lord will teach us his ways and enable us to walk in his paths. To come into God's presence is to recognize that God is Lord and that we are his. It is to allow God to define real peace for us and to shine upon us with the true light of life.

As we prepare our homes and lives for the coming of the Messiah, let us remember to come before the Lord daily that he might teach us how to live in peace and walk in light.

DECEMBER 3   THE POWER

Let us then lay aside the works of darkness and put on the
armor of light.
—Romans 13:12*b* (NRSV)

(Read Romans 13:11-14.)

I was baby-sitting my young nephew, Christopher, one day. We were watching late afternoon cartoons on television, and

Christopher became very excited by the presentation of "bad guys" in the shows. He turned to me and said, in response to what he was viewing on the television, "I've got the power!" I nodded in agreement thinking that he was simply mimicking what he was picking up from such programs. Noticing that he had not gotten his message across to me, Christopher repeated, "Aunt, I've got the power!"

Recognizing that he was frustrated by my lack of attention, I responded, asking him where he got the power from. His answer surprised me. He said, "Jesus gave me the power and those bad guys can't touch me."

Christopher, at the age of four, had learned the lesson of Romans 13:11-14. With the coming of Jesus we are given power to lay aside the works of darkness and be clothed in the protective armor of light.

DECEMBER 4   THE WAITING

> *Therefore you also must be ready, for the Son of Man is coming at an unexpected hour.*
> —Matthew 24:44 (NRSV)

(Read Matthew 24:36-44.)

Sometimes I wish Advent were twice as long. There is just so much to do in the four short weeks before Christmas Day—house cleaning, baking, preparing the Christmas tree, buying gifts, and sending all those cards to friends and loved ones. Every year it seems that before I know it, Christmas is here and I've not done all that I had hoped to do.

The writer of the Gospel of Matthew interrupts our busy days to remind us that the most important thing we can do during Advent is wait for the coming of the Lord. It is a patient and vigilant waiting, for we do not know when or how the Lord will come. The Gospel writer says simply that the Lord will come as unexpectedly as a thief in the night.

On that day, like men working the field, women grinding meal together, or a man asleep in his home, we will be about the daily tasks of life. But in the midst of the common and ordinary, and most especially in the middle of the festivity of special times, our hearts and minds must always be expectant of the coming Savior. To not expectantly wait for the Lord is to run the risk of missing him and being left behind.

To expectantly wait for the Lord, I find that during Advent, I must work even harder at the disciplines of prayer and meditation, for the distractions are greater. At the same time, it is through prayer and meditation that I am again to experience the joy of the coming of the Lord.

DECEMBER 5   THE TRUSTING

From ages past no one has heard,
no ear has perceived,
no eye has seen any God besides you,
who works for those who wait for him.
—Isaiah 64:4 (NRSV)

(Read Isaiah 63:16–64:4.)
I have spoken of waiting for the coming Lord with expectant hearts and through the assistance of prayer and meditation. Yet there is another aspect of our lives that we must consider for faithful waiting. We must be ready to confess our sin and let God reclaim us as his holy people.

It was the experience of the Israelites that when they allowed sin to lead them away from God, and when in sin they acted as other than God's people, they met with chaos and destruction at the hands of their every adversary. But when they looked for the Lord and trustingly waited upon his saving action, the Lord responded through awesome deeds beyond their expectations.

Our world is also filled with chaos and destruction, our own sin often contributing to the state of things. Yet with the Israelites, we too can call upon the Lord to come to us in our time of need. The God of ages past is our God, who continues to work for those who wait for him. Waiting requires that we turn to God anew, moving away from our sin and allowing God to rule in our lives. May our Advent prayers be ones of repentance that, with the prophet of old, shout out to the Lord, "Tear open the heavens and come down."

For in every way you have been enriched in him . . . so that you are not lacking in any spiritual gift as you wait for the revealing of our Lord Jesus Christ.
—I Corinthians 1:5a, 7 (NRSV)

(Read I Corinthians 1:3-9.)

I have a colleague who pastors a church in Argentina. Along with his pastoral abilities, he is also a gifted musician and composer. One Advent the director of his church's annual Christmas pageant came to him and said that he was preparing a chorus of angels, but they were lacking just the right song for the presentation of the birth of the Christ Child. Could he help?

My colleague accepted the challenge and wrote a song for the angels of his church's Christmas pageant that is now sung around the world. I once had the great joy of singing his composition in an international assembly of ten thousand women!

We don't all have the talent of my colleague in Argentina, but as I think of sisters and brothers from across the Christian community, I must say that we have each been given gifts that enrich and strengthen us all as we wait for the full revelation of our Lord Jesus Christ. Thanks be to God for the Christian community that makes Advent all the more blessed.

DECEMBER 7   THE PROMISE

And this is the name by which it will be called: "The LORD is our righteousness."
—Jeremiah 33:16b (NRSV)

(Read Jeremiah 33:14-16.)

In 1979 a Nicaraguan woman and her two children came to live with me. Advent that year was a time of sharing customs and saying prayers for our families who lived far from us. It was also a time of reflecting upon the state of our separate yet interrelated worlds. Her country was in the middle of civil war, and mine was providing funds for arms and ammunition for that war. Throughout the time we lived together, the politics of U.S.-Nicaraguan relations changed in sometimes clear ways and, at other times, in contradictory and confusing ways. We both kept expecting and hoping that our intelligent and experienced political leaders would find a just solution to the plight of the Nicaraguan people. We are still waiting for that day.

My Nicaraguan friend and I were often at odds in our political perspectives, but through dialogue, prayer, and the study of God's Word, we were led to agree that only the Lord's justice and righteousness can bring true peace to the land. We no longer live together, but every Advent we celebrate our faith in God's promise to send a righteous Branch who shall execute justice and righteousness, and save Judah, Jerusalem, Nicaragua, the United States of America, and all nations. In him we shall all find safety, and the world will proclaim that the Lord is our righteousness.

DECEMBER 8   THE PROPHECY

On that day the root of Jesse shall stand as a signal to the peoples; the nations shall inquire of him, and his dwelling shall be glorious.
—Isaiah 11:10 (NRSV)

(Read Isaiah 11:1-10.)

The oracle of Isaiah 11:1-10 is a messianic prophecy. The Christian community interprets it as a prophecy fulfilled in Jesus, the Christ. The Scripture passage describes the Messiah and the manner in which he will rule, and what a glorious sight it is! The poor and the meek will receive righteousness and equity; the wicked, death. Creatures weak and strong will feed and frolic together, led by a child. Pain and destruction will be no more. We all know the vision, perhaps so well that we set it aside as just another dream. But the Messiah has come. Why then are we not living the fulfillment of the prophecy?

Could it be that fulfillment of the prophecy requires the consent of those who are to be governed? The Messiah does not impose his leadership through force or violence, but rather calls to him those who are willing to live according to his ways. As he finds delight in the fear of the Lord, we who choose to follow him must also be committed to living lives that are rooted in faith in God. Only then will we be able to fully experience the promises of the coming of the Messiah.

DECEMBER 9 THE FAMILY

May the God of steadfastness and encouragement grant you to live in harmony with one another, in accordance with Christ Jesus.

—Romans 15:5 (NRSV)

(Read Romans 15:4-13.)

Three years ago I married a man from a different culture. Bringing our families together on that occasion made it a unique and special day. Two persons from our families who seemed to especially enjoy getting to know each other were our two young nieces, Sarah and Monica. In spite of their cultural and social differences they became great friends that day.

Several months after the wedding we gathered with my husband's family in his hometown for a reception to celebrate our marriage with those of his family who had not been able to travel the long distance to my home for the wedding. Sarah, who is my husband's niece, was there.

When we arrived, Sarah greeted us with hugs and kisses and said that she had an important question to ask me later on. Near the end of the celebration, Sarah came over and asked her question. She wanted to know if her uncle having married Monica's aunt made her and Monica cousins. I explained that things did not work that way, but that they certainly could be good friends. Sarah's face dropped in disappointment over the response, for she and Monica had talked and had decided that they wanted to be family for each other.

The passage from Romans calls us to have the spirit of Sarah and Monica. We are to welcome one another and live together in harmony as one family, as Christ has welcomed us. Christ comes for the salvation of all, that we might together glorify the name of God.

DECEMBER 10   THE PREPARATION

Prepare the way of the Lord, make his paths straight.
—Mark 1:3*b* (NRSV)

(Read Mark 1:1-8.)

I have read that in the time of John the Baptist and Jesus, little attention was given to the cleanliness of cities. There were no public works or sanitation departments, and often even the king's highways were used for the dumping of refuse.

The only time that there was a concerted effort to clean up was when an official visit was to be made by the king. The doors and windows of the shops and homes along the streets where the king would travel were adorned with the best carpets and finest tapestries. The citizens would even compete with one another in their efforts to make the greatest impression on the visiting royalty. And special attention would be given to cleaning up the king's highway so that nothing would impede his arrival.

This is the message of John the Baptist. It is time to clean house for the coming of the Lord. The refuse of our sin must be cleared from our lives through repentance, making way for the Lord of salvation.

DECEMBER 11   THE COMFORT

Comfort, O comfort my people, says your God.
—Isaiah 40:1 (NRSV)

(Read Isaiah 40:1-11.)

The people of God were in exile in Babylon. But God, who is sensitive to the cry of his people, is coming to comfort those who live in bondage and despair. They have suffered enough, says the Lord. This is God's promise to them. It is God's promise to all who suffer. Our suffering will not be eternal.

It is so easy to get caught up in our suffering that we lose sight and sound of God's presence and promise to be with us. The prophet Isaiah reminds us that unlike God, we are as fragile and as temporary as grass. In contrast, God and his Word are faithful and everlasting.

In whatever suffering we may be experiencing today, let us

set our hope on God, who, like a good shepherd, tenderly cares for us and calls us by name, saying, "Comfort, O comfort my people. . . ."

DECEMBER 12   THE OFFERING

Then the offering of Judah and Jerusalem will be pleasing to the LORD *as in the days of old and as in former years.*
—Malachi 3:4 (NRSV)

(Read Malachi 3:1-4.)

Growing up on a farm, my brothers, sisters, and I were often called upon to find twigs for the fire that would heat the water in the large basin that our grandmother liked to use to wash the linen. Into the boiling water she would drop bars of soap and when the soap had melted, she would place the linen in the steaming foamy mixture.

With great patience and care, grandmother would stir the linen in the basin with a long broom handle, occasionally lifting a piece of linen out of the soapy water to check on its condition. When the linen was spotless and brilliantly white, she would remove it from the hot basin and place it in another basin of cool, clean water for rinsing. As the linen dried on the clothesline, grandmother's pleasure with her work would be evident on her face.

Like a grandmother at her wash basin, God cleanses us of all our impurities. With care he makes us right again, so that we are pleasing to him and able to present him offerings of righteousness. The heart of the Advent message is that God, who cleanses and purifies us, is coming.

DECEMBER 13   THE LOVE

And this is my prayer, that your love may overflow more and more with knowledge and full insight to help you to determine what is best, so that in the day of Christ you may be pure and blameless.
—Philippians 1:9-10 (NRSV)

(Philippians 1:3-11.)

Advent is a time known as a season of love. Love is in the

songs we hear, the themes of the movies we see, and the gifts we give and receive. Love is the message of the season. As persons of faith, we wait for the One who is perfect Love—Christ Jesus—making every effort to love as we wait.

The apostle Paul reminds us that the love we are to strive to have is not a simple state of mind, however. It is a spiritual groundedness that leads us, in love for God and others, to seek after those things that are of ultimate good. It is a love reflected in the life of the church at Philippi. Throughout, the members had shared their companionship and possessions with Paul, as well as co-labored with him in the proclaiming of the gospel. They had shown fruits of righteousness through the constancy of their love for Paul, but above all, through their love for Christ and his work.

As I look at the community where I live, I become aware of the fact that if I am to express a discerning love that leads to goodness and fruits of righteousness, I must be concerned for the homeless, the refugees, the battered women, the neglected children, and others in need. To do this requires that I give of myself spiritually, physically, emotionally, and materially. These are not necessarily the persons with whom I want to share my love and time this season. I pray for God's forgiveness and the in-flow of Christ's love, that true love might fill my spirit and prove me pure and blameless for the day of Christ.

DECEMBER 14   THE HOPE

Happy are those whose help is the
God of Jacob,
whose hope is in the LORD their God.
   —Psalm 146:5 (NRSV)

(Read Psalm 146:5-10.)
I know a woman who lives in dire poverty. A two-room cinder-block structure serves as home for her, her husband, and their five children. Her husband works occasionally with a railroad company. His limited skills disqualify him from all but the most menial of jobs. To help her family

survive, our sister worked as a waitress, but a year ago left her job in order to devote all of her time to serving as a lay evangelist in her community. She did so with the support of her family. As she witnesses to her neighbors and friends of God's love, the saving grace of the Lord has touched many lives.

Next to this woman, my middle-class life seems to be one of great material wealth. My seminary education and years of pastoral practice seem, at points, superficial in comparison to her faith witness. In knowing this sister, my life has been enriched and my faith strengthened. She has become my mentor, for she has experienced in a direct and profound manner the God who executes justice for the oppressed, gives food to the hungry, sets the prisoner free, opens the eyes of the blind, and lifts up those who are bowed down. My sister is still economically poor, and she continues to suffer oppression, but she is no longer bowed down, for God has lifted her up and she does surely know God's help.

This Advent we might all do well to look toward persons who, in the midst of great suffering and oppression, are experiencing the deliverance of the God of history who keeps faith forever. Through their witness, our confidence in God's ongoing salvation might be renewed and our hope rekindled.

DECEMBER 15   LOVING ONE ANOTHER

I give you a new commandment, that you love one another. Just as I have loved you, you also should love one another.
—John 13:34 (NRSV)

(Read John 13:34-35.)

The coming of the Lord calls us to care for one another. How well we care for one other will determine the outcome of our own lives. I once read a tale in the Midrash that speaks to this truth.

There was a woodsman who went to a forest in search of material to fashion a handle for his axe. Standing before the trees of the forest, he presented his petition. It seemed such a modest petition that the oldest and grandest of the trees decided among themselves that it would be granted. Turning to the man, they offered him the wood of the humble ash. Well, no sooner had the man fashioned the handle for his axe than he began to cut down the noblest of the trees in the forest. Aghast at what he saw, the cedar turned to the oak and said, "The first concession has lost all. If we had not sacrificed our humblest neighbor, we might yet have stood for ages ourselves."

Advent reminds us of God's love for us through Jesus Christ. As God and Christ have loved us, we are called to love one another. Our expressions of care and love for one another will determine our relationship to him who makes possible our standing for ages to come.

DECEMBER 16   LA POSADA

And she gave birth to her firstborn son and wrapped him in bands of cloth, and laid him in a manger, because there was no place for them in the inn.
                                        —Luke 2:7 (NRSV)

(Read Luke 2:1-7.)

In the Mexican tradition of my foremothers and forefathers, a special Christmas celebration begins today. It is called *La Posada*, which means a dwelling house or place of lodging. In this celebration, persons depicting Mary and Joseph and persons from their time walk through their hometowns looking for lodging, remembering Mary and Joseph's journey to Bethlehem and their efforts at finding a place to lodge. As persons portray this ancient scene, they stop at the homes of townspeople, asking for lodging. At every home they are turned away until on Christmas Day, at a designated home, they are welcomed in and the birth of Jesus is celebrated with food and singing.

For nine days the persons participating in *La Posada* experience, if only through drama, the rejection that Mary and Joseph, and with them Jesus, received as they looked for safe haven in Bethlehem. Having participated in several *Posadas*, I can say that one does indeed begin to feel the pain of being turned away. One also begins to ponder the hearts of those who turned Mary and Joseph away.

There were of course persons who logistically had nothing to offer to the couple, for Bethlehem was overflowing with visitors at the time. But could it be that for some, the callousness of their hearts did not allow them to respond in more merciful ways to a woman about to give birth and her anxious husband? Could it be that in 1992 we too have become callous and unable to respond to the coming of the Christ Child who knocks at our door? May we today consider the condition of our hearts as we prepare for the coming of Christ.

DECEMBER 17   THE PRIVILEGE

And now, you will conceive in your womb and bear a son, and you will name him Jesus.
                                   —Luke 1:31 (NRSV)

(Read Luke 1:26-31.)

As I wait with Mary for the birth of the Christ Child, I too carry a child in my womb. I feel some of Mary's fear and anticipation. I have begun to experience the extraordinary sensation of having my child move within me, and have begun to speak aloud to this son or daughter of mine. I wonder if Mary spoke to Jesus growing within her?

I marvel at Mary's courage in birthing the Savior of the world, and am grateful for that courage as well as for God's decision to send Jesus to be born of woman. That God would deem a female body and person worthy of presenting divine salvation to the world is for me both affirming and challenging.

Affirming that contrary to ongoing belief, women are also called of God to be integral participants in the building of the new community of faith. Challenging, for with Mary we too are called to bear and rear children, physically and spiritually, whose lives will reflect the goodness and love of God.

There is only one Savior. Mary had the great privilege of presenting him to the world. Disciples of the one Savior are in our hands to nurture. May we have the courage and faithfulness of Mary.

DECEMBER 18   MIRACLES

For nothing will be impossible with God.
—Luke 1:37 (NRSV)

(Read Luke 1:32-37.)

Two women who could not possibly be pregnant, yet are. One young, one old, but both touched by God and filled with life—for God, nothing is impossible.

I think of all the situations in my life which seem impossible, barren of possibility, or simply beyond the time and means for change—broken relationships, unbreakable bad habits, debilitating fears, moments of spiritual emptiness. Herein the Good News: Nothing is beyond God's life-giving power.

God can create within us new life, regardless of our condition or circumstance. For our sisters, Mary and Elizabeth, new life came in the forms of sons, but no one can deny the life-transformation that surely occurred in them through the touch of the Holy. I believe that Mary was strengthened in her courage and Elizabeth in her hope. Both grew in faith. With them we, too, can experience transformation of all life's possibilities in the hands of God and be women of courage, hope, and faith.

DECEMBER 19   HERE AM I

Then Mary said, "Here am I, the servant of the Lord; let it
be with me according to your word."
—Luke 1:38a (NRSV)

(Read Luke 1:38.)

God can change our lives, even do the impossible. But God is not one who acts unilaterally. As we wait for God, God also awaits us. God's activity in our lives is experienced to its fullest when we acknowledge God's presence and invite God's participation with us. As servants of God, we also receive the divine invitation to take part in God's plan of redemption. Yet again, God leaves the choice of whether to participate to us.

Mary is one who acknowledges God's presence, inviting God to act in her life and offering herself to God in servanthood: "Here am I, the servant of the Lord." In this act of faith and commitment Mary is blessed.

On this day we may know what God is able to do in our lives and may be awaiting God's activity in our behalf. But have we truly invited God to act in our lives? Have we remembered to say with Mary, "Here am I . . ."?

DECEMBER 20   THE MESSAGE

> *But you, O Bethlehem of Ephrathah,*
> *who are one of the little clans of Judah,*
> *from you shall come forth for me*
> *one who is to rule in Israel,*
> *whose origin is from of old, from ancient days.*
> —Micah 5:2 (NRSV)

(Read Micah 5:1-5*a*.)

Jesus came to us at a moment in history when there were great nations led by royal households. God could have sent Jesus to the world as a member of one of those households, yet God chooses instead to send Jesus through the family of Bethlehem of Ephrathah, "one of the little clans of Judah." And rather than being born in a palace, Jesus is born in a stable. It is not what the Israelites expected, for they awaited a warrior-king who would save them. Instead, God sent a baby. While the world looked for power and might, God sent a powerless infant born in humility.

Today we are still often swept away by expectations of power and might. Christmas bonuses received at our workplaces validate our worth. Children compete with other children to see who will receive the most expensive gifts this Christmas. Even pastors check on one another to see whose Christmas programs have received the most participation, thus demonstrating who is the best pastor around. Sadly, these things blur our vision of the true meaning of Advent and Christmas.

God's message to us through the birth of the Christ Child is about love and humility. Unless we center our lives around these gifts and qualities of the Christian character, we miss the blessing of the coming of Jesus.

DECEMBER 21   THE REAL SPIRIT

May the God of peace himself sanctify you entirely; and may your spirit and soul and body be kept sound and blameless.
—I Thessalonians 5:23b (NRSV)

(Read I Thessalonians 5:16-24.)

Paul exhorts the Thessalonians to a life of joy, constancy in prayer, and thanksgiving. It is God's own desire in giving Christ Jesus for humanity's sake. In order to live this holy life, the Thessalonians are advised to test everything, holding fast to what is good and abstaining from every form of evil. It is this faithful living that will enable them to be prepared for the coming of Christ. Considering the fact that the Thessalonians lived in a society filled with paganism, this was no easy task.

As I prepare for Christ this Advent, I am struck by the fact that our world is still filled with paganism. Pagan values permeate even these holy days. Merchants and media join forces in commercialism that promotes materialism; businesses as well as individuals plan elaborate holiday parties to display their wealth and power; some of us look forward to days off during this time so that we might pamper ourselves, escaping from all responsibilities. These are pagan values indeed when we remember that central to the message of Advent is that Christian living requires that we empty ourselves to make room for the presence of Christ in our lives.

With the Thessalonians we, too, must continue to test everything, emptying our lives of all evil so that the goodness of Christ might come and abide with us. A spirit of joy, prayer, and thanksgiving can help us to focus on Christ and his goodness.

DECEMBER 22   THE COMING OF THE LORD

Be patient, therefore, beloved, until the coming of the Lord.
                    —James 5:7*a* (NRSV)

(Read James 5:7-10.)

Christmas Day is almost here. It has become more and more difficult to wait. Children and even some of us adults have begun to take peeks into the wrapped gifts lying under the Christmas tree. Our energy level is now ebbing low, spent on all the preparations for the big day. I catch myself wanting these days to be over so that I can take a rest. About this time, our nerves are also often strained affecting how we relate to one another and how we wait for the day of Jesus' birth. For these last days, the writer of James has some advice for us.

We are to be patient and remember that the Lord who is Judge is already standing at our door. Like the farmer who knows that the fruit of his field is coming, and like the prophets of old who knew that God was on his way to them and the people, we are reminded of that which we know: The coming of the Lord is imminent. Let us not be caught unprepared.

May we take time now to gather our thoughts and energy and set our hearts to the coming of the Lord, being patient with one another, with ourselves, and with the Lord, who is already in our midst.

DECEMBER 23   A NEW ORDER

And Mary said, "My soul magnifies the Lord."
                    —Luke 1:46 (NRSV)

(Read Luke 1:46-55.)

We have been preparing for the Christ, but have we given thought to what God, through Christ, has prepared for us? Mary, in the extraordinary Magnificat, tells us that the Lord has prepared for us a new world. Those who have prided themselves on their might will tumble down, while those who have been humbled in their low estate will be lifted up. The hungry will be filled, while those who have had every desire met will be left empty-handed. The old world order of pride and greed, of social status and class, will be destroyed in the coming of Christ to make room for a world in which love prevails. Examining our lives, where can we expect to find ourselves in this new world?

Letting go of the familiar will be difficult for those of us who have much. For those who suffer, God's new world order, revealed and initiated in the coming of Christ, brings hope. But for all, the coming of Christ will bring the ultimate well-being and peace for which generations of humanity and all creation have yearned. Divine mercy will descend upon the world, creating a new order in which all God's children will be cared for according to God's love, not according to human arrogance or structures. May it thus be.

DECEMBER 24   MAKING ROOM

And she gave birth to her firstborn son and wrapped him in bands of cloth, and laid him in a manger, because there was no place for them in the inn.
—Luke 2:7 (NRSV)

(Read Luke 2:7.)

The Messiah is coming, so let us be ready to receive him. To do this, our lives must have room for him.

I expect family members to visit me on Christmas Day. Already I have been preparing room in my home for them. My home is small, and at one point we had considered asking our family to stay in a hotel nearby. But I do not want to miss a single moment with them. I would rather make room in my home so that I can have them close to me, enjoying the full blessing of their visit.

We can do the same with Jesus. We can have him stay at a distance and enjoy his presence part of the time, or we can make room for him right in the middle of our homes and lives, and reap the full benefit of his coming.

344

DECEMBER 25   A SAVIOR IS BORN

"Do not be afraid; for see—I am bringing you good news of great joy for all the people: to you is born this day in the city of David a Savior, who is the Messiah, the Lord."
—Luke 2:10-11 (NRSV)

(Read Luke 2:8-20.)

Christmas Day is here! It is a day for great rejoicing. With the angels and shepherds we join in a song of joy and thanksgiving—"Glory to God in the highest heaven, and on earth peace among those whom he favors!" (Luke 2:14 NRSV). Our Savior is born and we celebrate.

But there are those who call into question our celebration. The world continues to be filled with death, destruction, and despair. Christmastime has been known to send many into such deep depression that they commit suicide. There is still hunger and hatred, prejudice and poverty. How can we celebrate?

May we remember on this day that in spite of the condition of the world, we can celebrate and rejoice, because the one who leads us out of darkness and heals our pain has come. We continue to struggle with the condition of our world, but we do it now with hope, for our Savior has been born.

DECEMBER 26   THE WORLD OF LIGHT

The people who walked in darkness
have seen a great light;
those who lived in a land of deep darkness—
on them light has shined.
—Isaiah 9:2 (NRSV)

(Read Isaiah 9:2-7.)

Because Jesus has been born, we can live in a new world where God's light shines. The birth of Jesus transforms all human history. There is a definite new point of departure for humankind that is marked by Jesus' birth and described by Isaiah as the coming out of deep darkness to light. Yet our world is not significantly different from the world in which the prophet Isaiah lived. What does this say to us?

The post-Christmas Day message seems to be that unless we choose to live in the new world made possible by Jesus, we will continue to live in darkness. It is not sufficient for Jesus to have been born in Bethlehem. He must be born in our own hearts, and we must decide to follow his teachings in order to participate in the world of light. To do otherwise is to remain in the land of deep darkness.

DECEMBER 27   THE ONE GIFT

For the grace of God has appeared, bringing salvation to all.
—Titus 2:11 (NRSV)

(Read Titus 2:11-14.)

Right about now, we are beginning to feel the full effects of our Christmas preparations—we are tired and weary; our pocketbooks are perhaps empty; and we wonder how we made it through another Advent and Christmas. Lest we become self-centered in our perception of who has given of themselves this Advent and Christmas season, let us remember God's gift of Jesus Christ. The grace of God and the salvation that he gives to us in Jesus is the measure of the greatest gift of all. God has given his most beloved for you and me and all creation. Glory be to God!

DECEMBER 28   MY EYES HAVE SEEN

Master, now you are dismissing your servant in peace, according to your word; for my eyes have seen your salvation.
—Luke 2:29-30 (NRSV)

(Read Luke 2:25-40.)

It has always been amazing to me that Simeon was able to recognize that in baby Jesus, he was seeing the Christ. There is no indication in Scripture that Simeon knew anything about Mary or Joseph or the birth of Jesus in Bethlehem. How then could he know that this child in his arms was the bearer of God's salvation?

The question becomes particularly relevant for us, who can know Jesus only in the spiritual sense. The witness of Simeon's life perhaps leads us to some answers.

Simeon was a righteous and devout man who looked for God's salvation and whose life was filled with the Holy Spirit. His was a disciplined life of faith and expectant hope. Simeon's closeness and devotion to the Lord enabled him to be prepared to recognize the Messiah. But it was the Spirit of God that revealed and guided Simeon to the discovery of the Christ Child.

If we are to recognize Christ in our midst, like Simeon, our lives must be lived in righteousness and devotion to God. We must also actively look for the Messiah among us, praying incessantly that the Spirit of God will lead us to him.

DECEMBER 29   THE FULLNESS OF TIME

But when the fullness of time had come, God sent his Son.
                    —Galatians 4:4a (NRSV)

(Read Galatians 4:4-7.)

There is a right time for all things. We must be aware of the timing as we make decisions in our lives. Is it the right time to make that financial investment we've been wanting to make? Is it the right time to consider another job? Is it the right time to let go of that relationship we've been in for so long? Is it the right time to commit ourselves to new tasks? We must carefully consider whether it is the right time before we make our decisions.

God, in sending Jesus, considered the time and decided that it was the right time. The fullness of time had come. God's chosen people were in bondage to the Romans and longed for the coming of the Messiah. Others found themselves in religious confusion, drawn every which way by the idols of their age. At the same time, the conquests and ideology of Alexander the Great had brought a unity to the world through the use of a common language and a highly developed system of highways. This unity would facilitate the spread of the Good News. In his

347

wisdom God declared that it was the right time to reveal himself to the world through his Son Jesus Christ.

At the right time Jesus came into the world. How have we responded? Is it not the right time for us to give ourselves completely to Jesus?

DECEMBER 30   THE GARMENTS OF SALVATION

I will greatly rejoice in the LORD,
  my whole being shall exult in my God;
for he has clothed me with the garments of salvation.
                    —Isaiah 61:10*b* (NRSV)

(Read Isaiah 61:10–62:3.)

The Christmas season is a time for elaborate dress. Our sanctuaries are adorned with Advent wreaths and Jesse trees. Our homes are equally decorated, and we ourselves dress up in special, and sometimes new, clothes to express our joy over the coming of the Lord. Yet nothing in which we dress ourselves or our surroundings can compare to what the Lord clothes us with.

While we dress up in clothing that will at some point be put away or worn out, the Lord dresses us in the eternal garments of his salvation and righteousness. Like those dressed for a wedding, we are adorned by God's vindication.

The beautiful decorations of the Christmas season are now being put away for next year. It will probably be some time before we have an opportunity to wear that lovely Christmas dress again. But throughout the year, God will clothe us majestically with his love and salvation.

DECEMBER 31   NEW WINESKINS

"One puts new wine into fresh wineskins."
                    —Mark 2:22*b* (NRSV)

(Read Mark 2:21-22.)

Throughout this Advent and Christmas season God has refreshed us with the new wine of the Good News: Unto us a

Savior is born! It is still news, even though the message is almost 2,000 years old, and new every day in the way that it daily transforms our lives.

As we reach the end of this calendar year, God blesses us again. He gives us a new year—a fresh wineskin for our new wine. God gives us new opportunities for living our faith and experiencing his salvation. Our past sin can be thrown away, discarded like old wineskins with the ending year. Like new wineskins, we can embody the new wine of the Good News. Filled with the Good News, our lives can be different and make a difference in the lives of others next year. Thanks be to God!

NOTES